*M*any important psychic personalities and events, especially those from countries other than the United States, England, and Europe, drop through the holes of parapsychology's history and are lost forever. In this great and interesting collection, Dr. Imich and colleagues gather and restore to visibility some very *different* and astonishing and even incredible phenomena. More than mere history, the tales are *exciting* and wonderful and mind-stretching—and perhaps a hint of future things to come.

Ingo Swann,
author of *To Kiss Earth Goodbye, Cosmic Art, Star Fire, Natural ESP,*
Your Nostradamus Factor, **and** *Purple Fables*

This is a book to remind us that there are more things in Heaven and Earth than are dreamt of in our parapsychology laboratories.

John Beloff, Ph.D.,
Hon. Fellow of the Department of Psychology, University of Edinburgh,
author of *The Existence of Mind, Psychological Sciences, The Relentless*
Question, Parapsychology: The Concise History,
and co-editor of *The Case for Dualism*

Cover art:
"Levitation in the Desert"
by Dr. Ingo Swann
from the collection of Trammell Crow

Incredible Tales of the Paranormal

Documented Accounts of Poltergeist, Levitations, Phantoms, and Other Phenomena

Edited by
Alexander Imich, Ph.D.

BRAMBLE ❖ BOOKS
New York

For information write to:
Bramble Books, 8 Route 212, Bearsville, NY 12409

Library of Congress Cataloging-in-Publication Data

Incredible tales of the paranormal : documented accounts of poltergeist,
  levitations, phantoms, and other phenomena / edited by Alexander Imich.
          p.   cm.
      Includes bibliographical references.
      ISBN 1-883647-03-7 (pbk. : alk. paper) : $14.95
      1. Parapsychology—Case studies. 2. Occultism—Case studies.
  I. Imich, Alexander.
  BF1031.I53 1995
  133—dc20   94-45013
                                        CIP

First Printing 1995
1 3 5 7 9 10 8 6 4 2

Printed in the United States of America

The paper used in this publication meets the minimum requirements
of American National Standard for Information Sciences—
Permanence of Paper for Printed Library Materials,
ANSI Z39.48-1984.

Contents

Mirabelli!!

Mediumship in Italy

Indridi Indridason

Matylda

Teofil Modrzejewski

Physical Mediumship in Russia

Psychic Phenomena in China

Preface

COLIN WILSON

Parapsychology is the most anomalous of all the scientific disciplines. There is simply no parallel case of a science which, after more than a century of experiment and observation, continues to be rejected by the majority of scientists.

The reason is straightforward enough. Humanity has always tended to allow its hopes and fears to blend with its observations about the world—so that, for example, primitive people see certain natural events as "omens." Early Greek scientists soon noticed that success depended upon forgetting their hopes and fears and concentrating on the objective world. The results were spectacular, and even included an accurate assessment of the size of the Earth.

But in the Christian era, religion continually stood in the way of scientific progress. It seemed impossible to teach popes and inquisitors that their beliefs about God, the vicarious atonement and eternal life were totally irrelevant to science. Finally, the popes and inquisitors had to be pitched out of the temple of science by the scruff of their necks. After that triumph, the scientists vowed never to let them in again.

When, in the late 1840s, some mysterious entity that made strange rapping noises in the house of the Fox family, in New York State, proceeded to dictate 'spirit messages' in code, the events became a nationwide sensation, and 'mediums' suddenly sprang up all over the place. Trumpets floated in the air, unseen hands stroked the sitters' faces, and tables occasionally soared to the ceiling. The initial response among scientists was to dismiss it as a revival of the medieval witchcraft hysteria which had still been around as late as 1700. But the craze persisted and—as Larissa Vilenskaya describes in this book—even reached the Russian royal family. (Queen Victoria herself fancied 'table turning.')

By the 1870s, respectable observers who could be persuaded to attend seances soon reported that some of the phenomena at least appeared to be genuine. What were scientists to do? Science, in theory, was 'democratic'; it was supposed to exclude nothing from its investigations. But 'spiritualism' was clearly beyond the pale. Dostoevsky had remarked that if there *is* survival after death, it would be the most important 'fact' known to humanity. Obviously, he was right. But if even one medium was admitted into the temple of science, what would prevent hordes of ragamuffins, charlatans and religious cranks from rushing in behind? The scientists quickly closed ranks. Undemocratic or not, they could not afford to take the risk. So psychical research was firmly pigeonholed under 'religion' (or possibly 'abnormal psychology'), where it could safely be ignored. And at the time I write this, a hundred and ten years after the formation of the Society for Psychical Research, that situation remains basically unchanged.

Most paranormal investigators will acknowledge that this is not entirely unfair. The trouble with psychical research is that its phenomena cannot be reproduced at will in the laboratory. But the unspoken taboo can lead to some outrageous absurdities. In August 1982, a globe of ball lightning floated through a window of the Cavendish Laboratory in Cambridge, England narrowly missing a secretary. At the time, many scientists doubted the existence of ball lightning.* The physicist Sir Brian Pippard collected many eye witness accounts and sent them to *Nature*. But when asked if this did not finally prove the existence of ball lightning, he replied: "Well, none of *us* actually saw it."

Again, when a benefactor recently left £100,000 to Darwin College, Cambridge, to finance a research fellowship in parapsychology, the college was embarrassed by the bequest, and finally awarded the fellowship to Dr. Nicholas Humphrey, a well-known enemy of parapsychology, who announced that he would devote the money to "exposing the fallacies of belief in the paranormal."

On the other hand, it must be admitted that the open-minded approach has proved to have one major disadvantage: it has so far failed to produce any positive results that are the justification of any science. In

---

* Since then, the Japanese scientist Yoshihiko Ohtsuki, of Waseda University in Tokyo, has demonstrated fairly conclusively that ball lightning consists of 'elastic plasma', a powerful form of ionized air, and has created it in the laboratory.

1882, the fiercely sceptical Professor Cesare Lombroso went to investigate a case of a girl who claimed to be able to see through her ear and smell through her chin. To his amazement, his tests indicated that she was genuine. He then attended a seance of the medium Eusapia Palladino, and watched a table float into the air. He went on to investigate a number of cases of precognition of future events and found himself convinced by them. Then, after investigating a poltergeist that smashed bottles in a tavern in Turin, witnessing the bottles rising from the shelves and smashing on the floor, he was forced to conclude that poltergeists really exist. He ended by writing a book in which he acknowledged that he had become convinced of the reality of life after death. But far from convincing his fellow scientists, he only undermined his own reputation. And when criminologists began to dismiss his early theories about 'criminal atavism' as crude and simplistic, his former colleagues hastened to applaud the views of his biographer, Hans Kurella, who dismissed Lombroso's 'spiritualistic researches' as sheer self-delusion.

Another converted sceptic, William James, put his finger on the problem when he remarked:

> I confess that at times I have been tempted to believe that the Creator has eternally intended this department of nature to remain *baffling*, to prompt our curiosities and hopes and suspicions all in equal measure, so that, although ghosts and clairvoyances and raps and messages from spirits ... can never be fully explained away, they can also never be susceptible of full corroboration.

In other words, James was suggesting, something in the very nature of psychical research prevents it from becoming a full-blown science. This notion—which we might call "James's Law"—seems to state that there will always be enough evidence to convince the believers but never quite enough to convert the sceptics.

If "James's Law" could be suspended, this present volume would cause an intellectual revolution. I doubt whether there has been a collection of documents on paranormal research that is so totally convincing. Taken all-in-all, it points to the inescapable conclusions that certain human beings possess 'paranormal powers,' and that these powers appear to include the ability to contact the dead. This is not to assert that fraud is an impossibility—in fact, the authors acknowledge that many 'great mediums' have been guilty of fraud. Even Carmine Mirabelli, one of the most powerful mediums of the 20th century, seems to have tacitly countenanced a faked photograph showing him levitating above his sitters. Yet researchers who have actually studied mediums at first hand—as Alexander Imich and Larissa Vilenskaya have—leave us in no doubt that they witnessed genuine 'miracles.' Imich's section on Matylda is a classic piece of psychical research that in itself would justify the existence of this volume.

Then why is it a foregone conclusion that this book will not produce the slightest effect on most members of CSICOP, that committee for the investigation of the paranormal which seems to take it for granted that the paranormal is not worth investigating? One reason, of course, is that they will take care not to read it. But the main reason is undoubtedly that most of the phenomena described in this book refuse to be fitted into any kind of scientific framework. Scientists get excited when a new theory—or observation—seems to offer a *key* to a whole range of unexplained phenomena. And the problem with these accounts of Mirabelli, Palladino, Indridason, Matylda, Modrzejewski, Kulagina and the rest is that they simply seem to contradict our normal assumptions about the physical universe without offering some intellectually consistent alternative.

In just a few cases, it seems possible to begin to formulate some kind of explanation. For example, Inge Gaiduchenko, who will be found in Chapter VI, is able to make objects stick to her as if she is a human magnet. There are many well-authenticated cases of 'human magnets' and 'human electric eels.' Frank McKinistry, a Missouri teenager, developed an electric charge during the night and lost it during the day: it could make his feet stick to the ground. Jennie Morgan of Sedalia could knock a man flat on his back with her electric charge. Caroline Clare of Ohio became a 'magnet' after a serious illness, and pieces of iron had to be pulled off her by force. Esther Cox, the 'focus' of a poltergeist occurrence in 1878, also became a human magnet who attracted all the knives and forks in the kitchen. Since we understand how electric eels develop their charge, all this is not too difficult to accept. But Inge Gaiduchenko seems to defy the laws of nature in that *books* stick to her, as well as metal objects. If this is static electricity, then it seems difficult to explain, even by invoking electric eels, since 'static' is produced by knocking off the outer electrons of a dry substance (like glass or bakelite) with silk or fur, and the human body is covered with a layer of moisture.

In any case, tests on the Russian woman Elvira Shevchuk have shown that electrostatic fields are *not* involved. Elvira's abilities, while startling, seem less remarkable than those of most of the mediums in this book. Vilenskaya describes how Elvira sat with a wooden stick resting at an angle on the floor, then slowly removed her hands—and the stick stayed where it was. She was also able to 'suspend' a knitting needle, a beaker of liquid and a glass filled with sand. It all sounds fairly unspectacular—until, of course, we try to explain it.

Boris Yermolayev, the film maker, can hold a pack of cigarettes between his palms, then separate the palms and leave the pack suspended in the air. He told Vilenskaya that he did this by "persuading" the object and "inducing a part of himself" into the object. This is obviously highly significant—but what does it mean? Ivan Dekhtyar can suspend a tennis ball between his open palms and explains that he engages in certain mental preparation that involves a sense of the enlargement of his hands and of the tennis ball.

As to the late Nina Kulagina, who has been called the Russian equivalent of Uri Geller, her remarkable powers included the ability to cause white mice to go into suspended animation, and to stop a frog's heart. She was also able to produce images on a sealed photographic plate—a feat also demonstrated by the American Ted Serious—and to move objects as large as matchboxes by 'psychokinesis.' Accused by a journalist of fraud, she convinced a Soviet court of her genuineness and won her case.

To evoke the name of Uri Geller in this connection may seem unwise, at least as far as English and American readers are concerned. Most are inclined to believe that Geller has been discredited by 'magicians' like James Randi and by scientific tests. This is, in fact, untrue. Guy Playfair, the author of the first chapter in this book, studied Geller in order to write a book about him and concluded that he was genuine. I myself spent some time with Geller in 1976 and saw certain things that could not be explained in terms of stage magic. On the first occasion, when I met Geller, he demolished my scepticism by reading my mind. We were facing one another at a table in a restaurant in London's West End. I was sitting in a corner, and there was a girl beside me. Geller told me to make a drawing on the back of the menu card, and as I did it, he turned his back to me. I kept glancing at him as I made the drawing—a kind of comic bogeyman I invented for my children; the girl beside me also watched him to make sure there was no mirror concealed in his hand. When I had finished, he told me to place my hand over the drawing; then he turned round. Next, he asked me to 'transmit' the drawing to him by staring into his eyes. He instructed me to 'draw it in my mind' as I looked at him. For several minutes he concentrated, then told me I was not trying hard enough. Then, just as I had decided the whole experiment was a flop, he seized a pencil and duplicated my sketch on the back of the menu card. I later published the two sketches side by side in a book on the paranormal.

When I had dinner with Randi, Geller's most vocal opponent, he demonstrated some amazing examples of stage magic; he not only bent a spoon by rubbing it—Geller's most famous 'trick'—but made one vanish in front of my eyes as he held it between two hands. Yet when I asked him if he could duplicate Geller's trick of reading my mind, he admitted that it would be impossible "without preparation." In fact, ordinary logic makes it plain that no amount of preparation could have enabled Randi to duplicate Geller's feat of reading my mind.

In any case, it seems abundantly obvious that few of the psychics described in the final chapters of this book required any kind of preparation. Twelve-year-old Hu Lian not only saw the position of a piece of shrapnel inside the body of Mr. Yao, a member of the Science Committee of Xuan Chen, but was able to describe its shape. Mr. Yao thought she was wrong about its shape, but an X-ray photograph proved her correct. Another schoolgirl was able to tell her aunt—in the presence of the investigator—that she had two tumors in her womb, not one, as the doctors had diagnosed; a womb operation proved her correct. The author then proceeds to give some accounts of children who can read through their ears, all of which seemed designed to provide sceptics with an object of ridicule—until we recall that this is precisely how Lombroso became 'converted.'

Now if parapsychology is to be accepted as a science, the most urgent necessity is clearly a paradigm that gives at least some illusion of understanding. And on the whole, it seems clear that these straightforward cases of 'supersensory perception' are probably the best starting point. We know, for example, that the human body is capable of feats that seem totally unbelievable. In the late 19th century, a hypnotist named Carl Hansen made a specialty of compelling his subjects to become as rigid as a board. Then the head would be placed on one chair and the feet on another, after which two men could stand on the stomach as if on a plank. One person who witnessed the same feat in recent years—the novelist Henry Green—describes how a commercial traveller hypnotized his wife, then invited Green and a friend to sit on her as she lay across two chairs. He comments that her muscles were completely rigid. A few seconds later, the commercial traveller snapped his fingers, and the woman instantly recovered, none the worse for her ordeal. In recent years, many scientists of Randi's sceptical persuasion have insisted that hypnosis is an illusion. These accounts make plain that it is not.

The Scottish poet Hugh McDiarmid once remarked that the basis of his life's work was the impression produced on him by the comment that we only use about one-fifth of our brains. He determined that he would spend his life trying to use at least *some* of the other four-fifths. Here again, we seem to have some kind of starting point for a theory of the paranormal.

We may begin, then, by assuming (as Lombroso did) that the explanation of these peculiar feats lies in some kind of perfectly normal extension of our physical powers. Lombroso pointed out that our senses all operate through the nerves, and therefore there is nothing so extraordinary about a girl being able to smell through her heel or read through her stomach.

Lombroso's nerve theory seems to fit the case of Hu Lian, as well as that of the schoolboy Tang Yu, who apparently possessed X-ray vision, so that he was able to see a packet of cigarettes in the pocket of a friend.

But then, Tang told the investigator that he did not see the cigarette packet with his eyes but "through his brain." It seems fairly clear that he would be unable to read the messages on balls of paper that were placed in his ear by any kind of 'X-ray' faculty. And this applies even more to Xiao Ping, who was able to read the message on balls of paper as he chewed them up.

These examples do not 'disprove' Lombroso's nerve theory, but they indicate that it is inadequete. What is involved seems to be a kind of 'screen' in the brain on which the psychic 'sees' the words or the cigarette packet. And this faculty has been traditionally labelled 'clairvoyance.' A clairvoyant is a person who 'knows' things that are happening in other times and other places. This definition can easily be stretched to include seeing the words on a ball of paper in one's ear or mouth.

Lombroso also tried to extend his 'nerve force' theory to mediums like Eusapia Palladino, who could cause objects to levitate. But he had to admit that it failed to explain the cases of precognition he studied for example, a doctor who foresaw the great fire of 1894 and persuaded his family to sell their shares in the insurance company that would have to meet the claims, or the woman who heard a voice telling her that her child was in danger and fetched her indoors half an hour before a train jumped the rails and plowed through the spot where her daughter had been playing. The woman herself believed that some dead relative had warned her of the danger, and on the whole, that explanation seemed just as reasonable as the notion that human beings *can* foresee the future and that therefore time is somehow unreal. But then, mediums have always maintained that time is unreal and that the dead are somehow 'above time.'

The penultimate case in this book makes us once again aware of the inadequacy of our usual paradigms. A girl called Xiong can apparently write on paper in a sealed box, using colored pens that lie in front of her (untouched) on the table. No theory of 'nerve force'—or any other kind of force known to science—can explain this. The same applies to the last case—the ability of a youth called Zhang to make pills fall through the bottom of a sealed bottle without breaking it. In the mid-19th century, pioneers of psychical research tried to explain such phenomena by positing a 'fourth dimension' that could overcome the problem of 'interpenetration of matter.' But even if Zhang is somehow making use of the fourth dimension as he shakes the bottle, this still fails to explain *how* he does it.

In spite of all his attempts to remain within the bounds of science, Lombroso found himself tumbling into the twilit world of the 'occult'—an experience that is common to most students of the paranormal, including myself. After studying mediums, he turned his attention to witchdoctors and shamans, who could produce the same phenomena. Without exception, they insisted that they did it with the help of 'spirits.' And there eventually came a point when Lombroso decided that this was, indeed, the simplest explanation.

If we turn to the other chapters in the present book, we can begin to understand why Lombroso capitulated to what Freud called "the black tide of occultism." Scepticism is the *sine qua non* of science, but explaining Mirabelli, Palladino, Indridason and Matylda in terms of Cartesian doubt is like trying to explain a television picture in terms of Cartesian mechanics. Alexander Imich's experience with Matylda is typical. When Imich—then in his late twenties—went to Wloclawek to see a medium in action, the phenomena were so violent that he had no doubt they were faked. Soon he had to revise his opinion.

> Thus, I suddenly found myself back in the true wonderland which I had left, with pride but also some regret, when I was seven or eight. I had left it, having discovered that the supernatural was but an invention of the grown-ups whose perfidy I got to know then. Now it appeared that people from my childhood were speaking the truth—though they did not know it. It appeared that all those negations of common sense—ghosts, phantoms, the supernatural—really did exist; it seemed that the power we were dreaming of was no fiction but truest reality. This thought made my eyes dilate with fear, my hair raise; a feeling of eeriness pervaded my whole being.

Chairs were pulled from under sitters and flew around the room, a hand scratched his head and pulled his hair, a girl was dragged on to the table, which was also shaken by blows like a cannonade, and 'apports' fell out of the air. It is hardly surprising that Imich's scepticism was soon vanquished.

But, typically, when Imich accompanied Matylda to London, to be studied by Harry Price—who could have given her worldwide publicity—nothing happened. Once again, James's Law came into operation. The likeliest assumption seems to be that Matylda's nervousness caused a blockage in the channel through which the manifestation occurred, like a nervous soprano who cannot sing a note. This is, of course, the problem that makes it so difficult to study mediums in the laboratory.

Let us suppose that, having read the chapters on Mirabelli, Matylda, Indridason and Modrzejewski—and had your fill of marvels—you concede that there *is* something to be explained. Where does that leave us? Here, I think, is the point at which we encounter the problem that has given the 'paranormal' such a bad name. The Fox sisters jumped straight from poltergeist phenomena into a new religion called Spiritualism, which was simply a 'Spirit-ized' version of Christianity. And the early Spiritualists believed implicitly in the connection between paranormal phenomena and Christianity. In Brazil, Kardec's *Spirits' Book* was accepted as a religious scripture, along with the Old and New Testaments. And since, in the eyes of science, Spiritualism is merely a belief-phenomenon, with no more *a priori* validity than Mormonism or Scientology, this religious dimension was quite unacceptable. As far as parapsychology is concerned, it was a case of guilt by association.

My own experience is sufficiently typical to be worth describing. As a child—during the Second World War—I was deeply impressed by newspaper accounts describing the 'return' of dead soldiers and airmen. An avid reader, I ransacked the local library for books on haunted houses and life after death. My grandmother, who was a Spiritualist, persuaded me to accompany her to the local Spiritualist church. This I found just as boring as the Sunday school that my parents forced me to attend (so they could sleep on Sunday afternoons) and failed to turn up a second time. At this point, my mother bought me a chemistry set—for my tenth birthday— and a book called *The Marvels and Mysteries of Science* which turned my attention from haunted houses to distant galaxies. The world of spirits fled like a ghost at cockcrow, and for the next six years or so, my only ambition was to become a scientist. I wrote my first book—*A Manual of General Science*—in my fourteenth year.

At the age of sixteen, a book on popular philosophy and a radio performance on Shaw's *Man and Superman* widened my horizons. I also began to read poetry and attend symphony concerts. By the age of seventeen, I had decided to abandon science and become a writer.

The period that followed was the hardest of my life. I became a kind of tramp or drifter, taking casual jobs; I spent six months in the RAF; I married and separated; and I went to London and began writing a book called *The Outsider* in the reading room of the British Museum. This study of 'alienated' romantics was published when I was twenty- four and brought me instant notoriety. Translated into a dozen or so languages, it also solved the problem of how to keep myself alive.

The central question of *The Outsider* has been expressed by H.G. Wells in his title *What Are We To Do With Our Lives*? This, it seemed to me, was the only question worth asking. Romantics like Goethe,

Wordsworth, Blake, Hoffman had experienced 'moments of vision' in which the meaning of human existence seemed suddenly obvious. It involved evolution, the attempt to become more than—as Nietzsche put it—"human, all too human." 'Outsiders' like Van Gogh experienced moments of pure affirmation in which life seemed self-evidently good, and Van Gogh expressed such a vision in paintings like 'The Starry Night.' Yet Van Gogh committed suicide, leaving a note that read, "Misery will never end." Was the vision of affirmation a delusion? Or was the suicide an act of stupidity?

When, in the late 1960s, I was commissioned to write a book on 'the occult,' I expected to find it 90% wishful thinking and self-delusion. In fact, I quickly realized that the evidence for telepathy, extra-sensory perception, clairvoyance, 'mind over matter' (PK), even precognition, was overwhelming. But, while keeping an open mind, I was strongly inclined to doubt the evidence for life after death. I accepted poltergeist phenomena because I accepted the current explanation of 'RSPK'— recurrent spontaneous psychokinesis—the notion that a 'poltergeist' is, in fact, the unconscious mind of a disturbed teenager. In general, writing *The Occult* confirmed my basic notion that human beings use only a small part of their potential.

When I came to write a book on poltergeists in 1981, I changed my mind. Guy Playfair's book, *The Flying Cow*, describing his researches in Brazil, argued that poltergeists are—in most cases—spirits. And when a girl in Pontefract described to me how she had been dragged upstairs by the throat by a poltergeist, I suddenly knew with total certainty that Playfair was correct: this was *not* her 'unconscious mind.'

I was still unhappy about believing in the existence of 'spirits'— much preferring the RSPK theory—but the facts forced me to accept it. Yet, oddly enough, I remained doubtful about the notion of life after death. Perhaps 'spirits' were simply disembodied energies of which we are ignorant. But when a publisher asked me to write a book called *Afterlife* and I settled down to study some of the immense literature on the subject, I soon had to admit that the evidence for 'survival' is overwhelming. I felt rather like the philosopher C.D. Broad, who said that while he accepted the evidence for survival, he didn't much care one way or the other. I still don't care much one way or the other, and 'Spiritualism'—as a religion—still leaves me cold. I accept the extinction of consciousness every night when I fall asleep, and see no reason why death should not be much the same. Yet the kind of evidence contained in this book seems to me to point fairly conclusively to the existence of 'spirits' and to some kind of survival of death.

This, I agree, still leaves me with the question that has preoccupied me since my teens: what are we doing here, and what are we supposed to do now we are here?

One thing seems to be very clear: that 'normal' human consciousness is, in fact, thoroughly subnormal. It is like a very dim bulb with which we do our best to illuminate a vast cave. For some odd reason, there are certain moments in which this bulb glows like a magnesium flare, and we glimpse remote corners of the cave. These we describe as 'mystical' experiences. In fact, mystical experiences are simply a recognition that there is something badly wrong with 'normal consciousness.' Where human beings are concerned, the main problem of life seems to be a kind of 'underfunding' of energy—like a business that never becomes successful because it is under-financed.

I suspect that the solution to this problem does not lie in religious belief or altruism but in a fundamental certainty of the *meaningfulness* of our existence, a certainty that leads to a continuous effort to extend our powers. The most important legacy that anyone can leave to his fellow human beings is a legacy of courage, purpose, optimism: the assertion that in spite of the weakness, stupidity and ignorance that are a part of our animal legacy, we only begin to understand ourselves when we recognize that the ultimate destiny of human beings is to evolve toward something altogether more godlike.

Which explains why, as I wrote *The Occult*, I became so fascinated by the paranormal. The problem with human consciousness is a certain narrowness, a certain 'close-upness,' which deprives us of meaning, just as standing too close to a canvas in a picture gallery would prevent us from actually seeing 'the picture.' We suffer from a 'worm's-eye view' of existence. Yet, in certain moments, this is suddenly transformed into a 'bird's-eye view' in which we see life as infinitely complex and infinitely exciting. Unfortunately, as the romantics discovered, the 'moments of vision' cannot be re-created at will; they come and go when they want to. What *can* be relied upon is the power of reason—that slow, plodding ability to add two and two to make four, which has led to the creation of our technological civilization. Reason—in the form of slide rules, maps, log tables—has created the most complex civilization the world has ever seen. It has taught us to 'pin down' knowledge with the use of words. Yet all our knowledge has failed to free us from waking up every morning to a worm's-eye view of existence. Intellectually, we are birds; 'existentially,' we remain worms.

The problem with the worm's-eye view is that it breeds a certain irritable scepticism. There is a mind-set in which a person who has spent his whole life in the same village *does not believe* in the existence of Hong Kong and Vladivostock. He may say he does; but deep down inside, he has no more reason to believe it than he has to believe in giants and fairies. And this narrowness—which is common to all of us—limits human imagination and, therefore, the human intellect.

In *The Outsider* I was concerned with romantic art and literature as instruments for the liberation of the human imagination—as well as with certain unpleasant side-effects, such as depression and suicide. Compared with this liberation, the question of spirits and ectoplasm and floating trumpets seemed trivial. I could perfectly well understand why Thomas Henry Huxley attended a seance, watched the extraordinary manifestations, then shrugged his shoulders and refused to discuss it further.

By the time I finished writing *The Occult*, I had recognized the nature of my error. If telepathy, clairvoyance, precognition and psychokinesis existed—as I was now certain they did—then they bore witness to the unrecognized potentialities of the human psyche just as much as the genius of Shakespeare or Mozart. Moreover, although I have always regarded myself as 'ESP-thick,' the study of these potentialities made me aware of how far they impinge on our everyday lives. For example, there was the day when I needed to check some reference to alchemy but was not sure where to find it. Moreover, I was tired—it was the end of a long day's writing—and disinclined to search through volume after volume. But I forced myself to get to my feet and look on the shelf of alchemical volumes facing my desk. In fact, I pulled out the wrong volume—but the right volume fell off the shelf and landed on the floor, open at the right page.

A few years later, when trying to decide whether I should write an article about Poe's *Mystery of Marie Roget* or about synchronicity, I opened Poe's story, and read:

> There are few persons ... who have not occasionally been startled into a vague yet thrilling half-credence in the supernatural, by *coincidences* of so seemingly marvelous a character that, as *mere* coincidences, the intellect has been unable to receive them.

I recognized immediately that this was a clear indication that I should write the article on synchronicity. And the moment I began to write, the most preposterous synchronic-ities began to occur—all of which I incorporated into the article. It was almost as if some power that was unable to reveal itself was determined to make me aware that it really existed.

This is why I believe that, at this point in human evolution, the paranormal has taken on a new importance. It is no longer a question of credulity or incredulity, but of understanding human potential. And no one who reads this volume will be able to lay it down without feeling an interesting—and perhaps frightening—enlargement of his sense of human potential.

Introduction

DR. ALEXANDER IMICH
NEW YORK, NY

The psychic world with its representatives—saints, prophets, yogis, shamans, witch doctors, other spiritual adepts, and psychics—is as old as the most primitive human societies. However, parapsychology—the science that studies these anomalous phenomena—is fairly young. It was born out of a remote sequence of events that took place in the last century not very far from New York City. In 1847, in Hydesville, a small town in New York state, raps in the walls and the furniture of a house inhabited by the Fox family were heard. Soon a communication with a mysterious power was established and questions answered by means of an established alphabet. The mysterious rapper presented himself as the spirit of a man who was murdered in the house. The rapping occurred in the presence of two Fox sisters; they were called mediums—intermediaries between our world and the world of 'spirits.'

Thus Spiritualism was born and rapidly gained wide popularity in the Western world. Soon other mediums appeared in several countries and became the object of public interest and scientific study. These great mediums of the Victorian era produced physical phenomena, i.e., movements and levitations of persons and objects, materializations of human beings or human shapes, apports of various objects, touches of the participants, a variety of light phenomena, playing of musical instruments, human and animal voices, noises and other acoustic phenomena, fragrances, etc. Such macro-phenomena, as opposed to micro-phenomena that can be detected only by means of statistical analysis, were the main subject of parapsychological investigation.

Mediums usually consider themselves merely as intermediaries between this world and the world of 'spirit.' They do not claim to have mastery over the phenomena they produce. As some state, the phenomena "just happen" in their presence. Many of these events occur more or less spontaneously; their study is consequently very difficult and tends to be more observational than experimental. Experiments are arranged to test a hypothesis or to answer a specific question. Parapsychology, as every beginning science, had to start by collecting facts and objects it intended to study; searching and observing were its first steps. Thus, the first period of metapsychology, as it was called in Europe, has to be best described as a semi-experimental phase. The close of this great phase of study came soon after Hitler seized power in Germany in early 1930. In the rest of Europe the events of World War II concluded the demise of organized parapsychological activities.

In 1927, Joseph B. Rhine at Duke University attempted a new beginning. The distinguished psychologist William McDougall called this new discipline "parapsychology." Parapsychology was not acknowledged by official science, therefore Rhine's immediate goal became its recognition by academic circles. Consequently, he had to accept the rigid procedural canons of experimental science. The achievements of the European past, since they did not carry enough evidential proof, were christened "anecdotal" and had to be ignored. Statistics became the chief test of veridicality in this second beginning. Card-guessing, then dice-throwing were the main subjects of experimentation. Under the false assumption that the paranormal phenomena can be produced on demand any time and anywhere, research was transferred to the laboratory.

As time passed, an important body of information about large-scale psychokinetic (PK) phenomena, gathered by European scientists during nearly half a century, and temporarily excluded for tactical reasons, has become forgotten by parapsychology researchers in this country. Because of the limitation of their pursuit, many present day psi researchers have never witnessed a genuine paranormal happening. Paradoxically, a leading researcher told me that the greatest event in his life would be to witness the bending of a spoon that is not being touched by the psychic.

It could be said that broader public interest in what are today called "parapsychological subjects" started in this country. Interest in the experimental study of macro-phenomena withered so much that when Uri Geller displayed an entirely new type of psychokinetic phenomena—the bending of cutlery—our parapsychological community did not show much enthusiasm for a serious study of his capacities. And after all of Geller's successful public performances and successes in mineral exploration, after dozens of children—called mini-Gellers—around the world were bending spoons even better than Uri, I still hear from psi professionals: "Do you really believe that Geller is a genuine psychic?"

Spontaneous paranormal phenomena appear in an uncounted variety of forms. Their elimination from research programs has meant limiting the investigation to a narrow, non-representational aspect of the field. Unraveling the enigmas of the paranormal is a task much different from, and possibly more difficult, than solving mysteries of the atom. Philosopher-parapsychologist, Stephen Braude, suggests that the cases of laboratory psi might be only degenerate cases of real-life psi, and presuming they are the true model of the psychokinetic phenomena is one of the reasons for the standstill of PK research. Braude does not think well of parapsychological experiments in general. In his words they "are designed merely to elicit contrived and artificially conspicuous manifestations of (psi) capacities."

As with other psychological traits, psychic capacities too are inheritable. Often in the family of a prominent psychic, some psychic events occurred in the life of his or her mother, grandfather or uncle. Geller's children seem to have inherited their father's talents. In Poland the medieval inquisition did not exterminate all psychically gifted individuals. Currently several Polish mediums, their remote heirs, are internationally known. I had the good and rare chance to witness there, in the country of my birth, physical phenomena considered today as legendary. It is clear to me that intelligent people—who have never experienced life-size paranormal events, utterly strange and eerie as they are, and so different from everyday reality—must be distrustful, suspicious, and hesitant to recognize their veracity. In a world full of swindlers, impostors, cheats, charlatans, and frauds, many of us think that only naive children can believe in the incredible tales of the paranormal.

This disbelief is harmful. It delays the intellectual and spiritual maturation of the human race. Why and how?

Parapsychology is the only scientific discipline studying the perennial question each thinking being asks: do we cease or do we still exist after the death of our body? Imagine for a moment how much human life would change if this question were answered in the positive! How much easier it would be to live through the pain and misery of our existence on this planet, if we were sure these were only temporary ills. This one task alone, among parapsychology's many others, is of such great importance—not for society's technical benefit or for any individual's material well-being, but for the mere happiness of each one of us—that I do not hesitate to consider the study of parapsychology to be more important than all other disciplines. In the following pages, my colleagues and I report to you, our readers, about the incredible events we and others have witnessed. It is our hope that these accounts will increase your awareness of and interest in the miraculous world that exists parallel to our everyday reality. To our professional colleagues we hope to convey the value and importance of the study of real-life phenomena even when this would require going out of the laboratory.

Isaak Bashevis-Singer, a modern mystic greatly interested in the scientific investigation of his mystical realm, wanted to write a preface to this book he knew I was editing. Unfortunately, the book was not ready when he left this world. The literary maverick, Colin Wilson, himself much involved in the paranormal, agreed to carry out the task; we, all co-authors, greatly appreciate his contribution.

Appendix of Photographs

Several of the phantoms shown in the following photographs, including the Pithecanthropus, as well as the phantoms depicted in the sketches, have been observed under conditions of full control by French, British, and Polish scientists. The veracity of these hard to believe phenomena will become evident, or, at least more plausible, after reading the Teofil Modrzejewski chapter in this book.

These photographs and sketches were taken from the book *Wspomnienia z Seansow z Medjum Frankiem Kluskim* (Reminiscences from the seances with the medium Franek Kluski) by Norbert Okolowicz, Warsaw Poland, 1926.

Alexander Imich

Fig. 1.

Fig. 2.

Figure 1 Pithecanthropus' crop of hair near medium's head.
Figure 2 Bird of prey on medium's shoulder.

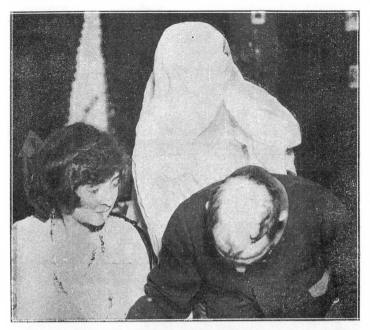

Fig. 3.

Fig. 4

Figure 3   White phantom behind the medium.
Figure 4   Pithecanthropus' crop of hair on medium's head.

TABLICA III

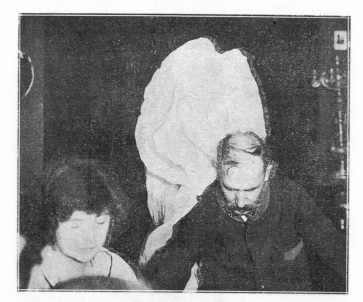

Fig. 5.

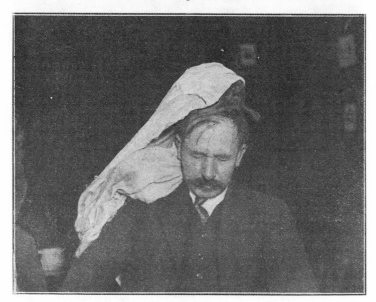

Fig. 6

Figure 5   White phantom behind the medium.
Figure 6   Top of Pithecanthropus' crop of hair on medium's head.

TABLICA IV

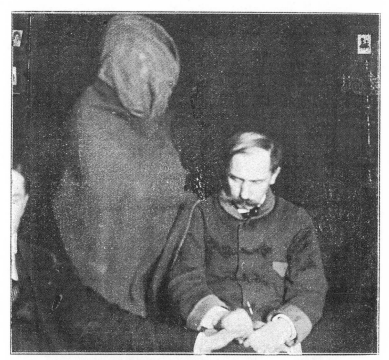

Fig. 7.

Fig. 8.

Figure 7 & 8   Phantom in grey clothing near the medium.

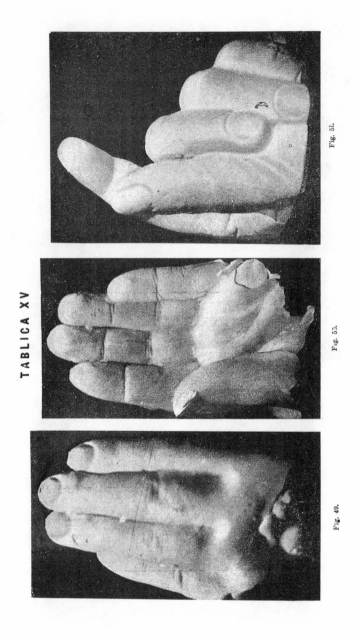

Figure 49-51   Plaster of Paris castings of paraffin wax forms.

TABLICA XVI.

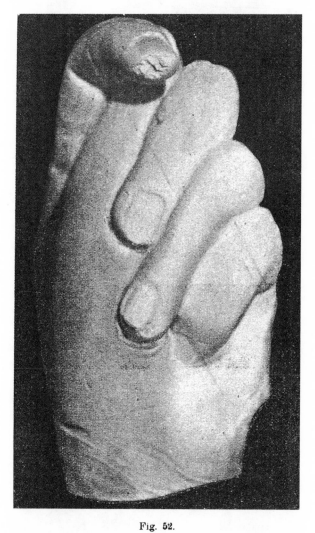

Fig. 52.

Figure 52   Plaster of Paris casting of paraffin wax form.

TABLICA XVII

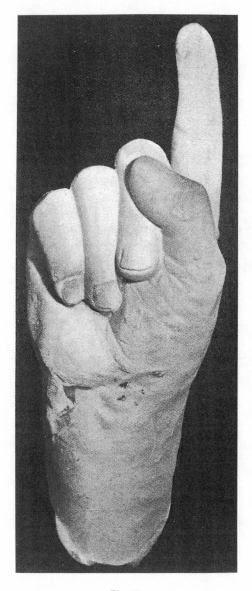

Fig. 53.

Figure 53   Plaster of Paris casting of paraffin wax form.

TABLICA XVIII

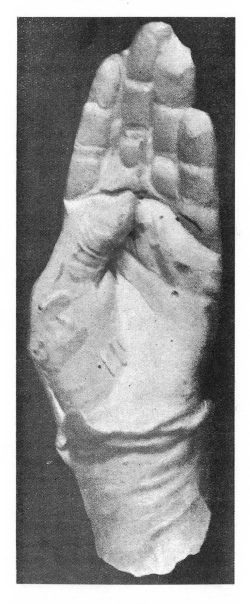

Fig. 54.

Figure 54   Plaster of Paris casting of paraffin wax form.

TABLICA XXIX

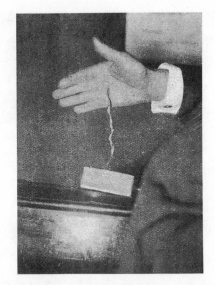

Fig. 77.

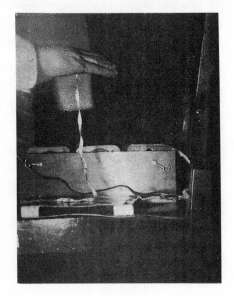

Fig. 78.

Figure 77 & 78
Ectoplasmic cord emerging from the palm of the medium.

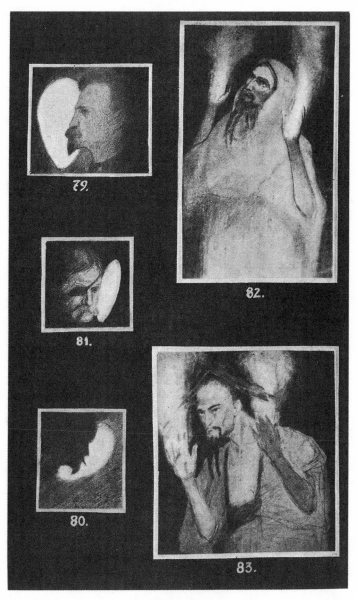

Fig. 79—83.

Figure 82 Picture of the "Assyrian high priest."

TABLICA XXXI

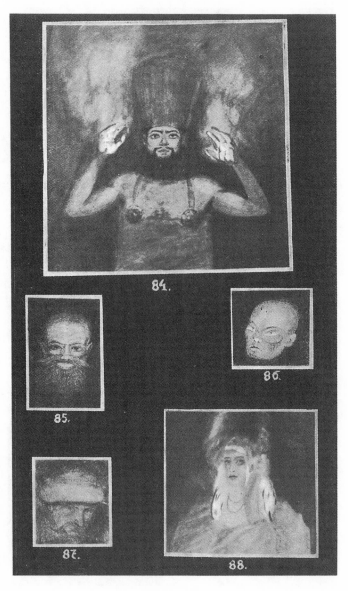

Fig. 84—88.

Figure 84   Picture of the "Chaldean priest."
Figure 85   Picture of an "exotic laughing man."
Figure 88   Picture of a "woman with pearls."

TABLICA XXXII

Fig. 89—93.

Figure 89   Picture of a "buddist."
Figure 90   Picture of a "young man with the sign of the cross."
Figure 91   Picture of a "hermit."
Figure 93   Picture of a "Polish knight."

Mirabelli!!

GUY LYON PLAYFAIR
LONDON, ENGLAND

*I*f everything they say about Carmine Mirabelli is true, he was without doubt the most spectacular physical effects medium in history. If *anything* they say about him is true, he should not be omitted from any survey of physical mediumship, and having heard some of the things they were still saying about him more than twenty years after his death, I find it difficult to think of his name without a pair of exclamation marks after it.

Mirabelli was surely the medium to end all mediums. You name it, and he is said to have done it: automatic writing in over thirty languages living or dead, speaking in numerous foreign tongues, materializing objects and people, transporting anything from a bunch of flowers to large pieces of furniture (including levitation of himself even when strapped to a chair), producing impressions of spirit hands in trays of flour or wax inside locked drawers, dematerializing anything in sight, himself included.

He could, they say, contact dead relatives of friends and paint portraits of them. He could sing and play the piano or violin with

1

considerable skill while in trance, although he had no musical training. He could write a message of several pages in a few minutes while chatting away at the same time—in another language. He did, in fact, just about everything any other medium had ever done, doing so for something like forty years.

Moreover, he normally did his thing in broad daylight or in a well-lit room in front of up to 500 witnesses. He seemed to have no objections to having his house searched or to being handcuffed and tied to a chair, or to being investigated (up to a point) by all and sundry.

Fortunately for posterity, many of his feats were witnessed by a great many people, some of whom were still able to recall them for me in detail. Two of his closest friends published a great deal of material about him, based on minutes of meetings at the various centers where he held forth. These were Miguel Karl, a businessman of German descent who divided his time between selling sewing machines and studying Vedanta, spending a year in India with Swami Yogananda Saraswati; and Eurico de Goes (pronounced *goyce*), a highly literate and intelligent man who became organizer and director of São Paulo's first municipal public library.

De Goes, one of Brazil's first serious psychical researchers, had a special reason for attaching himself to Mirabelli. His attractive wife had died young, and he was forever trying to make contact with her. Though he never managed a complete materialization, he satisfied himself that she really had contacted him through Mirabelli's mediumship on a number of occasions, in the course of which he witnessed and described more than a hundred materializations of other entities. Some of these lasted over an hour, allowing themselves to be examined by doctors and prodded all over. Mirabelli was, de Goes concluded, a 'veritable laboratory' for the researcher, and though he was not researched as thoroughly as he should have been, we must be grateful to his faithful Boswell for the great trouble he took to record his hero's feats. There is a large amount of literature on Mirabelli, but only de Goes's well-written 471-page tome[1] is of much value to modern researchers, and most of the information in this chapter is based on it, except where otherwise specified.

Mirabelli was in his lifetime, and remains today, a highly controversial figure, and since his death the legend has expanded in all directions. Many stories told about him are almost certainly untrue or gross exaggerations, yet even when these have been discounted (as many were before the writing of this chapter), a residue of evidence remains that suggests he deserves his place here.

The Beginning

Carmine Mirabelli (who later called himself Carlos to avoid confusion with the Brazilian girl's name Carmen) was born in 1889 in the town of Botucatu, some 160 miles from São Paulo. His father was a well-to-do Protestant pastor from Italy, whom de Goes generously describes as "a man with the kindest heart although imbued with Lutheran doctrines," and among his many illustrious ancestors were a president of the Italian royal court, an army general and a parliamentary deputy.

He was educated in his home town and at a primary school in the nearby town of Itu, where he showed a precocious intellect, although like many sons of immigrants he never quite mastered either his ancestors' or his adopted country's language. He learned some English and possibly also some German but certainly became no skilled linguist.

He showed an early ability, after leaving school, for making money in a deal involving a large consignment of gas mantles from Germany; and throughout his life he never had to rely on his mediumship to earn a good living—mostly by buying and selling land. He undoubtedly charged for his services on some occasions, one of his own leaflets clearly stating his very large fee for personal consultations, but it is also quite certain that he gave a lot of money away and was a generous and kind-hearted person.

His mediumship seems to have hit him (literally) while he was in his early twenties, working in the Clark shoe store in São Paulo. According to often repeated legend, boxes of shoes would fly off their shelves while the young salesman would be seized by bouts of chills, visions, depression, neurasthenia and assorted other fits. Obviously, he had to leave; and it is said that when he did, some of the shoe boxes went out into the street after him.

The general opinion was that young Carmine had gone crazy, and he was duly committed to the Juquery asylum for the insane, where he was closely observed by two doctors, Felipe Aché and Franco da Rocha, after whom the asylum is now named.

"He is not a normal man," Dr. Aché declared, "but nor is he sick." Referring to the strange things that were beginning to happen whenever Mirabelli was around, he decided they were "the result of the radiation of nervous forces that we all have, but that Mr. Mirabelli has in extraordinary excess."

Dr. Franco da Rocha later described what kind of a show Mirabelli could put on even at this early stage of his career:

"He placed a skull on top of a glass, and at my request it began to revolve, so that at a given moment both skull and glass fell over on the table. I replaced the objects in their former positions, and the phenomenon was repeated. I did so yet again, and the same thing happened. Nor was that all; as I held the skull I felt something strange in my hands, something fluid, as if a globular liquid were touching my palm. When I concentrated my attention further, I saw something similar to an irradiation pass over the skull, as when you rapidly expose a mirror to luminous rays."

After a stay of only nineteen days, Mirabelli was let out of Juquery asylum and went to live in the seaside town of Santos. Here, he became the representative of a homeopathic medicine company and opened his own charitable organization, the São Luiz House of Charity. Miguel Karl records that this was kept going for fourteen years at a total cost to its founder of 751,000 milreis, during which time donations amounted to only 12,628 milreis. Photographs of the center show that it was well attended by hordes of both rich and poor in search of physical or psychical diagnosis. For such an organization to last so long is quite a feat in Brazil, where Spiritist centers appear and disappear overnight.

Eurico de Goes knew Mirabelli well for over twenty years, after they first met by chance in a São Paulo hotel in 1916. He describes him as a typical Italian—excitable, impulsive and impatient; but also tolerant and warm-hearted, a lover of good food, animals and opera. He led a somewhat Bohemian life, being especially fond of going for long drives at night in the countryside. He was a big spender who would think nothing of buying ten suits or a dozen pairs of shoes at a time, only to give most of them away.

Despite his flamboyance and evident vanity, two qualities notably lacking in orthodox Brazilian Spiritists, Mirabelli fully embraced the Spiritist cause, founding and running a number of centers in São Paulo and Rio de Janeiro. One of these was nominally headed by a distinguished public health official, Dr. Thadeu de Medeiros. Though one of the main purposes of those various centers seems to have been to promote Mirabelli himself, many who attended them were converted to Spiritism as a result. Modern Spiritists in Brazil certainly do not approve of Mirabelli or his methods, but they grant that he was an effective evangelist.

Incredible Phenomena

Throughout his career as a medium, Mirabelli was regularly witnessed by doctors and scientists, several of whose names are attached to the minutes of meetings reprinted by de Goes. He was also watched at work by a popular conjuror, Carlos Gardonne Ramos, who stated that "it is entirely impossible for these (phenomena) to be achieved by sleight of hand."

Foreign observers who saw him in action at least once at various stages of his life included Bruno Heckmann and Johann Reichenbach from Berlin, Italian chemist Tito Guarnieri, envoys May Walker and Theodore Besterman from the American and British societies for psychical research respectively, and most important of all, the eminent Leipzig philosopher and Society for Psychical Research president (1926-27) Hans Driesch.

May Walker described "the best telekinesis I have ever seen" after a comparatively mild session in which rose petals floated from the ceiling, bottles jumped up and down on a table, and a fan began to "wriggle about, as if alive" in her hand, while her hat went round in circles on her head. She was convinced that some of the phenomena were real.

Mr. Besterman attended at least five sessions in August 1934, during which (according to the minutes, which de Goes reports him as having signed) flowers materialized, bottles on a table jumped around, one even hopping onto the floor, a picture left the wall to float in mid-air and land abruptly on someone's head, a chair slid along the floor for about ten feet, the front door key drifted out of its lock, and Mirabelli dashed off a learned written discourse in French, writing nearly 1800 words in fifty-three minutes.

All of this led Mr. Besterman to declare (again according to de Goes, who quotes him in English) that he found "Mr. Mirabelli's phenomena of the greatest interest.... Many of them were unique of their kind." Later, however, he changed his mind, as we shall see.

Eurico de Goes writes that phenomena like those mentioned above came to be mere routine, though now and then Mirabelli would introduce such novelties as asking witnesses to indicate an unripe orange growing in the garden, then to go and pick it and find a rare coin embedded inside.

On one occasion a businessman friend asked for advice about a letter he had sent to New York. Mirabelli told him exactly how his business deal was going, and when the reply came he sat down and dashed off translations in Portuguese, French, German and Hebrew without even looking at the original in English.

For a special session in 1933 held at nine in the morning, Mirabelli was handcuffed, his feet bound, and then asked to repeat phenomena he had produced at a previous meeting under artificial light. He promptly obliged; freshly plucked flowers floated in through a locked and sealed window, a religious statue weighing eight kilos drifted out again, while Mirabelli began to talk in Arabic to one of the investigators, who identified the voice as that of his mother who had died in Beirut twenty-eight years previously. He became a Spiritist on the spot.

A tray of flour was placed inside a drawer, which was locked and sealed, and after fifteen minutes three loud raps were heard. Opening the drawer, witnesses saw the clear impression of a human hand on the flour.

The lid of a water cooler took off and landed among the audience, and when one man went over to examine the cooler, it exploded in his face, soaking him with water.

Finally, it was time to read the minutes of the previous meeting, at which point the group secretary, the son of a German, found he had left his spectacles at home.

"Wait, son, I'll bring them right away from the room in your house where you left them," came a voice speaking German, adding: "I am your father and your protector." The spectacles promptly appeared in the secretary's hands.

Mirabelli seemed to run a kind of lost-property office for his friends. While driving from São Paulo down to Santos with him one day, Eurico de Goes remembered he had left his umbrella behind. As they arrived in the medium's house, it promptly dropped from the ceiling. Other property recovered via Mirabelli's unfathomable talents included a stolen gold crucifix, a fur wrap somebody had left on a bus, and several lost or stolen documents.

Some of his antics seemed no more than harmless jokes staged to prove the reality of such phenomena. When British poet and diplomat Sir Douglas Ainslie turned up for a session in a private São Paulo house in 1928, the first thing he saw on the hall table was the travelling clock he had left inside a suitcase in his hotel room. During the evening, the lady of the house mislaid her spectacles, which were later found in the home of one of her guests.

Many phenomena seemed entirely pointless—objects simply flying around the room or moving from one shelf to another, sometimes hitting people in the process and even hurting them quite badly. De Goes was once struck on the arm by a stone, while Mirabelli himself had a large picture smashed over his head, glass and all, at a public meeting (held in a center that was not one of his own).

Mirabelli himself would claim that inferior spirits were responsible for this sort of thing, using his power like a magnet or focal point for their pranks. This is a theory sometimes advanced today to account for poltergeist phenomena in general, and the concept of 'like attracts like' with regard to mediums and the spirits they attract is a widely held one. Had Mirabelli been a wicked man, which he most certainly was not, he might well have destroyed the whole of São Paulo in an earthquake of Biblical dimensions.

Sometimes the atmosphere was thoroughly gruesome. At one session, a human hand materialized, and Mirabelli announced that he saw the skeleton of a lady who had been buried minus her head. This, he explained, had been removed for study as she had been mentally disturbed before her death. He named the exact plot in São Paulo's Araçá cemetery where she had been buried, and said that her remains had been secretly removed and were being kept at her son's house.

At the following session, after the family in question had indeed found the box of remains to be missing from the grave, a terrible smell of decomposed corpse filled the room, as bones began to materialize one after the other and fall on people's heads.

De Goes managed to control his feelings, and his stomach, to note what appeared. There were, he meticulously recorded, "humeri, radii, ulnas, carpuses, a metacarpus, fingers, ribs, parts of the vertebral column, femurs, tibias, tarsi, metatarsi, anklebones—and hair."

It was, he recalled, like something out of Edgar Allan Poe.

Other Mirabellian feats read more like science fiction. One evening, after a long and tiring session, he asked for the lights to be switched off, and then with two men holding him firmly by the arms he began to glow all over, lighting up the whole room. Another time he levitated into the air while handcuffed, whereupon there was a sound of falling handcuffs as he disappeared altogether, reappearing in his nearby office which was locked from the outside, where startled witnesses burst in to find him stretched out on a chaise longue and chanting away in Latin.

But the most incredible Mirabelli feat of all—one that must strain anybody's frontiers of belief—concerns the occasion when he went with a group of friends to São Paulo's Luz railway station to catch the train to São Vicente, about fifty miles away. On the platform, he simply vanished and after fifteen minutes his worried friends managed to get through by telephone to the house they were heading for in São Vicente. Mirabelli, they were told, had been there for about fifteen minutes.

I cannot substantiate this story, but I am surprised at the number of people I have met who believe it. Eurico de Goes includes it in his book as if it were quite a normal thing for Mirabelli to do, and it should be mentioned that de Goes claimed to have investigated a number of mediums other than Mirabelli and been impressed by none of them. He was constantly on the lookout for fraud, he says, and records that whenever he was a guest at the medium's home he would always check everything personally before going to bed, searching the whole house to find an unlocked door or unbarred window.

De Goes had nothing to gain except ridicule for his championing of a well-known and controversial medium; for during the twenties and thirties there was a great deal of hostility in the press towards anything remotely psychic or occult, and Mirabelli bore the full brunt of it, though de Goes claims that no Brazilian who actually troubled to witness him ever said or wrote a word against him. Even some Catholic priests, often hostile then as now towards any form of Spiritism, could be won over by the medium's charm and apparent sincerity of purpose. A certain Father Jose Maria de Castro wrote in Mirabelli's private scrapbook: "Mirabelli is a man of faith whom the chiefs of the church in Brazil cannot condemn without knowing him."

Condemned he was, all the same, and he somehow survived no less than fifteen court appearances, all for allegedly illegal practice of medicine or witchcraft, the former usually consisting of doing no more than 'magnetizing' a bottle of water.

Although he could apparently produce accurate diagnoses of diseases while in trance, Mirabelli does not seem to have attempted to become a conventional Spiritist healer. There was one occasion when he claimed to have received the spirit of a former sufferer from tuberculosis; in front of witnesses he put on a realistic demonstration of a pulmonary hemorrhage, spitting half a litre of very real blood all over the floor, fully recovering in half an hour.

Dr. Thadeu de Medeiros testified that Mirabelli once spotted signs of incipient cardiac lesion and renal disturbance in a patient of his, which helped him considerably in effecting a cure. He also correctly diagnosed a serious condition in the solar plexus of another patient Dr. Medeiros had already examined, coming to the same independent conclusion.

But on the whole, having Mirabelli around the surgery seems to have been more liability than asset; bottles of expensive or even dangerous medicines were liable to leap out of glass-fronted cabinets and fly across the room. "Phenomena like this were frequently observed," the doctor noted. We can understand why he seems to have made little use of his medium friend's services.

As we might expect, Mirabelli's clinical methods during healing were unusual. A prominent society lady calling on him in 1933 reported feeling something invisible touching her near the heart. Oh yes, Mirabelli assured her at once, that would be Dr. Oswaldo Cruz, one of Brazil's most distinguished medical researchers.

"He is saying that you're taking too much of a medicine you're carrying with you," the medium announced. "He is going to..." There was a crash, as a bottle of Atophan was thrown violently against the wall, shattering into small pieces. It was the bottle the lady had been carrying inside her handbag.

"Oswaldo Cruz says," Mirabelli went on, unperturbed, "that you got a prescription from a medium. You can go on taking the medicine that the spirit prescribed for you." Whereupon another bottle, this time of

Antimopolis and also from the startled lady's handbag, was thrown onto the floor without breaking.

There seems to have been no limit to what the man could produce, in or out of trance. His artistic output in the latter condition was fairly impressive: he could paint in a number of different styles, produce portraits of dead people which were identified by surviving relatives (fifty paintings of his were once exhibited in Amsterdam), and also conjure musical phenomena out of thin air. Witnesses recall having heard ethereal concerts in his presence, ranging from snatches of opera to military fanfares, while the musically untrained Mirabelli (who was untrained in practically everything else as well, come to that) would sing lengthy arias in a number of languages, often while doing something else at the same time, like writing or painting. His inspiration could also take a practical turn: once he was lamenting the fact that his record player was out of action, whereupon the machine switched itself on and the needle placed itself on the disc—this before the invention of the automatic turntable.

Controversy over Messages

What, it may be asked, was the point of all this sort of thing? The apparent purpose behind the Mirabelli manifestations was to prove the existence of spirits and the validity of the Spiritist doctrine as formulated by Allan Kardec. This is the purpose of all Spiritist meetings, though nowadays physical phenomena are regarded as rather old-fashioned stuff, no longer needed to support the faith of veteran Kardecists.

The only evidence for Mirabelli's doctrinaire intentions comes from the examples of his automatic writing, many of which have been published in Brazil, and of which I have seen several photocopies but unfortunately no originals. These are thought to exist, but after his death there was some confusion in the family as to who inherited what, and even the two of Mirabelli's children I have been able to locate have no idea where they are.

At one typical 1928 session, Mirabelli dashed off messages purporting to come from Saint-Simon, St. Bernard of Clairvaux and Louis XII (all in French), Martin Luther (German) and a fellow who signs himself G. Knox The Quaker (English).

Saint-Simon comes across in elegant French, making an earnest plea for concentration on the principles of Spiritism and concluding "Voilà, mourir ... et revivre encore, cette est la Loi établie par Allan Kardec" [To die, then, and to live again, this is the law that Allan Kardec laid down].

The others say much the same thing in their own languages, while the final message, from Mr. Knox, concludes: "Therefore I can do no more than confirm all M. Bernard de Clairvaux's doctrines, for its author knows better than I what is truth, as he already reached the lightest places in the sky among the angels and nearer to God than I'm [*sic*]. Good bye. Bible and sword."

Messages would come through in all usual European languages, plus a few less usual ones such as Catalan, Albanian and Bulgarian; also in a number of oriental languages including Chinese. Most of them are neatly written, though spelling mistakes are common, and their subject matter varies enormously. De Goes lists discourses on Great Britain and the Irish Question, Slav psychology, the Russo-Japanese war, inhabitable planets and Buddha among several others. They contain nothing revelationary, but show evidence of more knowledge than a busy man with no special educational qualifications could be expected to have amassed in his spare time.

Some of the messages have an intriguing ring of authenticity. Cromwell, for instance, gives a long and rambling account of a nightmare he had in which King Charles had cut *his* head off, which is quite an entertaining little essay in its own right.

Joan of Arc comes over with a stirring denunciation of the church. "Je nie et renie mille fois," she writes, "la basse et noire croyance qui est l'église catholique, qui malgré avoir été causatrice de ma mort, joue le colin-maillard avec mes cendres et ossements!... La victime d'hier est sanctifiée par ses propres bourreaux et mise sur l'autel" [I deny and disown a thousand times the base and foul belief that is the Catholic church, which despite having been the cause of my death plays hide-and-seek with my ashes and my bones!... Yesterday's victim is sanctified by her own executioners and placed on the altar].

Messages such as these made little impression on the Society for Psychical Research, which noted a collection of them in its Journal for October 1927, dismissing them along with accounts of other Mirabelli miracles as 'preposterous'; hardly a scientific attitude, and especially curious coming from Mrs. Helen Salter, herself a prolific automatic writer and member of the team that produced the celebrated 'Myers cross-correspondences,' some of the best evidence for human survival of bodily death ever gathered.

Another collection of Mirabelliana was reviewed by Theodore Besterman in the SPR Journal.[2] He pointed out reasonably that the messages contained no evidence of supernormal knowledge, but over-stated his case by claiming there was nothing in them beyond the reach of Mirabelli's "linguistic associations and comparatively good education." All witnesses I have interviewed agree without hesitation that Mirabelli could not even speak either of his own languages (Italian and Portuguese) correctly.

A more open-minded attitude was expressed by Dr. E.J. Dingwall, in a review of a German translation of an early Mirabelli book that came out in 1960. He laments the fact that the Mirabelli case "remains another of those unsolved mysteries with which the history of parapsychology abounds," and takes his former SPR colleagues to task for not having collected evidence from eye-witnesses of the phenomena.[3]

Fortunately, I have been able to collect some evidence that might help at least partially solve the Great Mirabelli Mystery.

Eye-witness Testimonies

I set out in 1973 in the hope of finding people who reckoned they had witnessed paranormal phenomena in the presence of Mirabelli, and were prepared to talk about them on the record. It was no easy task. Though many of my friends in the Spiritist movement were able to produce a wealth of second-hand evidence (one eminent São Paulo surgeon assured me that his father had seen Mirabelli leave the floor while sitting in a chair), I could find only a handful of men who had known him over a long period of time, and most of these were too old to remember anything clearly except that the medium had been a source of inspiration to their spiritual development. This was comforting, but of little evidential value. It did suggest Mirabelli was an effective saver of souls after his unusual fashion, a point not to be overlooked.

The general picture that soon began to emerge was that Mirabelli definitely had abilities as a medium, though he did not develop them fully and very probably resorted to trickery on his off days. He also attracted a definitely second-rate variety of spirit, I was assured.

A leading São Paulo ophthalmologist, who should be able to believe his own eyes, described a partial materialization he had witnessed of a human figure that began to form inside a circle of people (including Mirabelli) holding hands, but suddenly vanished before it took identifiable shape.

This was an encouraging start, and after much further inquiry I was able to gather far more detailed evidence from two of Mirabelli's sons, insisting to each that he only describe what he saw with his own eyes, and allowing for the fact that no son is likely to denounce his own father as a fraud.

First, I sought out Regene Mirabelli, a businessman and accomplished amateur hypnotist with a keen interest in the scientific rather than the spiritual side of psychical research. Regene had no doubts whatsoever as to his father's abilities and flatly denied my suggestion that hypnotism had played any part in them.

Since his parents had separated amicably shortly after his birth, Regene saw little of his father until he was ten years old. Almost on their first meeting, things began to happen.

"I was sitting on the arm of a heavy renaissance-style sofa," Regene told me. "Father liked me to stroke his hair, and I was doing this when the sofa simply began to move, with both of us sitting on it. Then I clearly saw the shadow of a figure on the door in front of us; there was sunlight coming through a heavy glass window beside the sofa. Then the door of the cupboard across the room opened and a quill pen came out and was shot into the wooden floor like an arrow." All of this sent young Regene rushing out of the room in terror, screaming for his mother. But there was more to come.

"Out in the hallway there was a heavy brass cuspidor that had fallen over, blocking the passage. We heard loud bangs and crashes coming from a room beyond, and when I rushed in, there was Mother lying on the floor with every piece of the furniture in the room on top of her. She wasn't hurt because 'they' had the consideration to place a thick mattress over her first!"

One night, when Mirabelli's old friend Miguel Karl was staying in the house, Regene happened to peep through a crack in the door to have a look at the visitor, who was sitting on the bed with the light on, his arms folded in front of him in a position of meditation.

"As I watched him," he told me, "his body began to rise up in the air, without changing position. Then he just stayed there, in mid-air, about a meter off the bed, his arms and legs still crossed.... That was enough for me, and I ran off to tell Mother as fast as I could."

Mother, however, was quite used to this sort of thing, and one can appreciate why she had opted out of the family.

"You can imagine what it was like for her," Regene said, "spending half an hour laying the table, for instance, and then when her back was turned finding everything flung all over the room. How could you run a kitchen in a house like that?"

Another evening, Regene joined a session of the family and a dozen friends which was being held to help a bed-ridden invalid in another room. This was an occasion he will never forget.

"Father told us all to form a chain, and he said not to worry about any phenomena that might happen. I was sitting about two meters from a table where there were three corked bottles of water. This was to be 'fluidised' and used to treat the sick man. We all sat there, and suddenly the bottles rose about thirty centimeters into the air, and we heard three clinks as each struck the other. Then the bottles slowly began to turn over in mid-air, and stayed like that, upside down for a moment or two. I could see them very clearly, and the water inside seemed to have gone solid, for it stayed in position, with a gap just under the cork. Then all the bottles fell hard onto the table and rolled about, although they did not break."

Regene Mirabelli assured me that none of his family has inherited any of his father's talents, though there could be no doubt at all of those talents.

"He was the greatest medium since Jesus Christ," he summed up.

Cesar Augusto Mirabelli, the medium's youngest son, provided me with the kind of clear, straightforward evidence that would make research of this kind easy if there were more of it to be had from key witnesses. Providing clear evidence was indeed part of his job—as investigator in the São Paulo police force flying squad.

As we discussed his father's mediumship, Cesar would think hard before answering, choosing his words as if giving evidence in court. He made it clear at the start of our interview that he was far from sympathetic towards Spiritism in general.

"I have always accepted Spiritist facts," he told me. "But I never accepted the Spiritist religion. Ninety-nine percent of what is known as Spiritism is deceit, mystification or bad faith. If father were a fraud, I would certainly say so."

As an investigator himself, I asked, was he fully satisfied that his father had really caused paranormal phenomena without any possible collusion or trickery of any kind?

"Well," Cesar replied with a smile, "I'm a suspect when it comes to testifying to the authenticity and honesty of these phenomena, being his son. But, you may not believe it, I would never take part in a conspiracy aimed at deceiving so many people.

"The facts really were true. Fraud was impossible, bearing in mind the locations—even out in the street in broad daylight where there was no chance of previous preparation. The phenomena were often produced just for us, the family. Now, if there had been any intention to mystify people, this should have been done to others, but why us?"

One night, for instance, Cesar was coming home with his mother and father after a visit to friends. As they entered the house, a shower of rose petals fell on their heads just inside the door. This struck me as something that could easily have been prepared beforehand, but I could not say the same of the next phenomenon Cesar recalled for me:

"We had an ornamental porcelain vase, about sixty centimeters high, weighing I suppose three to four kilos, standing on a kind of tripod. We were the only people in the house. Suddenly, father started to look at the corner where the vase was, and I looked as well. Then the vase just rose into the air, about forty centimeters up. Then all at once it turned, picked up speed and smashed itself to pieces against the wall, two meters away."

Wasn't he curious about this sort of thing at the time? I wondered.

"Yes, I was," he replied, "but I thought it quite natural because of the frequency and the naturalness of the phenomena. They just happened almost every day, any time and any place."

"Were these phenomena connected with what your father was doing at the time?" I asked.

"Some things that happened were unforeseen, even by him," Cesar answered.

"Could he provoke a phenomenon deliberately?"

"Yes, he could if he concentrated. But sometimes they occurred independent of his will."

Finally, I mentioned the question of levitation, one of the most difficult of all phenomena to accept by anybody like myself who has never seen one. Cesar told me he had not been present on the celebrated occasion his father was supposed to have been levitated almost to the ceiling during a session at Rua Natal 9, the building constructed to house the Spiritist center next door to the family home at No. 11. (On a visit to this house, I checked the background of a photograph showing Mirabelli in mid-air and found it exactly matched, the same light fitting being still there today. Eurico de Goes accepted this photo as genuine, although recent research to be mentioned later indicates that it was almost certainly a deliberate fake.)

"But," Cesar went on, "since levitation means the displacement of the mass of any body with relation to its gravity...." Here again was the professional investigator speaking, rather than the son of a Spiritist medium. "...I did have the opportunity to witness other examples of objects that moved from one place to another."

He said he would never forget one particular occasion. Some building work was being done in the house, and a pile of bricks stood in the corridor.

"I started to imitate Father's gestures just for fun because at times I really used to think his attitudes were rather comic. Then a brick suddenly fell onto the floor beside me. I looked around— nobody was there—and then another brick fell, and another. I started to run, and bricks began to fly all over the place. I ran and ran, all around the house, and at the end of the passage there was a big iron door. As I was trying to get it open, another brick was flung against it...."

"Didn't that scare the life out of you?" I interrupted to ask.

"Well, although I was only a child, I distinctly felt the bricks were not exactly being aimed at me. Whoever was throwing them didn't want to hit me. Anyway, I finally got outside and ran across the road onto a small football pitch we had there. Then I started to yell; I was afraid to go home. Father appeared at the window, and I told him to stay there and keep a lookout while I went back into the house. At first, I thought he must have been playing tricks with me because he was covered with brick dust as well; he had been sitting on his rocking chair and bricks had been dropped all over him, though he wasn't hurt. He couldn't have been throwing them himself though, because I had really been running all over the place."

Cesar's most vivid memory of his father was a tragic one—that of the day he was killed.

It was April 30, 1951, and the two of them were on their way to the cinema when Mirabelli decided to cross the road to buy something. Cesar stayed chatting with a shoeshine boy, and as his father was walking across the road, a car came around a bend and hit him, causing a cranial lesion that put him into a coma from which he never recovered.

"It was a black 1938 Ford," said Cesar, ever the conscientious observer.

One man who will never forget Mirabelli is Fenelon Alves Feitosa, a courteous and kindly Brazilian of the old school now rapidly vanishing in ultra-materialistic São Paulo; he runs his real estate business from an office in the heart of the city's commercial district.

When I called to see him, he opened the top drawer of his desk and produced a small pile of literature on Mirabelli, as if it were the most urgent business of the day even now.

For my benefit, Fenelon recalled an outing he had spent with "the Professor," as Mirabelli was known to all during his lifetime, remembering it as clearly as if it had taken place the day before and giving a vivid impression of what life with Mirabelli had really been like.

One day in 1943, Mirabelli invited Fenelon to join him on a trip to Ibira, some 250 miles from São Paulo, to visit a certain Joaquim Seixas who lived there.

The two of them took the night train, arriving early in the morning and being warmly welcomed by Mr. Seixas and his family. Fenelon had slept little during the journey, and immediately went to take a bath and clean himself up. He was still in the bath and covered with soap when he heard Mirabelli calling:

"Fenelon! Fenelon! Come here quickly!"

"I dried myself and dressed hurriedly," Fenelon recalled, "and ran into the living room, where I found the Professor linked by a chain of hands to Mr. and Mrs. Seixas and two or three other members of their family. As I came in, the Professor cried: 'Fenelon! Fix your thoughts on Jesus, please!'

"Then he cried, 'Come!' in a loud voice, and we heard the sharp sound of something hitting a china bowl there in the room and falling onto the floor. Soon we saw what it was: a revolver bullet. Five more times, the Professor called out, 'Come!' and on each occasion bullets fell one by one until six of them lay on the floor.

"The Professor asked whose bullets they were, and Mr. Seixas picked them up and examined them. 'They look like the ones from my revolver,' he said, 'but they can't be because it's locked up in a drawer.'

"No sooner had he spoken when a revolver fell loudly onto the floor in front of our eyes. Mr. Seixas recognized it at once as his own, inexplicably transported from its locked drawer. He bent down, picked it up and was amazed to find there were no bullets in the chamber, whereas there should have been six."

At this point, amid general expressions of astonishment, Fenelon tried to persuade Mirabelli, who was sweating profusely and had turned pale, to have a rest or take a bath. But the Professor did not seem to hear him, and with a jerk he suddenly slumped into the chair, staring vaguely at the ceiling. Fenelon realized he had gone into a trance.

"Then," Fenelon continued, "he got to his feet as if drawn by an outside force and drew our attention to an object that was passing over our heads towards the master bedroom, connected by a door to the room we were in. We all ran into the next room and the first thing we saw was Mrs. Seixas, weeping and pointing to the bedside table, crying, 'Look! My St. Anthony has come back! Here he is!'

"There was indeed a statue of St. Anthony on the bedside table, and according to Mrs. Seixas, it had disappeared more than eight years previously. This was the object that had passed over our heads, on its way to its original position."

They returned to the living room, and a few moments later Mirabelli called out the words 'Schmidt! Long barrel, black handle!' They all joined hands again, and Mirabelli led them back into the bedroom; opening a drawer with one hand (while Mr. Seixas held the other), he produced a brand new Schmidt revolver, with a long barrel and black bakelite handle. He handed it to Mr. Seixas and told him to keep it.

Mirabelli then sat down again and asked who was in the habit of making up his bed.

"The maids see to that," Seixas replied. "Why do you ask?"

"I wanted to know," Mirabelli explained, "so as to be able to tell you that what we are about to see is not the work of your maids." Nobody understood what he was talking about, but I pulled the sheets and blankets aside and thrust the knife into the center of the mattress, prodding around with its point until it was heard to strike something metallic.

"Ah!" he said, "here it is." He put his hands inside the mattress and pulled out an old pair of scissors with both blades broken. "I just wanted you to know this was not put here by your maid," he observed. "You can throw it away; it's no longer of any use, especially for sleeping on!"

It was still early in the morning, and the party had not even had breakfast. As they went into the dining room, Mirabelli asked for a bottle of water. He began to make passes over it with his hands, explaining that he was receiving instructions to fluidify it.

"Look!" somebody exclaimed, "the water is turning pink!"

"We were surprised to see," said Fenelon, "that the water really was becoming discolored."

After that episode, the party set off to visit the farm belonging to Mr. Seixas's son-in-law, José Maria. Fenelon takes up the story.

"When we got there, we didn't even have time to sit down. José Maria introduced us to members of his family, including his own son-in-law, a boy of about twenty, telling us in confidence that he had been showing suicidal tendencies. The Professor at once went into one of the bedrooms, reached behind a wardrobe and pulled out a dusty picture, all covered with cobwebs.

"'Whose picture is that?' the Professor asked.

"'That's my late brother-in-law,' José Maria replied. 'He committed suicide.'

"'Exactly, and that's why the boy wants to do the same. You must pray hard for him and for your brother-in-law, so that he doesn't stay attached to him, influencing him with ideas of suicide without meaning to.'

"Then Mirabelli turned to me and said, 'Fenelon, put your hand on the boy's head, set your thoughts and don't move.' He left us and went into another room some distance away. I could hear him talking loudly at the other end of the house, and thinking something interesting might be happening that I didn't want to miss, I took my hand off the boy's head, telling him to stay where he was and think of Jesus. But I hadn't taken more than two or three steps when I heard the Professor call out 'Fenelon! Get back!', although we were in rooms far apart and there was no way he could be watching me."

At that moment, Fenelon learned later, a plaster saint from the nearby chapel had been flung against Mirabelli's legs, giving him a cut that took ten days to heal properly. He felt himself to blame fo this, by disobeying orders and taking his hand off the boy's head. But Mirabelli was in high spirits as the group sat down to lunch, in spite of the damage to his leg. He seemed to regard this as all part of the occupational hazards of his job.

"While we were eating," Fenelon continued, "something passed over our heads at tremendous speed and went into the next room. Then came a deafening crash. The Professor immediately got up, and we all followed him into the next room, where there was nobody else at the time. We saw the lid of a water cooler wobbling around on top of the table amid the shattered remains of the cooler itself, which was in pieces after spilling its water all over the table. We were still admiring this phenomenon when something heavy fell at the Professor's feet.

"José Maria stared at it and exclaimed, 'That's my revolver! But how on earth? It was safely put away inside its cover!' He picked it up, examined it and confirmed that it was indeed his. Just then, something hit the Professor on the back and fell to the floor. It was the cover of José Maria's revolver, no more, no less."

After lunch, the group went back to the center of Ibira and sat down on benches in the little town's main square. But Mirabelli—for all the entertainment he had already provided in two different houses, neither of which he had visited previously—was still not through for the day.

"Suddenly," Fenelon went on, "rifle bullets began to fall to the ground, one after the other. José Maria stared at them and said they must come from his farm because he had a store of bullets of the same calibre. Next, another object came floating out of nowhere and landed at our feet. It was a pen, which José Maria also recognized as his.

"'That's right, said the Professor, 'this pen was brought here so that we can sign the minutes this evening!'"

Fenelon himself wrote out this account of his memorable outing with Mirabelli, which he signed and presented to the Brazilian Institute for Psycho-Biophysical Research (IBPP).

Controversy Continues

Mirabelli's reported feats make an interesting comparison with those of the nineteenth-century medium D.D. Home, as painstakingly recorded by Sir William Crookes.[4]

Crookes divided the phenomena he had personally witnessed into thirteen classes. These were the production of sounds, alteration of weight of bodies, movements of heavy substances at a distance, levitation of objects and human beings, movement of objects without contact with any person, luminous appearances, materialization of hands, forms and faces and miscellaneous phenomena such as accordions playing themselves and bells ringing. The other class was of instances that, as Crookes put it, seemed to point to the agency of an exterior intelligence.

No scientist of Crookes's stature has ever made such thorough studies of so many of the physical phenomena of mediumship, although his research into what he called 'the phenomena of spiritualism' was restricted to the years 1870-1874, at which time he was at the height of his career. (He turned forty in 1872.) True, his greatest discovery, that of thallium, was behind him; but over the forty-five years *after* his psychical research period, his record does not read like that of a madman.

He became president of the Chemical Society (1887), the Institution of Electrical Engineers (1890), the British Association (1898), the Society of Chemical Industry (1913), and finally the Royal Society itself (1913). He was knighted in 1897 and awarded Britain's highest civil honor, the Order of Merit, in 1910. At the age of eighty-six he produced a paper for the Royal Society on the 'Arc Spectra of Scandium'. If he did go soft in the head, as has been suggested, he left it extremely late.

I mention all this to make the point that Mirabelli did very little that has not been witnessed elsewhere by a man with far more professional qualifications than any psychical researcher in history. A historical precedent is as useful in psychical research as in a court of law.

All the same, if anybody of Crookes's stature had investigated Mirabelli, I doubt if anybody would have believed him, just as few believed Crookes. As a contemporary of his observed, "Either the facts must be admitted to be such as are reported, or the possibility of certifying facts by human testimony must be given up."

Resisting the temptation to give up, I will end by summarizing what I consider the best evidence available both for and against Mirabelli.

Theodore Besterman's long report[5] on his August 1934 visit to Brazil contains allegations of outright fraud. Mr. Besterman states that he saw Mirabelli throw various small objects around the room after distracting everybody's attention by making them look at the ceiling. He also accuses Mirabelli's wife of being an accomplice in an act that involved the discovery of flowers draped around a chandelier in another room. Since the lady had left the room while her husband was making a speech, this does seem circumstantially possible. Some rather feeble bottle-clinking went on in the dark, spectacles moved on a table, a ruler was pulled from Mr. Besterman's hand and some paper torn while he was holding it. All this, he concluded, must be done by the use of threads, although "notwithstanding every effort" he never found any.

Next, a coin was made to appear in a pocket of Mr. Besterman's choice. Dropping coins in people's pockets is no harder than picking them, and as Dr. Dingwall pointed out,[6] what would have happened if Besterman had asked for the coin to appear in the heel of his shoe?

Then we come to what Mr. Besterman describes as "the only really impressive part" of the sittings he attended.

Mirabelli took a blackboard measuring 69.9 by 80.3 cm., one centimeter thick and weighing 3.65 kilos, and placed it on top of a bottle. A group of sitters, including the medium himself, then held their hands over the board, which after a minute or two began to revolve, turning about one and a half full circles before it fell off the bottle. On a second attempt, at another session, the board made three whole revolutions before falling, and the phenomenon was repeated with a cane 60.2 cm. long. All of this took place in a "brilliant" light, though not brilliant enough to enable Mr. Besterman to get good results with his movie camera, which Mirabelli allowed him to use without objection.

Mr. Besterman tried later to repeat the board-revolving effect by blowing and found he could not. He was satisfied at least on this occasion that no threads were used, and admits that "any other fraudulent method is difficult to conceive."

Finally, Mr. Besterman was treated to a display of Mirabelli's skill at automatic writing. He records that the medium produced just under 1800 words in French in fifty-three minutes, giving an average of thirty-four words per minute. This is not bad going; I can write fifty words in a minute in my own language, but I could not keep it up for fifty-three minutes, and I could certainly not do so in French although, unlike Mirabelli, I have a university degree in that language. Yet Mr. Besterman finds nothing difficult, let alone paranormal, about this feat.

He sums up his findings as follows: "He is either a fraud pure and simple, or else he possesses a certain narrowly-defined paranormal faculty, round which he has erected, for commercial purposes, an elaborate structure of fraud." There did appear to be, he admitted, "a *prima facie* case for the second possibility," subject to numerous reservations.

Mr. Besterman's evidence is inconclusive, but since it is almost all we have of its kind, it deserves some study. We must be grateful to him at least for providing good evidence that Mirabelli did cheat on occasions, though this is no proof whatsoever that he always did. (Many other well-known mediums have both been caught cheating and been pronounced genuine. William James gives a delightful account of how he himself once cheated during a physiology lecture, adding that he supposes everything he wrote since should therefore be discredited!)[7]

I suspect that Mirabelli was anxious to put on a good show for his foreign visitor, throwing in such extra tricks as he was able to manage for good measure. But I find it unlikely that he could have earned his reputation right from the start by relying on such trickery. You simply cannot fool so many people all the time for forty years.

One is reminded of Crookes's stern retort to his critics:

"Prove it to be an error by showing where the error lies, or, if a trick, by showing *how* the trick is performed. Try the experiment fully and fairly. If fraud be found, expose it; if it be a truth, proclaim it. This is the only true scientific procedure, and this it is that I purpose steadily to pursue."

Mr. Besterman duly exposed *some* fraud, but he was never able to show how the board trick was done. However, nearly forty years later he was able to state that "what I do remember very clearly was that Mirabelli left me in no doubt that he was purely and simply fraudulent."

"Once I had expressed this opinion," he added, "none of his followers would talk to me, so I was unable to get any firsthand impression of their role in his performance."[8] I am not surprised.

In fairness to Mr. Besterman, it must be said that little useful research can be done in two or three weeks in Brazil even today, even when one speaks Portuguese, as I do and he did not. In 1934 there was a strong tide of nationalism in Brazil in the wake of the 1930 revolution, and even if Mr. Besterman had interviewed witnesses *before* denouncing Mirabelli (which might have been worth trying), I doubt if they would have immediately described their personal experiences to an unknown foreigner. Enormous patience and very careful handling of sensibilities are called for if one is to get anything out of Brazilian Spiritists.

There is a curious discrepancy between Mr. Besterman's published account of the five special meetings Mirabelli held for his benefit and the official minutes of the same meetings, which Eurico de Goes prints in full in his book.

At the very first meeting, according to the minutes, Mirabelli announced that he could see an entity named Zabelle, whom he described in detail. Mr. Besterman said he had known a lady of that name in London who was now dead, and when he asked for a sign of her presence, bottles began to jump around on a table, one of them even falling onto the floor at his request. Besterman mentions the bottles, but not the mysterious Zabelle.

At the second meeting, Zabelle again dropped in and became visible enough for Dr. Thadeu de Medeiros to take a photograph of her. This is reproduced in deGoes's book—one of the more credible materialization photographs I have seen. (The lady is not even wearing an Arab headdress, for once!) According to the minutes, which deGoes reports Mr. Besterman as having signed, Zabelle performed a number of feats to prove her presence.

In the minutes of the third meeting, we are told Besterman examined the photograph of Zabelle, declaring a strong resemblance to the lady he had known. The face on the photograph is extremely clear, more so than in most pictures of this kind.

Surprisingly, Besterman makes no mention of this episode. It is clear from his lengthy published report that he was anxious to miss no opportunity to discredit Mirabelli's powers, and if the Zabelle story were untrue, here was an excellent opportunity to do so.

If, on the other hand, it was true, then Mr. Besterman is guilty of suppressing strong evidence in favor of the medium. As so often happens, an attempt to investigate paranormal phenomena led to raising more doubts instead of solving any problems.

Words of Two Scholars

Next, we turn to the brief but meticulously presented evidence of Professor Hans Driesch who, as I have already mentioned, was the most distinguished foreigner ever to see Mirabelli in action.

Driesch met him on a brief visit to São Paulo in August, 1928. His impressions were contained in a five-page letter[9] he wrote to an SPR colleague some three months later. This letter has never been published, and I am most grateful to the SPR Council for allowing me to quote from it here.

Mirabelli, says Driesch, was "quite a nice, jolly fellow, of an Italian or Spanish type"—although he surprised the multilingual German embryologist by claiming not to understand Italian, which was certainly not true. There followed, however, a long discourse in Italian, which Driesch found 'very indifferent,' purporting to come from the spirit of Mirabelli's deceased father.

After this unimpressive start, Mirabelli's performance improved somewhat when a mirror fell from a table with nobody less than six feet from it, a bottle moved and fell over in another room, and a metal pot did the same thing in the kitchen.

"There was also a vase with flowers," Driesch writes. "All the flowers fell to the ground; *one* of them moved towards Mrs. Driesch."

An enormous knife also fell to the ground, but "most impressive of all" was a double door that closed itself in response to Mirabelli's appeal to one of his favorite saints for "a sign."

Driesch made it clear that conditions were not scientific, but he was undoubtedly impressed by what he saw. The phenomena had taken place in the private house of a German banker ("who is personally beyond all doubts") in a good light, and though they were trivial compared to almost any of the sessions described by Eurico de Goes, they were enough for Driesch to invite Mirabelli on the spot to visit Europe to be investigated properly.

Mirabelli agreed at once, provided he could take his wife and his friend de Goes with him. He did not demand a fee. However, the project fell through, and the only further contact Mirabelli was to have with the SPR was through the inconclusive investigations of Theodore Besterman already described. A great opportunity was lost, but at least we have evidence that Mirabelli could be found "impressive" by a former president of the Society.

Now we consider the best published evidence available for the defense of Mirabelli, which comes from a wholly unexpected quarter; the late Carlos Imbassahy, one of the most widely respected pillars of orthodox Brazilian Spiritism and author of a monumental history of psychical phenomena that appeared in 1935.[10]

The 377 footnotes scattered through the pages of this well-written book show that its author was thoroughly familiar with psychical research in Britain, France and the U.S.A., though he has nothing to say about research in Brazil for the simple reason that there had never been any. He does however devote four pages to Mirabelli, making it quite clear at the start that he strongly disapproved of the man and had no desire at all even to meet him.

As a highly orthodox Spiritist, Imbassahy regarded Mirabelli as either a vulgar fraud, a skillful conjuror, or at most a medium who had become mixed up in the wrong company, both incarnate and discarnate. Worst of all, everything seemed to get smashed up when he was around, and Imbassahy had no wish to get involved in "this perilous mediumship."

One day, Imbassahy (who had made his opinion of Mirabelli well known to his friends) was at home with a businessman friend called Daniel de Brito, when who should turn up out of the blue but Mirabelli himself! He had been brought along by another friend of Imbassahy's who was convinced of the medium's genuineness.

"I must have looked like a farmer who has just seen a swarm of locusts on the horizon," he writes. A member of the household was ill at the time, and "there was nobody I less wanted to see."

Mirabelli nevertheless made himself at home at once, seating himself in a rocking chair and promptly launching into a speech in "detestable Italian mixed with Portuguese and Spanish words." This purported to come from Cesare Lombroso, and Imbassahy sat through it, deciding that the medium was a "grotesque charlatan," but consoling himself with the thought that at least his crockery was still intact on the shelves.

Upon finishing his speech, Mirabelli immediately turned to de Brito and proceeded to give the startled businessman an account of his life from the cradle onward. De Brito had never met him before, and was not a well known figure himself, but the medium seemed to know all there was to know about him. Imbassahy could not help being impressed.

"Once more, I began to worry about the fate of my plates," he writes.

Next, upon hearing that there was a sick person in the house, Mirabelli called for some bottles of water, which a housemaid brought in and placed on a table four or five meters from where he was sitting. He never touched them, and the four men joined hands to form a current to help the spirits 'fluidify' the water.

"Immediately, in full view of us all," Imbassahy writes, "one of the bottles rose halfway up the height of the others, and hit them with full force for five or ten seconds before returning to its place. We thought they must have been cracked. This was clearly seen and heard, with no shadow of hesitation. People in the next room also heard it, and the patient became extremely alarmed!"

So did everybody else, as Mirabelli then announced that a phalange of obsessing spirits had arrived. Oh Lord, Imbassahy thought, there goes the glassware! But at that point, the patient leaped out of bed and begged them to end the session, which they did. Mirabelli left soon afterwards.

Imbassahy slumped into an armchair, exhausted and sweating but relieved that his precious crockery had survived intact. The patient, incidentally, got worse at once.

"As consolation," he concludes, "we were left with the unshakable certainty of Mirabelli's mediumistic gifts." Trickery was out of the question; nobody had touched the bottles except the maid, the room was lit by two 100-watt bulbs, and there had been no time for Mirabelli to prepare any tricks. His hands had been held while the bottles moved, and he had been far back from the table.

Against his previous judgment, Imbassahy concluded that Mirabelli was a medium after all, though not one he ever wanted to have in the house again.

Conclusion

There are three possible verdicts on Mirabelli. One—he was a total fraud. Two—he was one of the greatest mediums of all time who produced examples of just about every mental and physical phenomenon known to psychical researchers. Three—he had mediumistic powers that came and went; and when they went, he sought to revive them with a spot of conjuring.

It is now virtually certain that he was party to deliberate deception on at least one occasion. Earlier, I mentioned the photograph that purports to show Mirabelli in mid-air. This was reproduced for the first time outside Brazil, as far as I know, in my 1975 book *The Flying Cow* (retitled *The Unknown Power* in the USA).[11] I noted in my original caption that "the author is unable to authenticate the photo" and that "it could have been faked." The discovery in 1990 of an original print, in the Society for Psychical Research collection in Cambridge University Library, suggests that indeed it was faked. There are clear signs of retouching, and it now looks very much as though Mirabelli was not in mid-air, but on top of a ladder. The print is signed by Mirabelli and inscribed to Theodore Besterman (who, surprisingly, does not mention it in the report I have quoted). I can hardly disagree with Gordon Stein, the American researcher who found it, that Mirabelli "knowingly passed off a fraudulent photo of himself as authentic."[12]

Once a cheat, always a cheat? Some will find this the easiest verdict to reach in the case of Mirabelli. Certainly Besterman, who met the man, considered him "purely and simply fraudulent," and if a man is known to have cheated once, it is reasonable to suppose that he cheated more than once.

In the case of Mirabelli, however, while this may be considered probable, it has not been proven. It is just as reasonable to assume that a medium whose powers have declined will try to perpetuate his reputation by any means available. Such behavior is common in the fields of sport and entertainment, after all. I find it unlikely that Mirabelli was always "purely and simply fraudulent." The testimony of his family and close friends is too consistent, as is that of at least one of his enemies, the orthodox Spiritist Carlos Imbassahy.

The best evidence in Mirabelli's favor is for psychokinetic feats at close range, repeatedly observed with others, most notably the late Nina Kulagina. She was not only thoroughly investigated on many occasions, but was also filmed in action and made history by suing a magazine that accused her of fraud for libel—and winning. If she could make objects move without physical contact, then it is easier to believe that somebody else could do the same.

Mirabelli broke basic Spiritist rules by charging for his services and allowing a personality cult to grow around him, yet he does not seem to have harmed anybody, and I met several Brazilians whose lives had clearly been enriched by their association with him. It is a pity he was never given the kind of scientific scrutiny as D.D. Home, Eusapia Palladino or Rudi Schneider, and that it will therefore never be possible to make a fair assessment of his talents. Even so, beyond a doubt, Mirabelli was one of the most colorful and intriguing characters in the history of psychical research.

Mediumship in Italy

DR. PAOLA GIOVETTI
MODENA, ITALY

Eusapia Palladino

ediumship has always had a great tradition in Italy. One of the most famous mediums of all times, Eusapia Palladino (1854-1918), was Italian. Her history is typical for the so-called *great mediumship* that characterized the last decades of the nineteenth century and the first ones of the twentieth.

Typical for this period were also the intensity of interest in psychic phenomena, an enthusiastic spirit of research, controversies about apparently incredible phenomena, and the involvement of important and famous

27

personalities with psychic research, especially scientists, e.g., Sir. Wm. Crookes, president of the British Royal Society; Sir Wm. Barrett, famous physicist; Charles Richet, Nobel Prize for physiology; Camille Flammarion, astronomer; Henry Bergson and Wm. James, philosophers; C.G. Jung, psychologist; as well as F.H. Myers, Walter Price and many other researchers who experimented with mediums, often risking their reputations.

A similar situation existed in Italy regarding Eusapia Palladino. After having tested her, scientists and neurologists like Enrico Morselli and Cesare Lombroso—very skeptical about such phenomena at the beginning—became convinced of their reality. Before describing in general the developments of mediumship in Italy, it is worthwhile to say more about Eusapia Palladino herself, the most researched and famous medium of her time.

Eusapia was born to a very poor family in Southern Italy near Bari, and her mother died at her birth. When she was one year old, she fell and fractured the parietal bone. In later years some sort of cold air current emanated from the scar, and a connection between that early accident and her mediumistic faculties was hypothezied.

When she was eight she was present at the death of her father who was killed by bandits. This traumatic event appeared to her frequently in later life in the form of visions and hallucinations. Intelligent but rebellious, Eusapia created difficulties for the people who were taking care of her. Until the age of sixteen, she worked as a baby sitter and a servant. Later she worked in Naples in the house of Mr. Murialdi, who used to experiment with the "turning table"—a general rage in those days. When Eusapia was present in the room, the phenomena became impressive: the table levitated, the piano moved by itself. Eusapia was then introduced to an expert spiritualist from Naples, Dr. Damiani, who had been studying spiritism in England. Recognizing the psychic faculties of the girl, he began a series of tests with her.

Soon Damiani brought Eusapia to the Roman society of spiritualism where controlled experiments took place. Eusapia produced raps, great movements of objects, cold currents, levitations of furniture and of the medium herself, and also sounds of music from instruments that were not in the room.

After one year Eusapia tired of this life and returned to Naples, where she worked as a seamstress. In 1885 she married and conducted a normal life for about a year. But normal life was not to be her destiny: in 1886 she met Ercole Chiaia, a medical doctor, who succeeded in bringing her back to mediumship. In 1888, Dr. Chiaia invited the famous scientist Cesare Lombroso, who so far was an active disbeliever, to take part in the seances with Eusapia Palladino. These experiments took place only three years later; but after seeing, among other instances, a large piece of furniture levitate at three meters' distance from Eusapia, Lombroso openly admitted: "I'm confused, and I regret having fought with such obstinacy the possibility of the so-called spiritistic facts: I say facts, because I'm still against the theory."

The seances at Naples, published by Lombroso, made Eusapia famous all over Europe: her road was marked. In 1892 a series of seances took place in Milano in the presence of Lombroso, Richet and Aksakov. Cold currents, contacts with invisible hands, raps, levitations of Eusapia, etc., were again observed.

In the following years Eusapia conducted seances in Warsaw, Cambridge (at the Myers' house), Paris, and St. Petersburg—always in the presence of scientists. In 1901, seances were with Enrico Morselli, with Madame Curie, Bergson and Ernesto Bozzano. In 1907, Eusapia came to New York where her mediumship was studied by James H. Hyslop and Hereward Carrington. During the last years of her life, Eusapia stayed in Italy; her last seance was held ten days before her death in Naples on April 22, 1918.

The phenomena produced by Eusapia Palladino had mostly psychokinetic character—levitations, movements of objects, cold currents, materializations and dematerializations, imprints of spirit hands on clay, various lights, manifestations of incredible strength. Without touching it, she once demonstrated the power of over 110 kilograms at the dynamometer. Less frequent but appearing occasionally were phantom figures, like the figure of Naldino Vassallo, son of the famous journalist Arnaldo Vassallo, who recognized his son.[1]

Gustavo Adolfi Rol

Times have changed, and the era of great mediumship is over, but we still have important mediums in Italy. I have been able to meet them, to witness their experiments, and what I report here is mostly first-hand material.

Gustavo Adolfi Rol of Turin is now over eighty and looks twenty years younger. For the last fifty years he has produced a collection of paranormal phenomena: telepathy and clairvoyance, booktests, materializations and apports, direct writing and painting, etc.—everything performed perfectly, with elegance and serenity.

In Italy he is considered some sort of a magician, and every parapsychologist dreams of experimenting with him. But Rol always refuses to submit to any controlled tests, for reasons I'll explain later. He makes his incredible experiments with only a small group of friends, as though it were a game. However, some of our best researchers have been present on certain occasions—also Prof. Hans Bender from Freiburg (Germany) and, many years ago, even Albert Einstein who was enthusiastic about Rol. No one has ever been able to find fault with his performance.

Rol never falls into trance; he always works in full light and never touches the material he's working with, as I have personally verified. I attended his experiments several times and have talked with many people who experimented with Rol, in the past as well as recently. He has told me many things about himself, confessing that he is almost afraid of his faculties, and still keeps asking: Who am I?

He is certainly a difficult person and he refuses to be categorized. He seldom agrees to interviews, so very little has appeared in public about him and his wonderful gifts.[2] I shall try to describe Rol and his phenomena, especially those which I have observed personally and those that are better documented, without, however, offering any interpretation—except what Rol offers himself, letting the reader draw his own conclusions.

Gustavo Adolfo Rol is a handsome, tall, distinguished man, with a magnetic, penetrating look. He is very cultivated, knows several languages, loves art and literature and can recite many of his favorite poems in whatever language they're written. He is a sociable man who enjoys company and likes beautiful women. His house is full of precious objects; as an enthusiastic admirer of Napoleon he has been able to collect many objects which once belonged to the emperor (including his own sword). Although he doesn't talk much about it, it is known that he considers himself Napoleon's reincarnation.

When Rol was young, he lived many years abroad, especially in France and England, working as a bank clerk. But when he had discovered his faculties, he renounced everything else, settled in Turin where he was born and became a painter; this is still his profession. But his "normal" painting has nothing to do with the paranormal one.

About his gifts Rol says:

Nothing was given to me free of charge, I have acquired it working years and years with myself. It was through will, faith and an unshakable confidence that I became what I am today. I started trying to guess the color of a covered card, for a long period without success; then, suddenly, looking at a rainbow, I experienced a flash of understanding.

Rol does not explain this "flash of light," but cards have always had and still have great importance in his experiments—a sort of ceremonial rite.

When he experiments with somebody for the first time, Rol just uses cards, i.e., he limits his experiments to what he calls "initiation games"—as he had when I first met him years ago. He generally carries several packs of cards, often new ones provided by his friends. As I have mentioned, he never touches them, and everything happens in full light as in a normal game. On that night some years ago when I was a new guest, Rol "played cards" with me, i.e., he was giving me instructions and I had to touch and move the cards. Here is an example:

> Choose one of these packs of cards, mix it well, cut it, then put it down on the table and keep your hand on it. Now let's choose a suit: pick up and cut another pack of cards. What did you find? Oh, well, hearts! Now let's remove all hearts from your pack; close your eyes and imagine you are taking all the hearts out and putting them on top of your pack. I'll be imagining with you. Now open your eyes and look at your cards.

I do as Rol tells me, and I begin to lay my cards on the table: the first 13 cards of the pack I had mixed and always kept under my hand are all hearts! I check the other ones, they are all mixed!

That was my first meeting with Rol. That night he made many of these card experiments, amused by my astonishment, always inventing new games. It should be mentioned that Rol never repeats an experiment. These "card experiments" are often used by Rol to "warm up and prepare the atmosphere" for his fabulous, great experiments. An important feature of those is their spontaneous character and the role of the people present who give suggestions often determining what kind of materialization, writing or picture Rol will produce. I'll describe some typical experiments.

An example of an apport, Rol conducted this experiment with a well known journalist from Turin, Dr. Remo Lugli, one of his best friends and a very good friend of mine as well. The apported object was an old quill pen that suddenly fell on the table during the following experiment. Rol told Lugli to imagine a scene in the past as though he had to write a short story; then Lugli started to describe a garret in Paris where a writer is living and, said Lugli, he is writing an important book that is to become his masterpiece. "With what is he writing?" asks Rol. "With a quill pen, a beautiful, long, colored feather." "There it is," cries Rol—and at the same moment a long, colored feather falls on the table. Five other people were present and confirmed this report; I myself had seen this quill in Lugli's house.

In this manner, i.e., through such "imaginary journeys into the past and into the future," always suggested by the people present, Rol has produced and still produces a lot of apported objects: old coins, letters, books, flowers, generally of little value.

Now an example of the complicated "book-test" at which I personally assisted: I was alone with Rol, in his house; we had a long talk about Rol himself, and at a certain point I noticed standing on a table a large crystal sphere that seemed to me very old. I asked Rol what it was, and he answered: "This is the divining sphere, I got it from an old lady..." Then suddenly Rol stands up and says: "Shall we see what it's used for?" We go to the table, Rol takes a pack of cards and tells me: "We'll find an explanation in the Encyclopedia Treccani (a huge Italian encyclopedia, like the Britannica); the cards will tell us where this explanation is; uncover some cards."

I mix my pack, cut it and, picking up some cards, I find the following numbers: 14, 396, 1, 4. Before looking at the cards, we had agreed that the first number should indicate the volume, second—the page, third—the line, etc. "Very well," says Rol, "there's our explanation, let's go and see if it's right."

Now he hesitates a moment: "Maybe we'll find it quicker?..." He takes a pen and a piece of paper, concentrates for a while, then with closed eyes he writes with automatic writing: "A contemplare la vita" (to contemplate the life). We check in the Freccani, vol. 14, page 396, first line and we find the words: "a contemplare la vita..." which is a proper explanation for a divining sphere.

Let's now consider the experiments of direct writing and painting, the fields where Rol obtains exceptional results. He says he obtains help from "intelligent spirits" of dead and living people. The most frequent "inspirer" for the painting is August Ravier, French painter of the last century. But frequently it is Rol's own "intelligent spirit" at work; that at least is Rol's interpretation.

A curious type of Rol's direct writing often happens as follows: Rol goes with friends to a restaurant, and then he amuses himself by "writing" words or phrases in the air, and then the words appear written on their napkins; or in the same way he makes the drawing of a rose appear, his favorite flower.

Whole pages covered with different handwriting appear during Rol's seances in the following manner: a piece of paper, folded several times, is put in the pocket of one of the persons present, or even shut in a drawer. After a certain time this piece of paper is examined and one finds on it various writings, some answering the questions put by a member of the group, others commenting on a subject similarly suggested. Unfortunately, Rol destroys almost all that is produced during his seances, especially drawings and paintings—in order to prevent the sale of any of those pieces, and because they frequently resemble in style the works of the dead masters. Consequently, very few drawings and paintings are preserved.

Various drawings are obtained in a similar way, as for instance a beautiful "Face of Christ." A sheet of paper was folded up, placed in a teapot, and the teapot put in a drawer that was then closed. Rol asked what should appear on the paper, someone said: "Face of Christ." Rol concentrated a few seconds, then said that it was ready. A beautiful drawing was found in the teapot, seemingly "inspired" by El Greco.

Another drawing, called "Life" appeared in the pocket of one gentleman present at the seance. Rol asked for a subject, someone said "life," and there appeared on the paper a drawing of hundreds of tiny figures doing various things. The "inspirer" in that case was apparently the "intelligent spirit" of Rol himself.

A different procedure is used for paintings. Four small paintings were obtained a few years ago in this way: A new canvas is signed by all those present at the experiment and put in a separate room. Through automatic writing Rol receives instructions about paints and brushes, and everything is placed near the canvas. Tubes with paints remain unopened. Then Rol asks each of the four women present to suggest the subject to be painted; one woman says, a country landscape in winter, another suggests a little house near the river. etc., etc. Rol remains with the group the whole time; he concentrates for a while and after a few minutes the picture in the other room is ready: four different subjects divided with lines, still wet—the subjects according to the suggestions of the four women. This "inspirer" was August Ravier who during his lifetime had painted many landscapes in the same style.

Many paintings appeared in the same way, apparently inspired by Kandinski, Modigliani, De Pisis, Picasso and other modern painters. One night several years ago Rol made the following experiment in full light, in the presence of myself and three other persons (including Dr. Gastone de Boni, one of our best researchers). Each of us got a sheet of white paper which we had to fold and put on the table. Then Rol told me to choose one of these sheets and to put it in my pocket. I did not have any pockets, so I slipped it under my blouse. Then he told me to suggest the name of a painter, I said: "Paolo" (like my own name). Rol responded: "Let's see if Paolo is here.... Oh, yes, we have a special Paolo, Pablo Picasso!"

Now Rol began to talk French with the invisible and not audible Picasso, who seemed to be willing to draw a picture for us, and indicated which paints and brushes were to be used (he wanted watercolors in four shades), he also needed a cup of water. Rol supplied everything; the watercolor paints were old and dry (Rol had not used them for many years), but he said: "If Picasso asked for these paints, it means he can use them even in this condition."

He left the tubes unopened, then he asked me what the painting should represent. I suggested a woman (the wife) in her bedroom, with flowers on a small round table, a man looking in at the door—and other complicated details. Rol made the gestures of painting, touching the closed tubes with the brush and moving the brush over another sheet of paper. When I finished my description, he said: "Take the sheet of paper you have on you and put it in the water." I did so, then I took the paper out of the water, unfolded it—and we found the picture according to my suggestions, in the characteristic style of Picasso. The paper was wet, but the colors were not blurred. Rol let us admire the picture, then he destroyed it.

These few examples should suffice to give us an idea of how great a medium Rol is. As I had mentioned before, he does not want to be tested by scientists. "My experiments develop suddenly, without planning," he says. "Therefore I can't produce them in a laboratory." As a matter of fact, everybody who attended his experiments could see their casual character.

Rol's favorite statement is as follows: "I pondered much about my role in what happens to me, and I call myself a gutter that gathers a rain from heaven. It is nonsense to study the gutter, what should be studied is the rain...." And then he adds: "Science cannot yet analyze the spirit!"

Roberto Setti

"Cerchio Firenze 77" is the name of a group which, for many years—until 1984—had periodically held seances with an extraordinary medium, Roberto Setti. To talk about him was allowed only after his death; as long as he lived he wished to remain unknown, since he was exceptionally modest and reticent about his private life. Only his relatives and the nearest friends had known his real identity and his activities. To everybody else he was just an employee in the administration of the city of Florence, and nothing more.

Many articles and even books were written about his seances and his phenomena, but his name was never mentioned.[3] His sister Luciana Campani and his nearest entourage protected his wish of remaining personally unknown and helped him develop his mission in the way he preferred.

The history of Roberto Setti as a medium started, as it often happens, in an unexpected way. When Roberto was 15, in 1945, his older brother Ruggero died dramatically, and their mother, in her despair, wanted to get in touch with her son by means of the "turning table." One member of the family was familiar with this field; they tried, and to everybody's surprise the table moved and answered questions on the very first occasion. Roberto was not present the second time, and nothing happened; the table did not move. The next time, Roberto was again participating in the experiment, the table moved and Ruggero, the dead brother, manifested himself. He gave convincing evidence of his identity, telling things no one could have known beforehand and which proved to be true, such as the existence of his diary. He quoted its first sentence before it had been found. This confirmed the assumption that Roberto was a medium.

His mediumship developed quickly. His family, unacquainted with mediumistic phenomena, soon directly experienced the most important ones: automatic writing, lights, sweet smells, materializations of people already dead but not previously known to those present, and many beautiful messages with a profound philosophical and ethical meaning.

Soon after Roberto learned he was a medium, he developed the gift of automatic writing with a different handwriting style for different "entities." Still later he developed the ability to fall into trance and speak with different voices. Until Roberto's death this had become the method the "entities"—if one accepts this interpretation—used to communicate their messages and lessons: each "entity" had a particular voice (which remained the same for years and years) and a particular teaching to give.

All the seances have been recorded, and during the long time while Roberto was active as a medium, a vast amount of material has been collected and partially published. The decision to publish was made after the "entities" suggested to the members of the group that the phenomena and the teachings might be useful to many people and therefore should be made available to the wider public. All books were signed "Cerchio Firenze 77."

Luciana Campani, Roberto's sister, who took care of editing the books and wrote a number of pages herself, had told me:

> The "entities" corrected the proofs themselves, of course
> through Roberto. He sat at a table with the pen in his hand and
> the proofs before him; in order not to influence the corrections
> he was blindfolded, then he would start writing automatically.
> The precision of the corrections was incredible: the notes
> between the lines, very exact reference marks, perfectly
> legible. The handwriting was not of Roberto, but of his "spirit-
> guide" called "Dali."

Roberto Setti and members of his group had always attached more importance to the teaching than to the phenomena: the latter, they said, were only demonstrating that something more than human was in action, but the real importance was in the messages. One should remember that Roberto was a young boy with little education when he was revealed as a medium; members of his family knew very little about religion and philosophy. Step by step, for over thirty years, they received teachings that could be called an initiation: teachings that explain great problems of life and comprise a wonderful synthesis of Western and Eastern philosophies. All this had been brought to light gradually—with patience, indulgence, love.

Let us see now what Roberto's seances were like. It must be said that for many years he worked only with a small group of friends and relatives, but in the last ten years, after the books started to be published, his case became famous and, through his sisters, many people could attend. Among these, Italy's leading parapsychologists: Dr. Gastone de Boni, Dr. Piero Cassoli, Dr. Alfredo Ferraro, Dr. Silvio Ravaldini, Prof. Giulio Cogni and others. I was present at those seances many times and became a good friend of Roberto.

The seances took place once a week, usually on a Saturday, with a small group of people, in total darkness. Roberto would fall in trance very soon and did not remember anything after waking up. Only the sweet smells that lingered for a long time, the materialized objects and the records gave him an idea of what had taken place during the seance. Only twice in his life was Roberto able to be an observer during his seance. Later he described what happened:

> I had an impression of sitting among the people. My body was sleeping as always, but my consciousness was vigilant. I was divided in two. One part was sitting in front of my sleeping body which spoke in trance, and the persons who sat next to me on the sofa felt as though someone was occupying the empty place; the whole time they had a clear sensation of a presence. I think this had been a gift for me from the "entities," in order to let me be present at my own seances!

As soon as Roberto fell into trance, his voice changed: different "entities" would start speaking through him with different voices. When he incorporated Lillie, a little girl of six who died of typhoid in the last century, Roberto stood up and moved gaily among the present people, making funny jokes for everybody. When I was at Roberto's seances for the first time, Lillie came to me and put her hands on my face. I can assure you, these hands were not the large hands of a man six feet tall, but the small and tender ones of the little girl: a transfiguration phenomenon, observed at Roberto's seance by several other persons. Then Lillie said to me: "You have a little girl as mischievous as I am!" That was true: my daughter was at that time a little girl, and even today, as an adult, she is playful and cheerful. Nobody in that group knew anything about my family; I had been invited as a researcher, and I met the medium and the members of the group for the first time.

Lillie was able to produce her picture, which was obtained in a very strange way: during a seance, at her suggestion, a plate of glass wrapped in paper, sealed and signed by the people present, was placed on the knees of Roberto in trance. Then the group was asked to concentrate strongly, visualizing in darkness the symbol of the cross. After a few minutes Lillie announced that the phenomenon took place. The plate, still wrapped, had been passed to a photographer to be developed—and the image, not perfectly clear but recognizable, shows a girl with the very short hair typical for someone sick with typhoid fever.

Michel, the "entity" who apparently takes care of the physical phenomena, announced that the picture was obtained by him by concentrating on Lillie when she was alive until he succeeded to materialize her face at the level of X-rays which had exposed the plate.

In recent years, shortly before Roberto's death, a similar phenomenon took place: the "entity" Michel asked to have the Polaroid camera directed in darkness at the face of Roberto in trance. A few pictures were shot, and on two of them there appeared the face of a bearded man, surrounded by a cloud of ectoplasmic formation. It was announced that the face represented a new "entity" François, who had started to communicate recently and who, during his life, had been a French medical man, François Broussais, a contemporary of Napoleon. Subsequently his portrait was identified on a painting by David, the famous French painter, and with the photograph it was possible to verify the resemblance.

Almost at every seance a very mystical personality was manifested who called herself "Teresa" and who talked about love for people and the importance of praying. On these occasions the medium levitated and produced a strong smell of roses that lingered for a long time. During the levitation his voice came from above. Then, as I could personally verify on several occasions, the medium would ask for hands and fall on his chair.

The spirit-guides at the seances were: (1) Dali, whose manifestation was always accompanied by a wonderful smell of violets; (2) Kempis, who gave deep, metaphysical teachings on God; (3) François who spoke with a French accent and answered personal questions, and (4) Claudio, the "oriental brother," who always started his speach with the Tibetan mantra

"Om Mani Padme Hum" and used to express himself with a certain detachment.

Another important entity was the "physical guide" Michel, who was responsible for the wonderful, inexplicable materializations produced at every seance. In such manner hundreds of objects had been materialized, frequently valuable, of silver or even gold, with precious stones: rings, brooches, bracelets, medals, old watches, crosses, miniatures, etc. All these objects were offered as presents to the participants; Roberto kept nothing for himself.

It is altogether impossible to suspect any tricks or manipulations; for many, many years the phenomena took place only in a small group of relatives and friends whom Roberto had no reason to impress in such manner. Besides, he was not rich and certainly could not afford to give away such valuable objects week after week, year after year. It should be remembered, moreover, that during the last four years of his life Roberto was partly paralyzed and confined to a wheelchair, while the number of objects he "materialized" in that period was over one hundred.

Moreover, the way the phenomena were happening excludes all doubts. I assisted at the materializations many times and can describe them in detail. At a certain moment the "physical guide" would announce that everybody should deeply concentrate to make possible a full manifestation of the phenomenon—then, in total darkness, the hands of the medium would gradually become visible. They became bright with a light blue color that seemed to come from inside his hands, and was accompanied by a smell of ozone. In a few seconds the hands seemed as if they were made of light, emitting abundant floating vapors that gushed out and up to the ceiling; it was a most impressive effect. Then you would suddenly realize that in those hands of light, opened and stretched before the medium, there appeared some transparent object, and this object would slowly acquire shape, solidity, compactness.

The persons present at the seance could sometimes control stages of materializations. I was sitting once in front of Roberto and during the process was asked to touch the object; I approached Roberto who gave me a small soft object of wax-like consistency. I gave it back to Roberto who continued to keep it in his hands still full of light and blue vapors. Shortly afterwards I received the object again; now it was denser and acquired a square shape. After another moment, in the hands of Roberto (still in trance), the object was ready: it was made of some polished, bright metal with a sacred image engraved upon it. The medal was then offered to one of the present friends, and in his hands, continued to emanate a blue light which slowly vanished.

When I was present for the first time at a seance of Cerchio Firenze

77, in 1978, I was sitting near Roberto and was able to follow perfectly a materialization of the beautiful silver filigree reliquary that was then given to me as a present. The light from the medium's hands was so strong it allowed me to follow distinctly the whole process: first the building of the central, more compact part, then the external part of filigree and the stones. When I received the object, it was still warm and pliant, as though it were alive. As a matter of fact, the materializations were always finished in the hands of the person to whom they were given.

These objects often had a symbolic and emotional meaning for the recipients. A priest, Padre Eugenio from Genova, received a small silver figure of an angel. He then revealed that this materialization had for him a particular importance: he had a gift of automatic writing and wrote messages signed "Your guardian angel." A certain woman who had recently lost her husband and came to the Roberto's seance for the first time, received a gold brooch with an emerald that formed a perfect set with a ring, also with an emerald, her husband gave her before he died.

Sometimes the objects appeared in a different way, that is, suddenly: they would fall from above and would also have a particular meaning. Once, for instance, someone received an old silver pocket watch. It was like the one his father had received as a present from his father before leaving for the war in 1917; he had lost it in the famous battle of Caporetto. Through the medium the grandfather brought the watch back and gave it to his grandson! The watch was recognized by his aunt who, as a daughter of the grandfather, had seen it many times.

On another occasion there was a new person at the seance, no one knew him, or his family, well. At a certain moment Lillie manifested herself, saying to this man that she was sent by his father recently deceased. At the same instant there was a light sound, as if a small piece of metal had fallen on the floor. "Your father," said Lillie, "sends you this present." After the seance an old button from a military uniform was found on the floor. Thereupon the new guest at the seance announced that his father had been a carabineri officer and his uniform had buttons like the one they had just found.

Explaining the phenomena, the "physical guide" Michel said that all apports (usually old) were objects once lost or forgotten which dematerialized and then materialized again in the hands of the medium. "We do not deprive anyone of anything," he said. On other occasions the materializations consisted of flowers. Once, at Easter time, olive tree leaves had fallen from above in such abundance, they covered the whole floor.

Through the mediumship of Roberto Setti, some very important identifications took place. Completely unknown entities manifested themselves, giving names and other information about themselves, subsequently checked and confirmed. In 1978, for instance, an entity described, with great emotion, his death that occurred on February 15, 1917, on board the steamship Minas, as the result of an explosion. His name, said the entity, was Antonio Teresia, born in a Sicilian village. Two of his friends, he added, died with him, and their names and age were also given. Dr. Alfredo Ferraro, a physicist who followed Roberto's experiments for a long period, wrote to the Ministry of the Navy and received an official confirmation of everything said at the seance: the sinking on that date of the SS Minas after the explosion, as well as the names of the three sailors from Sicily.

Another case: In 1975 an entity with the voice of a small girl with a characteristic Southern accent manifested itself and said that her name was Maria Renata Giorgino, born in Pietragalla near Potenza in Southern Italy; she had died at the age of nine in the hospital of St. Carlo in Potenza in 1969 after she had been kicked by a mule. None of the persons present had known the name of the hospital in Potenza or had ever heard of Maria Donata Giorgino. Dr. Ferraro wrote to the townhall of Pietragalla and received an answer that such a girl really existed and died in the described way on July 28, 1969. The entity, who called herself Maria Renata, said that she wanted to comfort her mother who was still grieving. Dr. Ferraro wrote to the woman informing her about the "return" of her daughter. The woman answered thanking Ferraro and the medium, but it was not evident from her letter whether she believed the story or not.

As I mentioned before, Roberto and the members of his group always gave more attention to the messages than to the phenomena, which only confirmed their supernatural origin. It must be said that these teachings still find a great following regardless of the fact that the medium has died and the seances are not held any more.

Still one point must be added: Roberto sustained his long illness with patience, serenity and great courage. He could smile until his last day. Such an attitude obviously was possible thanks to the extraordinary experience of his whole life.

Entity "A"

In the panorama of Italian mediumship of the last period, it is impossible to forget a case from Naples, studied for more than thirty years by Prof. Giorgio di Simone of Naples University, the president of the local Society for Parapsychology. The case in question is called "the case of Entity A"—a conventional name given to the personality manifesting itself through a medium who is still active; born in 1930, he is the same age as Roberto Setti.

In this case we do not have physical phenomena, only deep philosophical messages. The medium started his activity when he was still a boy of 15, falling into a trance and speaking with voices very different from his own. As time went on, control of the medium was taken by a "voice" of particular authority who answered any question and delivered metaphysical teachings.

From the point of view of psychic research the case is of special interest because of scientific experiments Prof. di Simone performed with the medium in order to verify the independence of the trance "voice" from the personal voice of the medium (whose name must remain undisclosed for reasons of privacy). Entity "A" has a different accent and a far greater education than the medium had had—a necessary consideration to properly understand this case.

In 1975 Prof. di Simone sent voice recordings to the Instituto di Elettroacustica G. Ferraria of Turin; their analyses often are used in judiciary cases. He recorded the voices of Entity "A" and of the medium who after waking up from the trance repeated the same sentences. The result according to the experts was that the two voices did not belong to the same person.

The second experiment was made in 1978 in the Clinic for Nervous Diseases at the Hospital of Naples; they have registered the brain wave activity of the medium before, after and during the trance. The result was that before and after the trance the brain activity of the medium was completely normal. During the trance, while Entity "A" was speaking with characteristic intensity, the presence of alpha activity was observed. As is known, alpha rhythm is typical for the brain in the state of relaxation, sleepiness, meditation with closed eyes and mental emptiness. It means that the brain of the medium was at rest—and the lively speaking voice of Entity "A" could be explained only by supposing an intervention of another mind. For the medical professionals analyzing this case, it was, however, inexplicable!

It is desirable that similar experiments be repeated with other mediums as well.

The Return of the Prince of Sansevero

One more case of mediumship in Italy I shall describe concerns the Prince of Sansevero and his "return." First let me tell you something about the Prince himself and his fascinating personality.

Raimondo di Sangro, Prince of Sansevero, was a very creative eighteenth century personality from Naples, a cultivated and enlightened man. He was, however, so badly treated by history that today his reputation is simply sinister. A freemason and alchemist, he invented new materials and machinery, he studied human anatomy, and was ahead of his time in many fields, including medicine. To mention only a few of his achievements: He succeeded in desalinating sea water; he invented drugs recognized as valuable today, a waterproof material for hunters which he offered to King Carlo III Borbone who greatly respected him, an automatic rifle and many other things.

Obviously exceptionally talented, the Prince could not be understood by the people of Naples who transformed him into a diabolical personality, his reputation enduring until this day. His masterpiece, the Sansevero Chapel in Naples, adorned with beautiful statues, is connected with terrifying legends. It is said, for instance, that the marble statue of the "veiled Christ" executed with some mysterious technique, has been made by the sculptor Sanmartino—after the Prince, with the aid of the devil, put the sculptor under hypnosis. People also assert that the Prince killed two of his servants in order to realize his most terrible invention, the famous "anatomical machine": two frightful bodies still preserved in the caves under the Chapel. It is said the Prince had injected in the veins of those two poor men a special "metalizing" liquid which would enable him to study the system of veins and arteries in the human body. This cruel legend is the prevalent opinion about Raimondo di Sangro—not only among the common people but the educated as well.

Apparently tired of this situation, it appears the Prince is trying now to repair his reputation by means of various extraordinary interventions with the unintentional cooperation of a young teacher in Naples, Clara Micinelli. Clara lives with her mother in an old palace in the historical quarter of Naples. In 1975 there began to appear in their apartment small pieces of old-looking paper with words written in an old-fashioned script—not with ink, rather with something looking like blood. They would hear strong raps in the walls after which they would find on the floor or table a short note mentioned above. The writing was still wet, as if executed a minute before. The notes were signed with the full name of the Prince of Sansevero or his initials "RDSS"; under his signature was a form of triangle, the Masonic symbol.

In these notes the Prince apparently wished to reveal the truth about himself and repeated that he had chosen Clara for this task; she had only to follow his instructions. One should know that Clara and her mother had no connection whatever with the Prince, nor any special interest in his legend. They only knew what everyone in Naples knew.

The phenomena continued to develop slowly in the following years. Many notes were found. Some of them suggested that Clara should go to the Notarial Archives of Naples where she would find the Prince's will and other documents that would be helpful in establishing the truth about him. Indeed the will and other documents were found and the graphological analysis of those, as well as of the notes found in Clara's apartment, demonstrated they were written by the same hand. The red color of the writing on the notes was also analyzed; it proved to be blood, but of a different type than the blood of Clara and her mother.

The Prince had "brought" to Clara several objects, among others a small statue of San Gennaro, the protector saint of Naples; the Prince was the Great Master of the Chivalrous Order of San Gennaro. This little statue was often covered with fresh blood. The blood seemed to be the most characteristic feature of this case—maybe, says Clara, because the Prince also belonged to the Order of Templars, the "guardians of the Holy Grail"; and the Grail, according to traditional legends, was the cup in which the blood of Christ on the cross had been collected.

There are many apports: watches from the eighteenth century, old manuscripts, jewels and other ancient objects. They materialized in the hands of Clara (who began some years ago to fall into trance), in full light and at unexpected moments. Sometimes they would fall from above—again in full light—and nobody could understand from where they came. One day the Prince drew his portrait, also in red, on the wall in Clara's apartment; when she discovered it, it was still wet.

When I first visited Clara in 1986, she was in a sudden trance, which I am going to describe to help readers understand this unusual case still going strong with, no doubt, many surprises to be produced in the future.

That day Clara invited me to her bedroom where she kept the notes from the Prince and the statue of San Gennaro. As soon as we entered the room, I noticed something dark dripping from the statue onto its crystal base. I came nearer and saw a red, sticky liquid, very similar to fresh blood. In a few minutes the liquid coagulated, sticking San Gennaro to the crystal. "Don't be surprised," says Clara. "It has happened on other occasions too. It signifies the presence of the Prince, and it means you are a welcome guest in this house...."

At the same time I noted that Clara's voice sounded strange; I looked at her and realized she was in an altered state of consciousness: her posture was more upright, her voice had a masculine timbre and no Neapolitan accent—the Prince, I remember, was born in the region of Pugli and educated in Rome. "She is in trance," said Clara's mother who had accepted the whole situation with some difficulty, but was getting accustomed to it. "Let's go to the living room."

Here we sat, around the table, in full light and talked for about an hour. The Prince's language was elegant, ironic, but with many expressions no longer in use today. He spoke of himself, of the injustice he suffered, and his wish to be rehabilitated. He explained that he was in advance of his time, did not care for the ceremonies of the Church and liked to live in an atmosphere of mystery. In such manner he came to be considered by people as damned. But, the Prince adds, God allows him to come back to Earth to establish his credibility through Clara. Other revelations, other discoveries, other surprises will come. I myself, he says, will contribute.... Then the Prince said to me: "Please accept this present." The medium opened her right hand before me and closed it for a second; when she opened it again, I saw on her palm something bright: a tiny piece of gold, shaped like a heart, the size of a fingernail. "It's a simple thing," the Prince added, "and of small value. But I give it to you with all my heart. Keep it! It will bring you luck."

As I received the little heart from the Prince, it was still hot. Finally, the Prince gave me his—the medium's—hand and said goodbye. The medium seemed to be asleep, but after two minutes she opened her eyes, and she was again Clara. She asked what had happened and complained about not having been able to hear the Prince's voice; her trances are always unexpected, and she does not remember anything. Besides, the Prince does not allow recordings because "these modern machines" bore him. Consequently I could only take notes.

In the meantime, through suggestions given by the Prince's notes or through Clara in trance, other old documents have been found in the State Archives. In addition to the original will, there emerged a document rehabilitating the Prince of the most defamatory accusation concerning the two bodies preserved in the caves under the Sansevero Chapel, the two skeletons with their circulatory systems perfectly conserved. The official explanation put in writing near the bodies, visible still today, says, "conversion into stone"—supporting the popular belief about a coagulating liquid injected by the Prince in his two living servants in order to demonstrate their veins and arteries.

A newly discovered document destroys this belief: a contract between the Prince and a medical doctor from Palermo who "made *with wax* the models of veins and arteries as they are in reality; these models," says the document, "will be of great utility to human society and will help doctors avoid mistakes..."—which were no doubt very frequent in those days. Evidently the Prince's only purpose had been to promote scientific research. Clara Micinelli, who follows this case with passion and intelligence, managed to obtain fragments of these "bodies" and had them analyzed. They were made from dyed wax with parts of iron and string to such perfection that until today people believed they were seeing two real human bodies.

But there is no end yet to the surprises: another document found in the Archives following a note from the Prince is a lease by the Prince of an apartment in the palace "with the use of the caves." The extraordinary circumstance is that this apartment (converted in the palace) is where Clara now lives! The apartment no doubt had been a studio of the Prince that had to be separate from his residence, and his laboratory was in the caves! Visiting the vast underground space of the palace that reached the real caves under the hills of Naples, Clara and the experts found old pieces of furniture, rusty instruments for chemical and medical research, and alchemist writings on the walls.

Maybe the fact that Clara by sheer accident came to live in that particular apartment, and had as yet unknown mediumistic faculties, is the reason she had been chosen to help the Prince re-establish his credibility?!

But this is not the end of the story: two years ago a note from the Prince announced that under the floor in a certain room of the apartment, the only room that remained intact since the time of the Prince's life, Clara would find his "treasure."

Actually, after the floor had been lifted, there was found a sealed, old box that contained several documents, an old watch and a portrait of the Prince at the age of 17. All documents were examined by graphological experts who confirmed they had been written by the Prince. They represent the whole alchemical work of the Prince, several medical prescriptions, including one against cancer; a spiritual testament of the Prince and the description of the complicated technique used by the sculptor to obtain the splendid effect on the statue of Christ in the Chapel—a technique completely lost today.

One of the documents also reveals that the Prince had discovered what he called the "active ray," i.e., radioactivity, which killed him. In fact, the Prince—according to this document—predicts his own death which happened in the way he had described. In his spiritual testament the Prince warns posterity "not to manipulate and use carelessly the minerals of 'active ray.'" These words are today a particularly valid admonition!

All the documents described above were displayed in 1987 in

Venice on the occasion of the *Biennale*, in the historical section—without, of course, mentioning the way in which they had been discovered!

Such is the story of Prince Sansevero and his medium Clara Micinelli: a story which is not yet finished and will surely offer still more surprises!

Indridi Indridason[1]

DR. LOFTUR R. GISSURARSON
DR. ERLENDUR HARALDSSON
REYKJAVIK, ICELAND

*I*ndridi Indridason (1883-1912) was investigated and tested extensively by members of the Experimental Society in Reykjavik, Iceland. Remarkable psychokinetic and mediumistic phenomena are described in detail in contemporary reports, from the beginning of Indridason's mediumship in 1905 to its end in June 1909. These phenomena, some of which occurred in full light, comprised movements and levitations of various objects, of furniture and of the medium himself, knocks on walls and clicks in the air, odor and light phenomena, materializations of human forms, playing of musical instruments, apports, direct voices often singing forcefully aloud, dematerializations, direct as well as automatic writing by the medium, and trance speech.

We probably have information about most kinds of phenomena which occurred with Indridason, and the sequence of their appearance, as there exists a substantial number of fairly extensive reports covering his five years of mediumship. The strength and variety of phenomena observed seem to resemble those associated with the famous Daniel Dunglas Home.

No reports can be found of any medium in Iceland before Indridason. Spiritualism was practically unknown in Iceland before his time, and those who experimented with Indridason faced the phenomena of physical mediumship for the first time. All investigators and observers maintain in their reports that the phenomena were not explainable in terms of fraud.

The Experimental Society

The Experimental Society was the first society in Iceland devoted to psychical research. Inspired by reading F.W.H. Myers' famous book, *Human Personality and Its Survival of Bodily Death*, Einar Kvaran established an experimentation circle in October 1904 to investigate the claims of mediumship.[2] This circle became a formal society in the autumn of 1905.[3] Kvaran was president of the society for the whole of its existence; he deserves the honor of having started psychical research in Iceland.[4]

Indridason is probably unique among great mediums in the way that his mediumship was discovered and developed by research-minded scholars and academics. Sittings were usually held once or twice a week from September to the end of June.[5] Indridason was paid a fixed, modest yearly salary from the Society and given free lodgings; in return he gave no seances without the Society's permission. Shortly after his death the Society was dissolved, but in 1918 it was resurrected as the Icelandic Society for Psychical Research.

The Experimental Society was in fact founded primarily to investigate the extraordinary phenomena that took place in Indridason's presence.[6] The Society was not spiritualistic in the ordinary sense of the word, although many of those who frequently took part in the experiments believed in spiritualistic explanations.[7] Among the founders were Haraldur Nielsson and Einar Kvaran, Bjorn Jonsson (later Prime Minister of Iceland) and several other prominent persons in Reykjavik. In 1907 the Society had become so impressed with Indridason they built a small house to be better able to study him. The building was on one floor and had a flat roof and shuttered windows. There were two rooms for meetings as well as the two rooms in which Indridason lived. The house was always referred to as "the Experimental House" (see sketch of house in Figure 1).

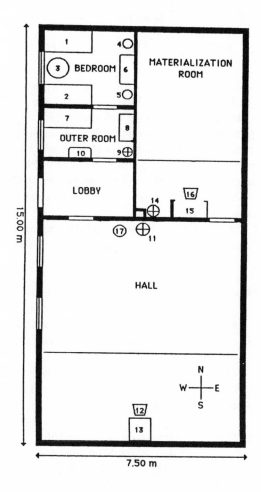

Figure 1. A plan of the Experimental House (adapted from Nielsson[8]). Independently, Thordarson also made a sketch of the House, which resembles Nielsson's in every detail. We have added No. 17 to the picture, as well as a few details to other items from Thordarson's sketch, which was made according to a drawing from the Building Office of Reykjavik and to Thorlaksson's and the carpenter's (Jon Gudmundsson's) accounts.[9]

1. Indridason's bed; 2. Oddgeirsson's bed; 3. Table; 4. Medium's wash-hand stand; 5. Oddgeirsson's wash-hand stand; 6. Chest of drawers; 11. Stove; 12. Indridason's medium chair; 13. Pulpit; 14. Stove beside a fireplace; 15. Cabinet with stone walls; 16. Indridason's medium chair; 17. Chair on which Thorlaksson was sitting when his hat was removed.

Important Events in the Life of Indridi Indridason

Indridi Indridason, born on 12th October, 1883, in a rural area in the western part of Iceland, came to Reykjavik at the age of 22 to learn typography. Nielsson[10] writes that Indridason had never heard of mediumistic phenomena before he came to Reykjavik. His extraordinary psychic gifts were discovered at the beginning of the year 1905,[11] when by chance he happened to visit a newly formed circle (probably the first of its kind in the country) which was attempting to produce table-tilting; he was invited to join. Kvaran describes this apparently initial incident as follows:

> ... Then Indridi arrived. He was a printer's apprentice in Isafold. He was related to Indridi Einarsson and lived at his home.
>
> Indridi Einarsson was interested in the experiments but his wife much more so. Once when she sat by a table [probably with others attempting to produce table-tilting] Indridi came along. She asked him to participate in that experiment.
>
> Indridi had hardly taken his seat, when the table reacted violently and trembled. Indridi became frightened and was going to run out of the house.
>
> From that time experiments with Indridi started.
> He came to my home and we sat down at a table. The table trembled, shook, and moved violently around the room and nearly broke. Once it was overturned....[12]

Nielsson writes that Indridason blushed and became almost frightened when he discovered what influence his presence seemed to have on the table at this sitting.[13] The table apparently made strong movements as soon as he touched it. This was the beginning of a continuing series of gross physical effects that occurred more or less undiminished for nearly five years. Shortly after this incident new phenomena appeared. On inquiry the members learned that Indridason had formerly had some "remarkable visions," but no details are given concerning the nature of these experiences.[14]

Indridason, uneducated, the son of a farmer, knew no foreign language except for a few Danish words. Nielsson writes that the young country boy had never seen a juggler,[15] and conjuring tricks were at the time quite unknown in Iceland. During his mediumistic career, Indridason was probably the biggest celebrity in Iceland, and he became a highly controversial figure: to some he was an object of scorn and derision, to others a source of the most extraordinary psychokinetic powers and/or a man who connected the living with the dead. Indridason himself always interpreted the phenomena that occurred with him as being related to spirits,[16] which he claimed to be able to see.

Indridason was primarily a physical medium, probably the only physical medium we have ever had in Iceland. According to existing reports, the vigor as well as the variety of his phenomena developed steadily from 1905 until they were at their height in the year 1909, when he held the last sitting.[17] Indridason's powers never decreased, and he stopped because of an illness. Apparently most of Indridason's phenomena occurred while he was in trance at seances, but violent phenomena were also reported to occur when he was in a waking state. Furthermore, many phenomena took place outside the formal sittings held in the Experimental House.

In the summer of 1909 Indridason went to visit his parents in the country.[18] During this trip he and his fiancee caught typhoid fever, from which his fiancee died. Shortly afterward Indridason married another girl, and they had one daughter who died when she was nearly two years of age. Indridason never regained his health after contracting typhoid, and no further sittings took place. Later it was found he had contracted tuberculosis, which resulted in his untimely death in a sanatorium at Vifilsstadir on 31st August, 1912, when he was only twenty-nine years old.

A Seance in the Experimental House

A typical seance in the Experimental House during the winter of 1908-1909 can be described as follows. The larger hall in the House (see Figure 1) could seat one hundred people. The benches were in rows (as in a church), with the main door at the rear of the hall. There was an empty space at the front of the hall, and in the middle of the wall was a pulpit-shaped lectern. In front of the first bench stood a small harmonium, and in the empty space close to the lectern were two chairs and a table. Trumpets and a music box had been placed on the table. At the beginning of each seance Indridason would sit down on one of the chairs; the person who was to watch him sat on the other. Let us quote Hannesson, one of the researchers who studied Indridason's phenomena:

People seat themselves on the benches and the room is soon filled. Then comes the medium, a young, handsome fellow. He sits down on one of the chairs in front of the lectern, and beside him on the other chair sits a man who is to watch him when the light is put out, and report if he finds that he resorts to imposture. The President scans the hall to see if everybody is present and that everything is in order. Then the door is locked and the lamp is put out, but a candle is lit for the man who is to play the harmonium, care being taken that the light does not fall on the medium. All conversation ceases. A hymn tune is played on the harmonium and several among the audience sing to it.

... There is now semi-darkness in the hall; nevertheless we see the medium plainly. He is sitting motionless on the chair with his hands clasped on his chest, as people saying their prayers are represented in pictures. After a little while he may be seen to make some starts, as if involuntary jerks. All of a sudden his head and his hands fall down and his body seems to become limp. He sits in a stooping position on the chair with his head drooping. The president makes a sign to the musician. The candle is put out and when the tune has been played through the music ceases. The medium has fallen into a trance and is unconscious. The hall is now pitch-dark and silent as the grave.[19]

When Indridason was in a trance, several of his spirit control personalities spoke through him and greeted the sitters. Then the physical phenomena seemed to start. The music box was heard playing a tune in the air, and voices were heard speaking through the trumpets in different parts of the hall. One person, called "the watchman," was chosen to sit close to the medium, usually holding one or both of his hands and even his feet, so that he could report if the medium were to try to produce phenomena by imposture or fraud. Later, he was also apparently responsible for ensuring that nothing dangerous happened to the medium. This person was frequently Prof. Nielsson. As the phenomena occurred the watchman would often call out Indridason's position and say how he was holding him.

Indridason's seances differed in some ways from most seances in other countries during this period—perhaps because none of those present had ever attended a mediumistic sitting abroad:

1. A large number of sitters witnessed the phenomena. To the best of our knowledge, in other countries the number of sitters rarely exceeded

ten. Nielsson says that even though sixty to seventy sitters were present, direct voices were heard, the levitation phenomena occurred and so did all the other telekinetic phenomena.[20] Hannesson writes that the larger experimental hall (seating about one hundred) was full at ordinary seances.[21]

2. The sitters were seated on rows of parallel straight benches with the medium in an empty space in front of them.[22] Other seances were held for the so-called "inner circle," a small group of specially chosen people. These seances, generally held in the smaller experimental hall, were to develop and "experiment" with some of the phenomena, such as the materializations and the light phenomena.[23]

Indridason's seances usually took place in darkness. Members of the Society seem to have tried a red light a few times, but it was abandoned because it caused the phenomena to diminish.[24] However, many violent phenomena were reported to have taken place in full light outside of Indridason's sittings. These occurred during what seemed to be poltergeist outbreaks in the winter of 1907-1908.[25] Furthermore, some table-tilting seances (at which, besides table movements, knocks on the table were reported) seem to have been held in light,[26] and various other phenomena were also reported to have occurred spontaneously now and then in full light.[27] We have described the light conditions in the accounts of Indridason's phenomena whenever our sources have mentioned them.

In this paper on Indridi Indridason, we have concentrated on the development of his physical phenomena. We have not tried to give a comprehensive account of everything alleged to have happened. Unfortunately, early reports frequently lack sufficient details of circumstances. Thus the first part of the paper, up to the description of Hannesson's investigation, does not provide evidence comparable, for example, to what is found in the classic investigations of D.D. Home and Eusapia Palladino. However, the latter part of this chapter describes rigorous control methods imposed by Dr. Gudmundur Hannesson when he started his investigation.

The Beginning of Indridason's Mediumship in 1905

The Experimental Society claimed to have trained Indridason as a medium. Some phenomena first occurred spontaneously, for example when the levitations of Indridason began.[28] Other phenomena, such as apports and materializations, were only obtained after experimentation.[29] We do not have any account of how the Society's members actually trained

Indridason, but apparently in the end they succeeded in producing all or most of the mediumistic phenomena they attempted.

Rev. J. Auduns states that Indridason seems to have had a potential for developing all phenomena known to be produced by physical mediums.[30] Several mediums, such as Rudi Schneider and Eusapia Palladino, suffered decreases in their ability to produce phenomena, but this apparently did not happen to the bulk of Indridason's phenomena. The reason may be that Schneider and Palladino were mediums for long periods whereas Indridason practiced his mediumship for only five years.

In October 1904 Kvaran started to have irregular sittings with a small group of friends and family members, where they attempted to produce table-tilting and automatic writing.[31] Some automatic writing was apparently produced, but its content made little sense. At this time Indridason had not been discovered. After Indridason joined this group, the Society's members spent many months experimenting with and developing the medium's automatic writing, table movements, mediumistic trance and trance speaking.

Indridason immediately produced automatic writing when he tried it.[32] It was difficult to read the writing at first, but it became easier to read as time passed. Finally, he wrote with much more speed than he could normally manage when he wrote in a conscious manner—he had only written a few letters in his whole life, according to Kvaran.[33] About then, Indridason's first spirit control appeared, probably through the writing. The control, who claimed to be a woman, constantly begged Indridason to seek God and "good manners."[34] At this time, members of the Society claimed some "proofs of identity" for deceased communicators manifesting through Indridason's automatic writing.[35]

Indridason fell into trance for the first time at a sitting at Kvaran's home on the Saturday evening before Easter 1905. Until then, mediumistic communications had been received only through automatic writing.[36] The trance started when Indridason, while writing automatically, made some jokes about the entity he believed was making him write. This seemed to cause some upset and the writing protested, "You should not make fun of me," and then declared, "Indridi shall now fall into trance." Indridason did not agree at first, but again the writing insisted, "He shall." He then agreed, and the light was turned off. A table with a pillow was put in front of his seat, and on a small table, paper and a pencil were placed by his right side. He put his head on the pillow; after a few minutes he lost consciousness and started to write on the paper. Kvaran reports on this first occasion:

> He [the medium] wrote a few sentences with harsh jerks, and
> sighed heavily and screamed from time to time. He spoke with

someone he obviously thought of as being with him, asked him not to treat him badly and expressed disagreement with what he thought was being said to him. Then, after about an hour, he was woken up, apparently by the same force that had put him to sleep. He was woken at our request; as we had never seen this state before and we were uneasy.[37]

Experiments with Indridason were continued occasionally until the summer of 1905. But, in the spring of 1905, Indridason became scared while in trance and said he saw shadowy beings; he cursed them, trembled and shivered with terror.[38] Eventually a personality claiming to be Indridason's deceased grandfather replaced the woman control and became his second chief spirit control—the first to speak through Indridason's lips.[39] Little was accomplished with this personality; he soon disappeared and other controls took over. Members of the Society tested Indridason's trance state many times without prior warning, by poking needles in several delicate spots in his body—in his hands, on the back of his neck, in the corner of his eyes and elsewhere—but he showed no reaction at all.[40] They opened Indridason's eyes to test his pupils' reaction to light, but there was no response.[41]

In the trance state Indridason often spoke in the first person as one of the personalities who appeared. Also at this time he started to speak with great astonishment about his own body—and he would frequently do so later on—as if he experienced himself out of the body and was viewing it as from outside. Nielsson writes how Indridason in trance state often described this split perception (the split between observer and the observed):

> "Oh, see me and me. ... You are there below with the body. The body is not me. I am up here. There are two Indridis. Oh, is it not strange to see the nerve [cord], which lies between me and me! The lips of the body move and they say what I say. The nerve [cord] becomes thinner, the further away I leave the body."[42]

Nielsson adds that nobody at that time had heard of this 'cord' except Kvaran, who had read about it but had mentioned it neither to Indridason nor to anyone else. Indridason, during these experiments, was the first man in Iceland known to fall into mediumistic trance, so Nielsson doubted if he could have heard of it from others. Later, when Indridason's left arm apparently dematerialized, we notice again a similar split perception in his trance speaking.

The sections that follow deal chronologically with Indridason's phenomena in order to describe the sequences in his development as a medium. Readers who are primarily interested in the evidential value of the reports on Indridason's phenomena might want to turn next to the section on Dr. Gudmundur Hannesson's investigations during the winter of 1908-1909. In the next few sections, observations of phenomena are described: these are highly interesting accounts of extraordinary phenomena but do not provide such detailed descriptions of controls and conditions as are reported in Hannesson's careful investigations.

Further Development During the Winter of 1905-1906

In the spring of 1905, the number of sitters became so great, circle members decided to establish the Experimental Society on a formal basis. The members started to experiment with levitations of the medium, light phenomena and healing, and they attempted to get "proofs of identity" from alleged deceased communicators. Other phenomena reported during this period included levitations and movements of objects, knocks on walls and the floor, clicks in the air, dematerializations of Indridason's left arm and odor phenomena.

Levitations and Knocks

Indridason was at the home of two friends in Reykjavik on Sunday evening, November 12, 1905.[43] Nielsson reports that this incident took place in twilight and that three or four men were sitting around a table.[44] Indridason's friends suggested that he should try to "lift" the table, and after a short while the table suddenly levitated very high and "bumped" into the faces of those who stood by it.[45] Three men tried to keep the table down by force, but it was still raised from the floor and lifted up to the level of their faces. Additionally, the table lifted itself up to Indridason's and the sitters' hands while they kept their hands some distance above it but with none of them touching it.[46]

A new control personality now appeared and instructed the sitters to have seances every evening for a while in order to produce other phenomena. This third control said he was Konrad Gislason, the brother of Indridason's grandfather, who in his earthly life had been a professor of Icelandic language at the University of Copenhagen. This intelligence was to become Indridason's principal control throughout his mediumistic career.

The table experiment was repeated at Kvaran's house on Monday evening, November 13th.[47] A small table on three legs levitated so high that it "bumped" into the sitters' faces (probably in the sense of 'lifted to their faces'), while they touched the table-top. The table was also raised to some height when the sitters held their hands together at some distance above it, without touching it. The sitters then tried with a very heavy table, which tilted a few times without being touched and once levitated completely off the floor.

In this period a small table was abruptly levitated off the floor and up onto another table. This happened twice and apparently without Indridason attempting to make them levitate.[48] The first time, Indridason was sitting by a table with two other people. He was not in a trance and his hands rested on the table. Then another table behind Indridason levitated and landed on the table they were sitting at. Kvaran reports that the three of them had their hands together, so it was "unthinkable that the medium could have stretched his hand behind himself."[49]

On the other occasion Indridason sat "still as the grave" in a trance state and was speaking with an unfamiliar voice.[50] One of the sitters placed his arm on a small table which was situated in front of the sitter's chair. He noticed that the table started to make movements. He pushed the table down but it was nevertheless "snatched" away. A few moments later, the experimenters heard sounds as if the table had landed on another, bigger table, a fact which was confirmed when the light was lit. When the light was turned off, the table moved, in the same manner, to its original place. "Those who were present assert that Indridason could by no means have transported the table by himself," writes Kvaran.[51] Tables also moved on a few occasions during a "brightly lit day" and in the presence of observers.[52] The tables were moved a "great distance" across the floor to Indridason.

Nielsson reports that at first the experimenters had sat in the dark during meetings, but afterwards they tried a red light.[53] The red light seemed to reduce the power of the phenomena to a great extent, so they abandoned it. Nielsson further elucidates:

> In accordance with the wishes of the controls, who complained of the limiting influences of the light, we gave it up. On the other hand, they emphasized the importance of the greatest possible caution in order to exclude the slightest vestige of fraud on the part of the medium. That is why it soon

became a custom that one of us sat down beside the medium and watched him carefully, placing an arm around his waist or holding one or both of his hands.[54]

Most often Kvaran or Nielsson sat by the medium.[55]

Knocks on walls were heard for the first time during the third meeting in November 1905 while Indridason was in trance.[56] The knocks started in the vicinity of Inridason and were heard on walls or objects and sometimes close to the ceiling. They developed and moved around the room according to the sitters' requests. The knocks appeared as affirmative or negative replies to questions from the sitters. Kvaran states that this phenomenon was checked many times so carefully for fraud that the sitters were in no doubt Indridason could not have produced it by any normal means.[57] Knocks were also heard at the same time as Indridason was writing automatically or speaking in trance. Later, when the Society started to use a special hall for the seances, the knocks "increased."[58] (It is unclear from the Icelandic text whether the knocks increased in *strength* or *frequency*.) They even seemed to come from the ceiling, which was about ten feet above the floor.

One evening, at the end of a sitting, only Kvaran and Nielsson were present. They heard very strong knocks or strokes.[59] Indridason was lying in such a deep trance, according to Nielsson, that his pulse could hardly be detected. "Then the strokes roared on the panels round him and replied very promptly to questions."[60] Meanwhile not a word came from Indridason's own lips.

The Period of Light Phenomena

Two new phenomena started during the fourth seance in November 1905. Clicks were heard in the air, as when fingers are snapped aloud, but with a sharper sound. These clicks were heard every evening for some time, moving all around the room. Indridason was observed to be sitting completely still.[61] Nielsson writes that they had "obtained" peculiar cracking sounds in the air.[62]

There were also light phenomena.[63] The sitters first saw flashes of light or light spots in the air or on the walls in the seance room. Most of the lights appeared to be "tongue-shaped."[64] During the evenings that followed, the flashes grew in strength and had different forms and colors. Just before the clearest lights appeared, Indridason was heard to groan painfully.

One evening, at Kvaran's home, the sitters counted 58 appearances of lights during a single seance.[65] Kvaran writes:

They [the self-luminous lights] had somewhat different colors; some were very white; others were more reddish. Once, during an experimental seance at my home, fifty-eight lights were counted. These lights were of various shapes: some of the lights were round, while others were oblong. They were of different sizes: some were small, about an inch in diameter, but others were stripes of light around two to four feet long.[66]

During one evening Nielsson counted more than sixty lights while Indridason was sitting in the middle of a circle of sitters.[67] Tongues of light of different colors were seen at various locations in the room. The light spots developed into large flashes with a strong reddish tinge, which spread all over one wall of a large room. Nielsson reports that later on the whole wall behind Indridason became a "glow of light."[68] Kvaran writes:

There were a few times when a light spread on a whole wall behind the medium, which was twelve feet wide and ten feet high. Sometimes it looked like a sort of net of light, with circular meshes: slightly darker circles around bright flashes. Again, the light was sometimes continous, similar to the glow from a great fire. Those spreads of light were never as white as the small lights, but were more reddish.[69]

Often peculiar clicks accompanied the lights.[70] The clicks followed each other very fast. Nielsson also reports that strong gusts of wind seldom failed to blow through the room before the lights appeared.[71] The wind was so strong that the hair waved on the sitters' heads and the pages of notebooks, lying open on their knees, flapped vigorously. Three years later Hannesson also observed a strong wind blowing across the hall.[72] Indridason's controls told him that the gust had "to accompany the light phenomena."

Kvaran[73] reports that the guarantee for the genuineness of those lights was:

1. Lamps or equipment which could possibly produce the same kind of flashes were not available in Iceland.

2. Indridason had moved into Kvaran's home before the strongest light phenomena began. Kvaran's wife kept Indridason's belongings. Kvaran states that he and his wife were familiar with everything that Indridason owned. Indridason had only one trunk, which could not be locked, and therefore he could not hide things from the Kvarans in their own home, and there is no evidence he tried to do so. (The seances were being held in Kvaran's home at the time.)

3. According to Kvaran the sitters made a careful body-search of Indridason and also searched the room on some of the evenings at which most of the lights were seen.

4. Nielsson states that when the light phenomena were occurring, the sitters "kept a good eye" on Indridason.[74]

From our sources it seems the purported spirit controls were attempting to produce materializations, the lights being a part of that procedure. The light phenomena continued until eventually, on December 6 and 7, 1905, there appeared for the first time in the light the full form of a man, whose identity was not recognized by those present.[75] Kvaran describes this:

> On two evenings one could clearly see a man standing in the light. He was slightly above average height, muscular, well built, with broad shoulders. His back was turned towards us.
>
> Now one would naturally think that it was the medium that we saw in the light. I would assert that it was not. I was certain, at least the other time when this vision was seen, that the medium was in the corner, crying out loudly and screaming, some eight to ten feet from the place where we saw the man standing. The lights, as in all his major phenomena, seemed to cause him much pain. He began to shriek and scream when the lights were coming, and he continued to do so as long as the lights continued. They came in bursts, with small pauses in between, and during the pauses the medium was calm. After the seances he said he felt as if he had been beaten up.[76]

Nielsson reports that many members of the Society had first seen the materialized being (who later identified himself through Indridason as "Jensen") against a strong reddish glow, in the middle of the radiance which appeared on the wall.[77] He himself saw very distinctly the shape of the head and shoulders of the being. These light phenomena were observed several times, but then ceased around Christmas 1905 and reappeared around Christmas the next year.[78]

Levitations of Indridason Start

A new phenomenon occurred in November 1905, ten days after the experiments started after the summer break. Kvaran describes Indridason's alleged first levitation, which apparently took place in darkness, as follows:

The medium was then in a trance, and suddenly it started complaining that now he was going to be "dragged." Indridason was then "dragged" prostrate back and forth along the floor. ... After a short while I noticed that his neck was resting on the top edge of a small table in front of me. A few moments later another sitter noted that his feet were resting on the living-room table. We were then allowed [probably by the controls] to light a match, and we all saw him in this position, with nothing else holding him off the floor. As we put out the match, he fell down on the floor, overturning the living-room table. One sitter noticed that the table raised itself again.... The medium complained about the treatment.[79]

During the period when the seances were held in members' homes, Indridason is reported to have levitated sometimes to the ceiling, which he touched with his head.[80] Sometimes he even bumped his head harshly against the ceiling and complained about "pain in his head" after the sitting.[81] According to Kvaran, it was difficult at first to observe the levitations of the medium because of the darkness. But the noise, especially when he crashed down on the floor, resulted in complaints from neighbors, and at least twice the Society had to find another flat to hold their seances.[82]

There were several reports of a sofa (or at times a chair), with Indridason on it, levitating during the seances. Thorlaksson states that Indridason was once sitting in a trance state on a small sofa in darkness. The sofa levitated and stood at the "height of a person's chest" above the floor for "such a long time" that some of the sitters were able to feel with their hands the space under the sofa and all the way round it with Indridason still sitting on it. Then it moved slowly down to the floor.[83]

Nielsson described attempts by the sitters to test the early levitations:

In order to substantiate these phenomena, we placed him [the medium] in a basket chair, which creaked conveniently upon the least movement. We placed this at one end of the room and tight rows of chairs all across the room, so that any passage between the chairs was made impossible. Then the sitters— and it must be remembered that we were sometimes 50 or more in number—sat down on all the chairs, the light being put out. Very soon the medium was levitated in the basket chair at a great distance from the floor—the creaking in the chair being heard while it glided ... above our heads—and was eventually rather noisily deposited on the floor behind the chairs. Then the light was immediately lit and there sat the medium unconscious (in a deep trance) in the chair.[84]

Around Christmas 1905 Indridason performed some "remarkable" physical exercises or gymnastic feats in a trance state, which were so complex and difficult that Olafur Rosinkrans, who was a gymnastics education instructor, could not repeat them.[85] The Society members had the lights turned on while Indridason did the exercises.[86]

Dematerialization of Indridason's Arm

Perhaps the most mysterious phenomenon observed with Indridason started on December 18, 1905[87] when the sitters heard some creaking sounds in his arm while he was in a trance state. At Kvaran's home the next day, Indridason, while awake, wrote automatically about the serious concern the controls had about the experimental seance that was to be held the following evening. The controls stressed in automatic writing that the sitters would have to be very calm and quiet, otherwise the medium's life could be in danger. An "operation" would be carried out on him but he was not to have any knowledge about that beforehand so he would not be worried. At the seance during the evening, Indridason's left arm apparently became invisible and intangible for a while. Here is Kvaran's description, based on extensive notes taken during the seance:

> Then I shall allow you to hear what happened at the seance the next evening (Dec. 19th). After the usual seance beginning, a song from us and a prayer from the control, the control seemed to go away for a while. Then the medium said:
>
> "Hi! I am glad to see you came. But what are you going to do with all those knives?—No, no no!" (Goes into the cabinet). "No, no, this is not allowed."
>
> The control's voice: "You be careful!"
>
> Now for a while one could hear cries of pain from the medium coming from the cabinet. Then he came out of the cabinet and said, as if very unhappy:
>
> "When are you coming back with it?"
>
> Then the medium came to me (I sat at the back of the hall),

handed me the empty left sleeve of his jacket and said with the control's voice:

"Take hold here, carefully! You can touch with caution."

I touched but could not find the left arm.

The control: "Take the jacket and be careful! Take it from the right side! [Probably, start by taking the jacket off the right shoulder.] I will put him outside; the air is more refreshing there. [Probably, take Indridason out of the seance room.] ..."

The medium then went out into an empty room at the front of the hall and stayed there for a while. Then he came back in and went into the cabinet. ...

I asked if I could then light a match.

"Yes, but you may not have the light on for a very long time."

I lit a match and saw that it was not bleeding. The medium was lying on his right side on a mattress inside the cabinet. I checked again to see if I could find the arm. But the result was the same.

The medium: "Ah, where are you going with it? Where is it?"

The control: "Check now carefully whether you can see any phenomenon in front of you; perhaps someone will be able to see something waved; my relative's arm, for example."

We searched carefully around us in the hall, but didn't see anything. However, two sitters felt a cold, soft hand touch their faces.

I was again invited to search the shoulder, and I did it as carefully as I could, but did not find the arm.

The control: "In time, you will see this in full light..."[88]

The next evening this same phenomenon occurred again and also one evening later during the same winter, much to the surprise of all the sitters. When the phenomenon occurred on the evening of December 20th, five men searched many times for the missing arm by feeling Indridason's body all over. They did this repeatedly, and matches were lit many times during the search, but no one found the arm.[89] Three sitters out in the hall felt a hand touch their faces at the same time as Indridason was lying in the cabinet. Nielsson was one of the five who searched Indridason that evening.[90] The arm disappeared entirely, he reports, and it was not found, even though a light was lit and Indridason's body was carefully searched.[91]

Nielsson states that seven persons observed the phenomenon the third evening that Indridason's left arm disappeared.[92] They shone light all around Indridason while the empty sleeve hung down. They were permitted (probably by the controls) to touch and feel him all around the shoulder. Unfortunately, they were not allowed to undress the shoulder and see it bare in the light. Kvaran says he then observed this a second time and became more convinced.[93] Indridason stood on the floor and Kvaran felt from Indridason's "shoulder down along his side and back and the same on his front."[94] He also felt "all around him and high and low over the trunk." He thought that with such careful checking he would have noticed the arm if it had been there. All the seven witnesses signed a document at the end of this seance, stating that they had not been able to feel or find Indridason's arm and were prepared to certify this under oath. Thorlaksson was one of the seven who searched for Indridason's left arm and signed the document.[95] Nielsson reports that he was also one of those seven who searched Indridason while he stood in full light without his left arm being visible to any of the people present.[96] Half an hour later, the arm reappeared on Indridason. Nielsson helped Indridason to get his clothing on afterwards, "as the controls had pushed his shirt, waistcoat and jacket up above the shoulder on the left side [probably while 'replacing' it], the arm hanging down bare."[97]

Indridason's chief control personality, "Konrad Gislason," said that the levitations, light phenomena, physical exercises and dematerialization experiments were preparations for the materialization of human forms.[98] Indridason does not seem to have been undressed while the sitters were searching for his left arm, and we are not informed whether it was his jacket sleeve or shirt sleeve that hung down empty. It would obviously have been easier to feel and probe in order to find the arm if Indridason had been wearing only his shirt.

Reports of dematerializations of a medium's body are extremely rare in the literature of physical mediumship. Aksakow, the well-known Russian psychical researcher, reports extensively on the case of the dematerialization of the lower part of the body of the medium Madame d'Esperance, which allegedly took place in December 1893 in Helsinki, Finland.[99] Reportedly the light was sufficient for the eleven persons who were present to see by, and five persons verified by passage of hands that Mme. d'Esperance's body from the waist downward had disappeared. A few more cases of this kind can be found in literature.[100]

Other Phenomena

In February 1906, Indridason was suddenly taken seriously ill.[101] The references do not tell us what the problem was. It was decided to stop the dematerialization experiments. The Society then turned to healing experiments.[102] These experiments commenced with attempts to heal Indridason himself and developed after that into healing others. Indridason disliked these experiments; he had no belief in himself as a psychic healer, and he thought this would be turned against him.[103] At this time light taps, such as a doctor might make during his examination, were reportedly heard on Indridason's chest. Those present held both his hands, but the taps or thumps continued. Similar thumps on his breast were heard while he lay in a trance very ill in his bed.

It even happened that a control personality, called "the Norwegian doctor," would, so the sitters thought, let clear knocks be heard in the bedrooms of those sitters he claimed to visit at night.[104] This personality later revealed at seances what had happened, though these incidents were reportedly known neither to the medium nor to other sitters besides the people who had been "visited."

In February 1906, while Indridason was very sick in bed, a strong, fragrance was experienced coming from his head. Kvaran writes that Indridason could "not possibly" have had with him any drugs that could have emitted this odor.[105] The odor from Indridason's hands and arms was sometimes so strong that it spread over the whole Experimental hall, and when he touched the sitters' faces, the odor would linger there for a good while. Indridason was carefully searched many times before the seances when the fragrance came forth, to rule out the possibility that he had brought some perfume with him, but nothing was ever found. Each and every sitter experienced the odor, sometimes twenty to thirty sitters at the same time.

Many other phenomena occurred during healing experiments with Indridason. For instance, in February 1906, Indridason was in a trance state and massaging the back of one of his patients when Kvaran and other members saw some substance covering most of the patient's back (we are not told how the sitters were able to see the substance). It looked like "dried dew; in some places it was whitish grey but in other places it had a greenish gloss."[106] Kvaran asserts firmly that Indridason "did not have any chemical like that on him and would not have had any idea how to obtain it."[107]

Materializations and Apports during the Winter of 1906-1907

During the winter of 1906-1907 the Society worked mostly with apports, light phenomena and materializations, which reached their climax, while other phenomena were put aside.[108]

The Beginning of Materializations

Kvaran[109] and Nielsson[110] report that shortly before Christmas 1906 sittings were being held in two rooms in Kvaran's house (one fairly large room and a small adjoining bedroom). During sittings in the large room, the smaller seance room was becoming illumined with very strong whitish light. In this light appeared a human being that purported to be the discarnate Mr. Jensen. He first appeared between the curtains (probably curtains between the rooms), in the small room, and shouted, in a genuine and typical Copenhagen Danish accent, "Ka' De se mig?" (in English: "Can you see me?").[111] The control personalities had said they required the small room for their own use. Kvaran's wife and Thorlakson say that Jensen always asked as he appeared, "Can you see me?"[112] Kvaran continues:

> Then Jensen became visible in the [self-luminous] light. In the New Year he showed himself in the living room, where we sat. He was dressed in a white, very fine robe, which reached down to the floor. The light radiated from him and we saw him in various locations in the room. Sometimes he stood very close to one of us. Once he stood on a sofa and behind his shoulders was something like a tiny sun on the wall. This was a very beautiful sight. Sometimes he stood on the chair-back behind the medium. Once he sat with the medium on his knees. He could not stay more than a few moments each time, but he showed himself several times at each seance.[113]

Kvaran reports that on one occasion Jensen appeared 11 times in one hour.[114] Kvaran tells of an occasion when Jensen appeared and stood upright on a sofa which was next to Indridason's chair.[115] The light which radiated from this materialized being seemed quite bright, but somehow it did not penetrate far into the room, with the result that only people sitting closest to the entity could be seen in the light. On one occasion Jensen stood behind the chair in which Indridason was sitting. In the light from the materialized being the sitters could clearly see Indridason in a trance state.

Brynjolfur Thorlaksson described the materialization of Jensen. He says:

> ... it always appeared as a luminous, beautiful light-pillar, just above the average height of a human figure and slightly broader. Inside this light we saw a human form but it was not clear enough, for example, for the facial expression to be distinctly seen. This light-pillar was white but with a little tinge of blue. It was very luminous and did not flicker. However, it did not radiate much light. We saw the medium in a trance when the light-pillar stood near him, although otherwise there was darkness in the room.[116]

The appearance of the light-pillar lasted only very briefly each time and was always accompanied by a low buzzing sound.[117] Our source says that Jensen "often" touched the sitters when he materialized.[118]

Thorlakur Thorlaksson, Brynjolfur Thorlaksson's brother, is reported to have seen Jensen materialize during only one seance at Kvaran's home.[119] He saw Jensen five times the same evening, each time just for a brief period. The light-pillar resembled moonlight shinning but was translucent at the edges, where folds could be seen as on clothes. Jensen seemed to be of average height but "hardly as thick" as an average man. His figure did not emit much light, but Indridason could be seen when the pillar was close to him. Jensen became visible in different places in the seance room and once on a sofa where Indridason was sitting.

Kvaran reports that at one seance 40 people simultaneously saw Jensen appear a number of times.[120] Three witnesses, Hallgrimur Sveinsson (Bishop of Iceland), the Magistrate of Reykjavik and the British Consul, were invited to attend a seance one evening in 1907.[121] The Magistrate was later to become one of the five Supreme Court Judges in the country. He undertook to examine the two rooms and the medium to prevent fraud. Unfortunately, no description is given about the details of his investigation. Forty people attended and many of them had to stand. But all these 40, among them the three "highly esteemed men in whose evidence people could trust,"[122] saw Jensen appear 11 times that evening in bright, luminous light. Nielsson writes that the three reliable witnesses were unable to find any indication of fraud.[123]

The bishop asked for a seance to be held in his own house, and seances were held at his home from time to time during a three-year period. The sittings were held in the bishop's library, and there the different phenomena occurred with even greater ease. Sometimes the control personalities brought Indridason, walking in a trance state, directly from the seance room to the bishop's home, Indridason at such times being always under Nielsson's close attention.[124] The bishop declared later that he was completely convinced that what he had observed was genuine.

Kvaran writes that sitters had on occasion spoken with the materialized beings, touched them and been embraced and kissed by them.[125] However, it is not stated whether these "conversations" with the materialized beings were of a responsive nature. Kvaran says that these materializations lasted for a few weeks altogether.[126] The lights that accompanied the materialized beings disappeared after the beginning of 1907, according to Thorlaksson.[127] It was thought at the time that Indridason's poor health was the reason for the deterioration of his materialization ability. After this period it seems probable that complete human beings never appeared again, but parts of human forms were often seen and felt. Thorlaksson reports an example of a typical materialization that predominated from this time on.[128] Rev. Sigurdur Gunnarsson was once at a seance with the inner circle in the smaller hall of the Experimental House. A hand materialized and was recognized by Gunnarsson as his deceased wife's. He claimed that the hand had a scar on the same finger of the same hand, and in the same place, as his wife had. The hand touched Gunnarsson, and then the voice of his wife reportedly spoke to him.

Apport Experiments

Thorlaksson says that during the winter of 1906-1907 members had special sittings in Kvaran's home which they called "apport seances." Sitters sat by Indridason and guarded him while he was in trance and the room was in darkness. Sometimes objects mysteriously appeared in the room, seemingly teleported from other locations in Reykjavik. Thorlaksson attended only one such seance. At this, a viper preserved in a bottle of spirit was, he reports, allegedly transported through matter. Sitters heard sounds as of something being placed on the table which stood in the room. A light was immediately turned on and the sitters saw a bottle with the viper in it. After three days they managed to find the owner, who reported that the viper had belonged to a small collection which was kept in the attic of the owner's house. The relation, if any, of the owner to Indridason is not known. According to Nielsson, this type of phenomenon was frequently observed.[129] Space limitations do not allow us to list more examples.

One evening Indridason was himself reportedly taken into another room, which was locked and in darkness.[130] Rev. Jakob Jonsson remembers that Nielsson described this incident in a lecture at the theological faculty at the University of Iceland.[131] Tarchini reports a similar incident from a seance, where the sitters thought an (unidentified) Italian medium had been dematerialized and apported from one place (the cabinet) to another (the seance room).[132]

Poltergeist Phenomena During the Winter of 1907-1908

During the winter of 1907-1908, the Society's work was mostly devoted to levitations and large-scale movements of objects, levitations of Indridason himself, flight of objects, knocks, and sitters being touched by apparently materialized arms. In addition, members were trying to develop the phenomenon of direct voice, and music box, trumpet and light phenomena. It is noteworthy that many of these phenomena occurred under good lighting conditions and no evidence of fraud was found. Often, during psychokinetic attacks described below, Indridason was not in a trance.

In the autumn of 1907, strange disturbances started, also outside of seances, in the rooms of the Experimental House—which the medium shared with the theology student, Thordur Oddgeirsson. The phenomena intensified and reached their peak in December. For example, on the evening of December 7th, Indridason and Oddgeirsson had gone to bed in the Experimental House, with a lamp burning on a table between the beds. Suddenly a plate, which had been standing on a bookshelf in the front room, was thrown onto the floor.[133] It came down in the inner room, the bedroom, just inside the door curtains. Indridason's bed was pulled about one foot away from the wall. Indridason was terror-stricken; Society members had to stay with him at night for some time, and all regular sittings stopped.

On the evening of December 9th, a few members of the Society agreed to spend the night in the Experimental House. Nielsson, Gudmundur Jonsson, Gudmundur Jakobsson and Bjorn Jonsson arrived with Indridason at the Experimental House around 11:30 p.m.[134] After Indridason had gone to bed, he went into a trance, but after a short while, when the controls had spoken through him, he came out of the trance. During that night a small table standing between the beds at the head of Indridason's bed was lifted and fell on his bed, making a loud noise. It had apparently smashed against the wall and had broken into two pieces. Indridason's bed was shifted away from the wall, even though Jakobsson sat on the edge of it and Nielsson sat on a chair by Indridason's feet and leaned forward, pressing on the bedstead with both hands. According to

Nielsson, the foot of the bed was shifted "quite the width of a hand"[135] but the head-piece much more. A cardboard box fell down in the inner room at the feet of G. Jonsson, who was sitting close to the threshold. Indridason said the cardboard box had been under a couch in the outer room. At the same instant the lid of the box fell down on Oddgeirsson's bed in which Bjorn Jonsson was lying. No other phenomena took place that night.

Thorlaksson stayed in the Experimental House the next night.[136] Oddgeirsson and Indridason went to their beds, but Thorlaksson lay on a couch in the front room. Indridason fell into a trance, and through him the controls said that during the day Jon (a spirit personality which reportedly caused the phenomena) had collected considerable "power." The controls ordered that no lights should be on. Indridason then came out of the trance. Two candlesticks which had been standing on the harmonium in the front room suddenly fell on the floor. A brush, which was under a chest of drawers in the same room, was thrown into the inner room. Indridason screamed that Jon was there. Thorlaksson then came in and lay on top of Indridason on the bed. The table between the beds lifted onto Oddgeirsson's bed.

Then the situation calmed down for a while, and Thorlaksson returned to the couch in the front room. Again Indridason shouted that Jon was coming. Thorlaksson came into the doorway between the rooms and received a splash of water in his face, while simultaneously a water-bowl fell in front of his feet. It had stood under the washstand four to six feet from the foot of Indridason's bed. Thorlaksson went to Indridason, who lay kicking in his bed asking Thorlaksson to hold him down. Thorlaksson again laid himself on top of him. At the same time a chamber pot from under Indridason's bed was thrown into the outer room. The bed in which the two of them were lying suddenly moved about a foot from the wall, although Thorlaksson pushed with his foot with all his might against the other bed. At the same time, he had to use all his strength to hold Indridason down on the bed. Oddgeirsson came to help, but the table between the beds levitated high up and came down on his shoulders. Oddgeirsson caught hold of one of the legs of the table and held it while he went back to his bed and pulled the quilt over his head. He then received continual knocks on his head from the table top.

They lit an oil lamp—which stood on the chest of drawers between the washing tables in Indridason's bedroom—and also three candles in the front room. At this point they decided to leave the house. Thorlaksson was standing in the doorway between the rooms and Oddgeirsson was sitting on the couch in the front room. Indridason was standing on his bed and beginning to dress. Thorlaksson was looking at Indridason and saw him suddenly flung down on the bed. Thorlaksson rushed to him, but at the same time, he reported, a bowl, which had stood on the chest of drawers in the bedroom, flew toward him. It did not hit Thorlaksson but, according to his account, went past him, altered its direction and took a direct line to the southeast corner of the outer room, where it smashed against a stove. Then Thorlaksson went into the outer room and stood there. Again Indridason started to put on his trousers, and according to Thorlaksson,

> Then Indridi screams for help once more. I run into the bedroom. But then I see a picture that I shall never forget. Indridi is lying in the air in a horizontal position, at about the height of my [Thorlaksson's] chest, and swaying there to and fro, with his feet pointing towards the window, and it seems to me that the invisible power that is holding him in the air is trying to swing him out of the window. I don't hesitate a moment, but grab the medium, and push him down onto the bed and hold him there. But then I notice that both of us are being lifted up. I scream to Thordur Oddgeirsson and ask him to come and help.[137]

Nielsson reported in his paper on the same incident:

> The medium again started to dress, and having got his trousers on, he once more screamed for help. Mr. Thorlaksson had been standing in the outer room, but now rushed to the medium and saw him balancing in the air with his feet towards the window. Mr. Thorlaksson took hold of him, pulled him down onto the bed and held him there. He then felt the medium and himself lifted up. Mr. Thorlaksson shouted to Mr. Oddgeirsson to help him. Mr. Oddgeirsson went into the bedroom, but a chair was hurled at him and fell beside the stove in the outer room. Mr. Thorlaksson was then lying on the medium's chest. Mr. Oddgeirsson lay down on the knees of the medium, whose whole body was in motion on the bed. Then a bolster, which was under the medium's pillow, was thrown into the air; it fell on the bedroom floor. Simultaneously the candlesticks which were in the outer room came through the air and were flung down in the bedroom.[138]

Then all three of them stood side by side and walked backwards out of the room in order to be able to defend themselves against more assaults. Oddgeirsson held the lighted lamp in his left hand and had his right arm around Indridason's left arm. Thorlaksson held his left arm around

Indridason's right arm. Then they all saw a hand basin, which had stood on a washing table in the bedroom, come flying straight toward them nearly at a man's height. Suddenly, when it came into the outer room, it altered its direction and flew past them and broke into pieces on the stove. Then they all rushed out. Finally, they closed the outer room, but Indridason said he saw Jon take a water bottle and throw it at Oddgeirsson, who went out last (the next morning, Oddgeirsson's water bottle lay in pieces on the floor). It was 2:30 a.m. when they left the house and went to Kvaran's home. Soon after they arrived there, small things were thrown down from the walls, and a table made small movements, but no violent disturbances took place.

The readers should bear in mind that the main witness, Thorlaksson, did not become a member of the Experimental Society, nor did he start to attend seances, until after Indridason had been a medium for some time. He claimed not to have known Indridason before that time. There is no evidence, to our knowledge, that Thorlaksson was ever suspected of being an accomplice in faking the phenomena, and Indridason's phenomena were reported to occur with or without Thorlaksson being around.

Dr. Gudmundur Hannesson's Investigations During the Winter of 1908-1909

In the winter of 1908-1909, the phenomena were mostly the same as those of the winter before, except that the light phenomena apparently continued only as nebulous fog-like lights. There are reports of direct voices (frequently singing aloud), levitations and movements of objects, musical instruments being played and touches as if by invisible hands. Other phenomena, such as blows or air currents and direct writing (as if by invisible hands), were also reported to occur.

During this period, Dr. Gudmundur Hannesson asked the Society for permission to attend seances in order to investigate Indridason and his phenomena.[139] Two years after his investigation, in 1911, Hannesson was appointed Professor of Medicine at the University of Iceland, and he held his position until his death in 1946. Hannesson was held in the highest regard in Iceland as a scientist. He had conducted medical, as well as anthropological, research; he founded the Icelandic Scientific Society; and he served two periods as president of the University of Iceland. He was also a member of the Reykjavik City Council. He was an Honorary Member of both the Icelandic and Danish Associations of Physicians. The University of Iceland awarded him an honorary doctorate after his retirement. Hannesson had a greater reputation as a scientist in Iceland than any of his contemporaries, and he was known for his integrity and impartiality.

Dr. Hannesson's request was accepted, and he chose as his assistant an ophthalmic surgeon, Bjorn Olafsson.[140] Hannesson seems to have been known for his disbelief and his skepticism about the reports of the phenomena.[141] Hannesson's report was published as a serial in an Icelandic newspaper (weekly)[142] and much later it appeared in the *Journal of the American Society for Psychical Research*.[143]

Experimental Controls at Hannesson's Sitting

During the first seance attended by Hannesson (which was conducted at the Experimental House) objects were moved, voices were heard, and knocks were audible on the walls.[144] Since no experimental controls were employed by Hannesson on this occasion,[145] we are not going to discuss this sitting here. The next seance also took place at the Experimental House.

As described earlier, the Experimental House had been built according to the Society's specifications (see Figure 1). Hannesson convinced himself that there was neither a cellar below the floor nor space above the ceiling, the roof being flat. It would be easy to discover any meddling with the wooden floor, as it was covered with linoleum, which would "soon betray any interference."[146] Hannesson divided the hall into two parts by firmly nailing down a net from the ceiling down to the floor and out to the walls on both sides. Thus the sitters' benches were separated by the net from where the medium and the watchman should sit. (This area was about one-third of the hall.) Hannesson describes the net as follows:

> It is made of strong yarn and the meshes are so small that it is quite impossible to get a hand through them. It is fastened on all sides with laths [strips of wood], which are threaded through the meshes and screwed firmly to the walls, the ceiling and the floor.[147]

Shortly before the next seance began, Hannesson checked that the laths were securely fastened and the knots of the meshes were firm and did not slide. In the middle of the net, down by the floor, a slit provided an entrance to the inside (we are not told the size of the slit). Hannesson continues:

We [Hannesson and his assistant] examine the floor [inside the net]. It is covered with linoleum, which is apparently sound, with closely joined edges. Then the walls. They are ordinary unpainted panels. No suspicious joinings or movable parts are detected. The panel is nailed down in the ordinary manner. In one corner there is a cupboard in the wall containing a miscellany of small things. We examine it, lock the door and seal it. Finally there is the ceiling. It is of panels like the walls and nailed in the usual way. We examine the lectern, the chairs, the table, and the few other things that are in the place: every movable article is carefully searched for secret contrivances, but nothing of a suspicious nature is found. And no hidden cords are to be found.

We now take the table and other movable articles which were so close to the medium that he might have reached them with his hands or feet. These we move eight to ten feet away. There are then left in the center only the two chairs on which the medium and the watchman are to sit.[148]

In the Icelandic report on this seance, a more detailed description is given, mentioning further precautions, such as: Hannesson examined all crevices in the walls, the floor and elsewhere for hidden threads, and scraped with iron into the crevices when they (Hannesson and his assistant) could not see clearly into them.[149] No strings were found. After Indridason and his watchman were seated behind the net, the slit in the net was carefully threaded together with string, which was tied with a knot and the ends sealed with a seal that Hannesson kept in his pocket.

This second seance which Hannesson attended was similar to the first one, i.e., the same number of people attended—the large hall (having about one hundred seats) again became full—and similar phenomena occurred. Nielsson, who acted as watchman, was repeatedly asked about Indridason's position, especially when something was taking place. He always stated that he was holding one or both of Indridason's hands and that Indridason was sitting still. Once or twice a match was lit, and sitters could then see the medium sitting in the same position as the watchman had described.

One incident is of particular interest here. Hannesson reports:

Suddenly we are startled by hearing the music-box [which was placed in the empty area but out of reach of Indridason] play a tune and circle around in the air at a great speed.

We at once ask the watchman [Prof. Nielsson] what the medium is doing. He says that the medium is sitting motionless in the chair and that he is holding both his hands.

If the watchman were not a man of unquestionable integrity we should have no hesitation in calling him a liar....

It [the music-box] now falls on the table with a great thump. The old familiar voice roars through the trumpet that he has not been at a loss to move the music-box, though it was further away from the medium than usual. He is proud of it and asks us what we think of his performance.[150]

Then began "the same game as the previous seance: every movable thing goes mad and tumbles about. It is anything but quieter [i.e., it is even noisier] than it was on the former occasion."[151]

An examination of the seals, as soon as a lamp was lit at the end of the seance, revealed that they were intact. Hannesson and his assistant went inside to the empty space and carefully examined everything to see if they could spot something that could possibly give them a clue to the source of movements, but they found nothing.

Hannesson Imposes Stricter Controls

At the third seance Hannesson imposed stricter controls. Again the hall, and every item in it, was carefully searched from floor to ceiling:

No effort is now spared in examining everything as minutely as possible. The hall is searched from floor to ceiling, and also every article that is in it. Nothing seems too trivial to be suspected that it may in some way serve the purpose of the impostors.

This is no joke, either. It is a life-and-death struggle for sound reason and one's own conviction against the most execrable form of superstition and idiocy. No, certainly nothing must be allowed to escape.

We undress the medium and examine his clothes. The watchman invites us to examine him. Also the door is locked and sealed and also the cupboard in the wall. The slit in the net is not fastened this time. We are sitting close in front of it, and can watch it.[152]

The Icelandic version provides us with a few additional details, such as: the whole hall was carefully investigated, as well as all the benches, tables, etc.[153] Furthermore, Hannesson reports that the doors of the hall were locked and sealed, thus referring to both doors of the hall: one providing entrance to the materialization room and the other leading to the lobby. Only five persons were allowed to attend this seance. Indridason and his watchman sat inside the net on two chairs, but Hannesson and his assistant sat outside, with Kvaran seated between them. Neither singing nor music was allowed, so that possible footsteps, opening of shutters and other movements could be heard more easily.

The following occurred:[154]

1. Objects were thrown to and fro with great force. The two researchers lit a match and saw the watchman, Prof. Nielsson, and Indridason in the same position as the watchman had reported when things were thrown. They were sitting, and Nielsson was holding both Indridason's hands.

2. The chair was roughly snatched from under Indridason and thrown into a corner: it sounded as if it had broken. Nielsson got up to support Indridason, who appeared to be very weak. Nielsson's chair was immediately thrown away.

3. Hanneson reports:

The watchman asks for the chairs to be brought back to him, so that he need not leave hold of the medium. I offer to go in and fetch the chairs, and a match is lit while I slip through the [slit in the] net. I can see the two men standing in the center, and every article inside the net. The chair is lying out in the corner. I make for it, and in spite of the dark I find it at once. The very moment that I turn round to take the chair *I am struck a heavy blow in the back* [Hannesson's emphasis], as it were with a closed fist. Yet a few seconds previously there was nothing to be seen in that corner. I forthwith take the chair to the men and find them standing exactly as before.[155]

When asked, the watchman said that they stood there all the time without moving. Then Hannesson fetched the other chair and left the empty space via the net.

4. Hannesson continues:

Some moments later the watchman shouts, saying that things are getting serious, for the medium is now drawn up into the air with his feet turned toward the ceiling and his head downwards; and that he is pulling at both his (the medium's) shoulders. We hear a good deal of struggling going on, the combatants shifting backwards and forwards about the floor. The watchman says that the medium is pulled with such force that he is put to the limit of his strength to keep hold of him.

After a while the pull is slackened, the medium sinks slowly down and the watchman manages to put him on the chair.[156]

Then what seemed to be direct voices of the "uninvited visitors" ("spirits") said that they were going away to get more power.

5. When the uninvited visitors "returned," Indridason's and the watchman's chairs were repeatedly snatched away and finally broken to pieces. Hannesson continues:

Suddenly the commotion starts afresh and the voices speak again. The chairs under the medium and the watchman are time after time snatched away and finally broken to pieces. The medium is pulled up into the air with so much force that the watchman, as he says, is repeatedly almost lifted off the ground. All this is accompanied by so much scuffling and struggling that apparently it is going to be unavoidable to go to the aid of the watchman, who is exerting himself not to let the medium go—up into the air!

The scuffle is now carried toward the lectern. Suddenly the watchman shouts that things have taken a dangerous turn, for the medium's legs have been quickly pulled down into the lectern while the small of his back is resting on the edge. He fears that the medium will not be able to stand this and that it will result in disaster, for while he is pulling at his shoulders with all his strength "the others" are pulling at his legs.

We are about to go inside to give assistance, when we hear some still rougher shuffling and the watchman says that everything is again all right. He has, he explains, put one foot against the lectern and in that way been able to pull the medium out and get him on the floor.

The tumult now ceases.[157]

Direct voices were frequently heard speaking, using rude language and threatening the medium. At this point (according to the voices), the "uninvited visitors" went away again to fetch more power. The watchman said he had clasped his arms around Indridason's waist and pinioned his arms down. Additionally, he said, he was squeezing both Indridason's knees tightly between his own. Hannesson lit a match and saw them on the lectern step, in the position described.

6. The uninvited visitors "returned" and the pulpit was pulled once or twice so that it sounded as if everything was breaking.

7. A terrific crash was heard and a heavy thump. The watchman and Indridason had been thrown up in the air and fallen on the floor. The whole lectern had been torn loose. It had been built at the same time as the house and firmly nailed to the end wall. The upper part of the step (to the lectern) was equally firmly nailed to the lectern, but not quite so securely fastened to the floor. Nielsson, the watchman, reported on this instance:

> After a terrible struggle with two vulgar entities, while I kept my arms round the shoulders of the medium, pressing his legs between my knees, a pulpit situated near the wall inside the net and solidly fastened by nails to the floor had its panels all of a sudden jerked upwards from the floor and flung outwards to the net. It will be observed that this involved wrenching the woodwork out of the floor as well as from the wall, the pulpit being firmly fixed to both. After this I myself while continuing to hold the medium was thrown with him into the air, so that we crashed to the floor violently, I with swollen hands, he with a little perceptible sore caused by a nail upon which he fell.[158]

8. Hannesson found something bulging through the net near the bottom, and noticed it was the corner of the lectern. He grasped hold of it with his hands and challenged the "spook" to pull it away. "Eat hell," replied a voice, and the lectern was dragged, with considerable force, a little along the floor.

9. Hannesson reports:

> I cannot refrain from retorting in some uncomplimentary term. By way of reply I get some broken glass, and other rubbish that was lying on the floor, thrown into my face. This was thrown from the empty quarter and from a *different direction* [Hannesson's emphasis] entirely to that of the medium and the watchman, who were lying on the floor close to my feet.

Who in the world was it that threw these things?[159]

10. The watchman, lying on the floor, took hold of one of the table legs with one hand and held the other tightly around Indridason. The table suddenly levitated, and the leg was wrenched out of the watchman's hand. The table crashed noisily upside down on the floor close by them. After that the disturbances stopped.

When the lights had been turned on, the sitters saw the wreckage of the lectern lying broken on the floor, and an unpainted panel where it had previously stood. Pieces of broken chairs, glass from a water-bottle, which had been on a shelf above the lectern, and other items were strewn over the floor. Hannesson reports:

> We suggest that everything be photographed in its present condition and be left untouched. But we take the opportunity of examining the lectern and the floor underneath it, for these seemed the likeliest place for concealment of secret devices. Unfortunately we gain nothing by this, except the certainty that nothing was, nor could have been, hidden there. We also examine the nailing, which seems to have been quite secure....
>
> We rehearse the phenomena in every detail, and recognize that there is no possibility of explaining the lifting of the medium by supposed cords from the ceiling.[160]

On the one hand, the primary weakness of this report can be said to be the darkness and the fact that Hannesson did not actually witness the levitations himself. But on the other hand, Nielsson had an impeccable reputation as a professor at the University of Iceland, as well as a highly respectable minister of the church. Nielsson was, and still is, considered to be one of the greatest theologians and preachers that Iceland has had. It seems extremely unlikely that he was reporting something other than what he thought he was witnessing. Hannesson ends his report on Indridason's phenomena by stating:

> But finally I want to mention that in spite of all observations I never discovered any dishonesty on the part of the watchman [Nielsson], who as a rule was in charge of the medium and to whom I have repeatedly referred above. On the contrary, as far as I was able to judge, his observations were very keen and accurate. On a single occasion only I found a slight and excusable misunderstanding due to the darkness of the room.

This man has had better opportunities than any other to observe the phenomena. To be constantly deceived he would therefore have had to be more than blind. His verdict of the phenomena is that there can be no doubt whatever of their actuality, and he is a trustworthy man, highly respected by everybody.[161]

Levitation of a human body has sometimes been observed at seances of various celebrated mediums, but reports of such phenomena have often been hotly debated. The levitations of Eusapia Palladino (1854-1918) are among the best-observed cases, and the historic levitations of D.D. Home (1833-1886) have been frequently quoted and referred to in the literature of psychical research. Some of the most astounding cases of levitation of which there are any records, however, are probably those of St. Joseph of Copertino (1603-1663). His elevations, and flights over some distance, were reported on something approaching a hundred separate occasions under a variety of conditions and in many different surroundings.[162] Indridason's levitations must be considered an important addition to these reports.

Unpublished Notes by Hannesson

We discovered with Hannesson's descendants handwritten unpublished notes made by him and describing some seances.[163] The most remarkable of these occurred on December 12, 1908. Present were Indridason, Kvaran, Bjorn Olafsson, Hannesson, Nielsson and Mrs. Karolina Isleifsdottir (Hannesson's wife, who had indicated her disbelief in the happenings). Description of the following phenomena was written down in darkness, and the draft rewritten next morning. This is evidently a more detailed account of the seance Hannesson described in his article in *Nordurland*[164] and JASPR,[165] neither of which mention some important experimental precautions he took.

This seance was held in Hannesson's recently built house, to control for possible fraud by accomplices and equipment that might possibly be hidden in the Experimental House; although, after having examined the hall thoroughly, he reports that he had been convinced that it contained no secret door or contrivances.[166] Indridason had never visited this house, states Hannesson. The room was chosen by Hannesson only thirty minutes before the seance started. Prior to the sitting, Hannesson and his wife, who lived alone in the house, moved every loose object into one corner of the room and made sure that they were out of reach. The curtains were removed and the windows covered with blankets.

When the sitters arrived, Indridason undressed in bright light in the presence of Hannesson and put Hannesson's clothes on. The only clothes he got back after examination were socks, which had been turned inside out, a neckcloth made of silk, and suspenders. Indridason's hair was examined. The watchman, Nielsson, was also examined (although we are not told how). Doors were locked and sealed. "All round" Indridason's body was "sewed strong string," and this was fastened "quite well to the jacket" he was wearing. The jacket was sewed together (the notes do not say where or how). The watchman was to "hold the string" (probably the string which was left over from the string around the medium). If the string was not loosened, and not pulled out further than his knee could stretch, then Indridason could not reach anything except his own and the watchman's chair. Phosphorescent tape was put on Nielsson's shoulder. (Hannesson had obtained from abroad some phosphorescent tape which was glowing in the dark. To the best of his knowledge, nobody in Iceland had such tape at the time. The phosphorescent tape was then usually placed on the zither and other objects to observe their movements in the darkness. Sometimes the tape was attached to Indridason and the watchman to see if they moved.) To make it easier to follow any movements by the medium, Indridason was seated in a wicker-chair which creaked as soon as he moved. A red "photographic lantern" was lit, other lights being turned off, and the seance began at 8:45 p.m.

Some of the phenomena which took place were as follows:

> ... Silence at the beginning of the seance. Konrad [Indridason's chief control personality] greeted and was satisfied with the environment. [The personality] Jon, speaking as a direct voice, ordered that the red light should be turned off, but not until after a matchbox was thrown.

> Matchbox thrown. At 8:57 a matchbox thrown on the table to us. H.N. [Nielsson] thought it had been in his pocket, but did not notice it being removed. After this there was no light and therefore it was not possible to see what time it was. ...

> Unclear knocks in the north side of the living room, quite far away from medium. ...

> Medium levitates. [Such that] his hips [were] at the same height as H.N.'s shoulders [who was] sitting. ...

> Clear knocks on the north side of the living room further away from the medium, approximately over the buffet. Moved

horizontally closer and closer. ...

Now the phosphorescent star is no longer seen. As long as it was illuminated it was clear that H.N. was sitting still.

A piece of bread thrown to me. Unknown from where.

Whistling close to the ceiling.

A Norwegian man (the doctor) [a control personality] speaks very clearly outside medium.

Twice blown on H.N. such that it was heard. He asserts that it is not the medium.

... At this point the medium became restless and was felt to levitate [probably by Nielsson]. The chairs of H. [Nielsson] and medium fall over. After permission [probably from the controls] I (G.H.) move my chair to the other side of the medium, and raise up the [other two] chairs. The medium is then blocked in the corner of the living room between me and H.N.

Neither of them moved away. The medium's chair levitates a few times, but not with so much force that it could not be held down with one hand. The chair felt as if it kind of sprawled or was alive when it was held. The medium was raised up and H.N. thought that he was being pulled up on [by?] his head. He did not levitate, though, from the floor. I found nothing on the head when I felt around it.

I heard many times amazingly clear speech outside medium, very close to me, mostly swear-words and curses of the disturbing visitors. Most of the time the voices came from the corner behind medium or from the north side of him. 2 x [twice] somebody screamed suddenly and quite loudly about a palm's distance from my head such that I was startled and punched automatically in that direction, but didn't feel my fist come across anything.

Once [air] was blown very clearly in my face and, according to what I thought, quite far away from medium's head (ca. 1

alin) [two feet] and from a different direction. *Meanwhile the medium was talking* (Sigmundur] [a control personality], and I heard the controller [Nielsson] on the other side.

Apart from that nothing in particular happened. Afterwards, when the house and the string around medium were examined, nothing suspicious [was] found. The sewing not disarranged.
...

Damage or a scratch [noticed on the wall] from medium's chair in the corner indicates that the chair has levitated at least 35 cm.[167]

One of Indridason's Last Sittings in 1909

Reports of two seances that Hannesson published in *Morgunn*[168] describe well his precise method of observation. We shall briefly describe the seance which took place on June 8, 1909. Shortly before the seance started, Hannesson examined the net to ensure it was secure and undamaged—which it was. The slit was threaded together and Bjorn Kristjansson and Gisli Petursson sealed the ends together. Both Skafti Brynjolfsson and Prof. Nielsson sat inside the net, with Indridason, to guard the medium, in addition to Petursson and Hannesson, who were going to take notes of the directions of the movements of a phosphorescent tape, if it moved. Things were arranged as shown in Figure 2. One trumpet and an open envelope, on which was glued phosphorescent tape were placed inside the pulpit (door X in Figure 2). On the large table lay zither (on which about three inches of phosphorescent tape had been fastened), and one trumpet. On the small table lay a few sheets of paper and a pencil. Hannesson and Petursson checked to see if anything had been written on the sheets, and they marked the two top ones by tearing off (and keeping) a corner. The whole space inside the net was searched and examined by Hannesson and Petursson. Nothing suspicious or new was discovered.

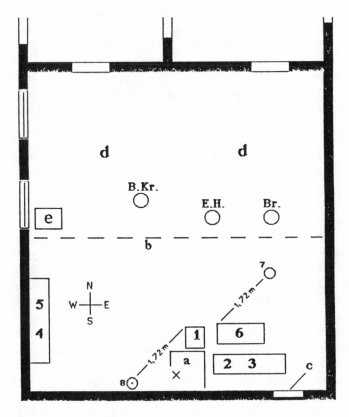

Figure 2. Location of objects and sitters at Hannesson's seance with Indridason on June 8, 1909.[169]

    a the pulpit (immovable since it had been nailed to the wall)
    b the net
    c the cupboard (closed, but not locked)
    d audience space
    e harmonium
    1 Indridason's chair
    2 Nielsson's chair
    3 Brynjolfsson's seat
    4 Petursson's seat
    5 Hannesson's seat
    6 the big table
    7 the large trumpet on a lattice
    8 the small table, on which writing implements had been placed
    Br. Mrs. Brynjolfsson's seat
    E.H. Kvaran's seat
    B.Kr. Kristjansson's seat

The following phenomena occurred:[170]

1. As sitters were singing at the beginning of the seance, Hannesson heard a female voice accompanying them after Indridason had fallen into trance. The voice seemed to originate from inside the enclosed area.

2. The zither levitated many times. It was seen flying at different speeds in various directions (the phosphorescent tape indicating this). There is no doubt that some of the movements were so far away from Indridason they were out of his reach.

3. The strings of the zither were touched and played upon a little a few times, both while it was in the air and when it was on the table.

4. Once the zither lightly touched Brynjolfsson forehead.

5. The phosphorescent tape was apparently taken off the zither and moved around in the air.

6. The end of the large table which was further away from Indridason tilted and moved in small jerks towards the net, then to the right, close to Hannesson; in the end it rolled over on its side.

(a) Brynjolfsson held firmly onto its end (the one further away from Indridason) but it tilted nonetheless.

(b) Indridason was sitting at the other end of the table and Nielsson was holding his right arm.

7. The big trumpet and the iron leg followed the table around from the left side of the hall to the west side and ended on the east side of the table.

8. The little table was turned upside down.

9. Shortly before the large table moved, a crack was heard in the pulpit as if something was pulling at it very forcefully.

10. Indridason's chair was thrown across the floor in Petursson's direction.

11. Hannesson reports:

> The shelf (nailed down firmly) was torn off the pulpit with a loud cracking noise. Thrown on to the floor. *Both* medium's hands were held while this happened (H.N. only or, rather, Sk.Br. and H.N.*).

> * *When the shelf of the pulpit was thrown*: the medium was held, but not clear whether both [watchmen] were holding or only H.N. Sk. Brynjolfsson asserted that the medium could not have reached the pulpit with his arms.[171]

12. The open envelope suddenly appeared out of the pulpit, went a bit higher up in the air, then moved to the net and swung in an arc west to

the wall. Brynjolfson saw the envelope when it appeared in front of him to the left.

13. The net, close to the harmonium, began to shake violently, and this was repeated many times. Indridason was standing between Nielsson's knees and both his hands were held while this occurred. Hannesson could feel the harmonium shaking. This was repeated many times. Meanwhile only "usual" shivering and no strong movements of Indridason's body were felt.[172]

14. Various things from inside the wall cupboard were moved out onto the floor. The medium stated that the objects had been apported through solid matter. Brynjolfsson, who sat next to the cupboard, had not noticed the door opening or closing. No sitter heard it open or close.

In conclusion, Hannesson remarks, after continuous attempts to prevent trickery during the sittings:

> I continued to attend the seances of the Society for a whole winter, and there was hardly one at which I did not try to detect fraud in one way or other. At almost every seance I noticed something which I considered suspicious, sometimes very suspicious, and at the next one I would be specially vigilant on that particular point. But in spite of all, I was never able to ascertain any fraud. On the contrary, the bulk of the phenomena were, as far as I could judge, quite genuine, whatever their cause may have been. A great many things I had no means of investigating, and so can pass no judgment as to whether they were genuine or not.[173]

Nielsson writes[174] that after this winter Hannesson had declared himself convinced of the genuineness of the phenomena. When Nielsson was leaving for the first International Congress for Psychical Research at Copenhagen in 1921, Hannesson told him: "You may state as my firm conviction that the phenomena are unquestionable realities."[175]

Accounts from Other Observers During the Winter of 1908-1909

From this winter we have an account of an object changing its position from one place to another without being seen moving between them. Indridason and Thorlaksson had just arrived at the Experimental House one evening early in the autumn of 1908 and were standing in the lobby when the voice of the control personality "Sigmundur" called to them, coming apparently from the large hall through closed doors.[176] When Indridason and Thorlaksson had entered the Experimental hall, Thorlaksson said, "Sigmundur, can you take the hat off my head and put it on the pulpit where I can see it?" No sooner had Thorlaksson finished the sentence than he saw the hat on the lectern upside down. The hat was not seen being transported across the hall. Apparently it had been placed on the pulpit at the same moment it disappeared from his head. At Thorlaksson's request the hat was moved back on to his head, and this was repeated once more to and fro. Bright moonlight from an almost full moon flooded the hall, and there were no clouds (the shutters of the windows must have been open). While this was taking place, Indridason sat motionless by the wall on the south side of the window at Thorlaksson's request. Thorlaksson sat by the wall on the east side of the door leading to the lobby. The pulpit was at the southern end of the hall opposite Thorlaksson, with a desk on top of it (see Figure 1).

Direct Writing

Thorlaksson describes a case of direct writing which occurred when he visited Indridason in his living quarters in the Experimental House.[177] Only Thorlaksson and Indridason (not in trance) were present. Thorlaksson tore a page from his pocket-book and placed it and a pencil on a table in Indridason's bedroom. There was no light on in the room, but an oil lamp was burning in the adjacent room, where Indridason and Thorlaksson were, with the door open between the rooms. After two minutes they heard "clear sounds as if the pencil had fallen down on the table and as if it had come down with one end first." Thorlaksson went in and saw the pencil not on the paper as he had left it but beside it. He took the paper and the pencil out into the light. On the paper had been written "singa sola mina vina." This text is broken Icelandic and probably means "sing solo my friend(s)." Thorlaksson repeated this procedure and again direct writing was obtained. They "felt sure" that on the first sheet they had obtained the handwriting of a personality called "Malibran," a communicator purported to be a French female singer, as Indridason had asked her "in his mind" to write something on the paper. The second sheet was signed "Edward Grieg" (the famous Norwegian composer). Thorlaksson managed to find an example of Grieg's signature: it appeared to be identical to the one from his diary. According to Thorlaksson,[178] Indridason had sat motionless in a chair in the outer room and never entered the bedroom while this was taking place.

Levitations During the Winter of 1908-1909

Powerful levitation of objects was not unusual. During a public seance in the Experimental House, the harmonium started moving away from Thorlaksson, who was playing it.[179] He said he had thrust his left foot against the floor but kept his right foot on one pedal of the harmonium and "followed it" in that fashion "jumping" along the floor. As this was happening Thorlaksson simultaneously told the sitters what was going on. Suddenly the harmonium was snatched away from him. Light was immediately turned on and the sitters saw that the harmonium had been moved onto a table on the east side of the hall. The harmonium was quite large and firmly built, its height being about that of a man's hip and its feet fitted with small wheels. The levitation was done so that no sound was heard when it landed on the table. Two men had great trouble bringing it down off the table and onto the floor; this was accompanied with a lot of noise.

Krisjan Linnet was sitting close to the end of the harmonium when this happened, and he confirmed Thorlaksson's account.[180] Linnet estimated the harmonium weighed around 150 pounds. Kvaran also describes this phenomenon, stating that the table had been a few meters from Thorlaksson.[181]

Let us look at one apparently powerful levitation of Indridason himself after a seance in January 1909 (probably taking place in darkness). Nielsson reports:

> This time (January 18, 1909) I and two others remained alone by the medium at the end of the sitting. Then the operators seemed to have difficulty in waking him.... In a kind of semi-trance... he said: "Where are you going to take me?" A little later we three heard his voice coming from close to the ceiling and made some remarks about it. Then one of the control's assistants was heard to say, loud and directly from the ceiling: "Don't be afraid." Next all three of us clearly heard the medium being drawn along the ceiling of the room, the height of the room being twelve feet, and made to knock his fingers on it. After a while he was taken down and we were asked for light. He was lying prostrate on the table, still being in trance.[182]

According to our sources, levitations of participating persons other than Indridason occurred rarely. Thorlaksson says he once challenged the personality called "Jon" to take him up during a seance in darkness:

> ...Once, as so often, I was sitting by the harmonium after I had finished playing. Then I said to Jon from the Westman Islands:

"It is not more than a man's job for you, Jon, to take me up."

Immediately—just as I finished the last word—I felt as if something covered me completely but did not grasp me in any particular part of the body. At the same moment I crashed down on the floor on my hands and feet behind the harmonium. This happened at such lightning speed that I had no time to realize the route. I had no awareness until I fell down on the floor. It was a complete mystery to me whether I was thrown over the harmonium, shoved past it or pushed through it. I was not conscious of anything until I fell down rather heavily on the floor.[183]

This occurred in the Experimental House during a seance in darkness. The lights were turned on when the sitters heard Thorlaksson fall down on the floor, and they saw him crawling on his hands and feet behind the harmonium.

Concluding Remarks

Most of the contemporary reports leave many questions unanswered, as they often lack sufficiently detailed descriptions of circumstances that may be crucial for a thorough and fully satisfactory assessment of the genuineness of the phenomena.[184] However, on the basis of the several contemporary reports that do exist, we can point out the following arguments that support the hypothesis that the phenomena are likely to be genuine:

1. In his well controlled seances in the winter of 1908-1909, Hannesson did not succeed in finding any evidence of fraud, in spite of a thorough and sustained effort to do so. The phenomena were then at their height. Besides, there is no evidence to suggest that Indridason's phenomena were fraudulently produced before that time. (A summary of the methods that Dr. Hannesson used in his investigation is given in Appendix A.)

2. Most of Kvaran's and Nielsson's articles were written on the basis of contemporary notes. Some apparently were written from their memory of events, but usually in both instances they also checked the Minutes Books. Thordarson also used the Minutes Books to check Thorlaksson's reports. Hence it is not perhaps surprising that our sources correspond in detail, as most of the authors consulted, and based their accounts on, the Minute Books. However, we also have reports of witnesses describing

certain events in the same manner, even though it is not mentioned that the Minutes Books had been consulted (e.g., accounts of Gislina Kvaran, Kristjan Linnet and Thorlakur Thorlaksson). Hannesson's reports were independently written.

3. The Experimental Society invited many outsiders to attend seances and witness Indridason's phenomena. Among them were strong disbelievers and specially qualified or highly respected citizens, such as the Bishop of Iceland, the British Consul, Dr. Gudmundur Hannesson, Bjorn Olafsson, and the magistrate who later became a Supreme Court judge, to mention a few. Those who were invited, and accepted the invitation, apparently became convinced the phenomena were not produced by fraud. Hannesson became convinced of the genuineness of the phenomena, although he apparently never made any statement supporting their spiritualistic interpretation.

4. All that we know indicates it was the sincere wish of the Experimental Society to have the genuineness of the phenomena fully examined. The leaders of the Society were generally considered men of integrity and were among the most educated citizens in Iceland at that time—most of them academics and some holding the highest offices of the country.

5. Many of the macro-psychokinetic phenomena were 'unwelcome,' so to speak. For instance, the phenomena occurring in connection with "Jon." According to our reports, Indridason seems to have been genuinely frightened by these ostensible telekinetic assaults.

6. Some of Indridason's phenomena occurred in full light and when he was not in trance.

In this chapter we have mainly confined ourselves to describing Indridason's physical phenomena. Not all the phenomena were violent and rough. Nielsson writes, for example:

> It should be remembered by the reader that Professor G. Hannesson has only described one side of these phenomena and the roughest one, and those were the things most convincing to him. But the phenomena had also a different side, an amiable one, and I have never met with such loving kindness as was shown by some of the intelligences of the fixed group. If this all originated from the medium's subconsciousness, then he was a wonderful man.[185]

We have chosen only seldom to refer to the voluminous literature on research with other physical mediums. We considered it outside the scope of this chapter to do so. However, in Appendix B, we have provided a comparison between phenomena that are reported to have taken place in the presence of Indridason and those that were observed and reported with Daniel Dunglas Home, the most famous of all physical mediums.

Appendix A

SUMMARY OF MAJOR METHODS
WHICH GUDMUNDUR HANNESSON
USED IN HIS INVESTIGATION.

G.H. = Dr. Gudmundur Hannesson;
H.N. = Prof. Harldur Nielsson;
I.I. = the medium, Indridi Indridason.

Item	Short Description
The empty area of the Experimental House was isolated.	The area where I.I. sat and in which various objects (trumpets, tables, etc.) were placed was isolated from the rest of the hall. G.H. nailed down a net reaching from the ceiling to the floor, which was made of strong yarn with meshes too small for a hand to get through. The net was fastened on all sides with wooden slats threaded through the meshes. The slats were firmly screwed into the ceiling, walls and floor.
Entrances were locked and sealed.	Doors leading to the seance hall were locked from the inside and sealed. The slit in the net, which provided entrance into the empty area, was also tied together and sealed.
The hall was examined.	The whole hall was carefully searched shortly before and immediately after experimental sittings, and the ceiling, walls and floor, the panel and all crevices carefully examined for possible clues to fraud.
Sittings were held in other houses.	The phenomena occurred at seances in other houses, e.g., at the homes of the bishop and G.H. This supported the opinion that the Experimental House was 'clean.' In his own home, G.H. chose the seance room shortly before the sitting.
Phosphorescent tape was put on most of the objects.	G.H. put phosphorescent tape on the objects that moved in the darkness at seances to observe their movements. He reported that the movements were odd, not like the movements that one would expect if I.I. (or an accomplice) had produced them by swinging the objects around with string and/or a pole.

'Multiple effects.'	G.H. tried to notice whether two or more of the phenomena occurred simultaneously, in such a way that a single person could hardly have faked them. He reported several such simultaneous occurrences, e.g., when he felt a strong blow coming from a different direction than that of I.I. and the watchman. On at least two occasions he was sure he heard two different direct voices simultaneously singing the same tune.
Excluding accomplices.	G.H. selected disbelievers to attend some of the sittings to control for a possible deceiver among members of the Society. For the same reason G.H. had sittings where only a few persons he trusted were allowed to attend.
Silence.	G.H. had sittings with only a few selected people and without playing the harmonium, to be better able to notice if someone moved around the hall. He observed many phenomena occurring during silence.
Sudden unprepared actions.	(i) Sometimes a sitter asked for a knock somewhere in the hall, and immediately the knock was heard coming from the spot. G.H. reported that the agility of an impostor would have to be amazing. (ii) Sitters often turned on a light immediately after asking for permission. Nothing suspicious was seen at these moments. (iii) Sometimes lights were suddenly lit without permission.
I.I. searched before sittings.	(i) I.I.'s clothes and hair were carefully examined. (ii) I.I. had to change clothes before at least some of the sittings with G.H. G.H. watched him while he was doing this. (iii) I.I.'s clothes were sewn together.
I.I. watched.	(i) A watchman sat by I.I. during seances holding all his limbs. (ii) Sometimes two watchmen held I.I. (iii) I.I. was blocked up in one corner of the seance room with two watchmen, one on each side, holding him. (iv) A string was sewn around I.I. H.N. held the end of the string. He had the string so short that I.I. could not reach the objects that were expected to move without him noticing.

(v) G.H. put phosphorescent tape on I.I. to see where he was.

(vi) I.I. was seated in a wicker chair, to hear if he moved in the chair or out of it.

The watchman searched.

(i) In our sources we are told that the watchman (H.N.) was often searched before sittings.

(ii) The watchman was held like I.I. during seances. G.H. held his hands and felt his knees while the phenomena took place.

(iii) G.H. put phosphorescent tape on the watchman to see where he was.

Ruling out possibilities.

(i) G.H. used various methods of producing light spots, to see if the lights that moved at seances were for certain the phosphorescent tape on the objects. These light spots never resembled the light spots coming from the phosphorescent tape.

(ii) The phosphorescent tape was bought abroad. It was not possible to buy it in Iceland at the time.

(iii) Hannesson argued that nothing could explain many of the phenomena, except that an able-bodied man was free inside the net. Three strong men were not able to shake the pulpit which later at a seance was torn loose by invisible power.

The objects that moved.

G.H. examined the objects that moved during sittings, both before and after seances. He found no hidden cells in them. Some of the objects were not owned by the Society; for example, the zither, which was often moved through the air, was borrowed from Thorlaksson. I.I. did not own any of the objects.

Appendix B

COMPARISON OF ALLEGED PHENOMENA
OBSERVED IN THE PRESENCE OF INDRIDI INDRIDASON
AND DANIEL DUNGLAS HOME[186]

H: denotes phenomena occurring in the presence of D.D. Home
I: denotes phenomena occurring in the presence of Indridi Indridason

Type of Phenomena

H	I	Medium falls into trance
H	I	Trance speaking

Knocks

H		Raps, like stream of electric sparks
H	I	Clicks/cracking sound in the air
H	I	Knocks respond to sitters' questions and requests
H	I	Knocks heard on the medium himself
H	I	Loud and heavy knocks

Blows

H	I	Cold/hot gusts of wind
H	I	Gusts of wind strong enough to blow paper
	I	Gusts of wind as if someone is blowing

Odor Phenomena

H	I	Sudden fragrance in presence of medium
H	I	Other smells, e.g., smell of seaweed
H	I	Odor 'clings' to sitters after touch by medium

Phenomena in Connection with Attempted Healing

H		Strange heat radiates from medium
	I	Operation without equipment*
	I	Wound heals completely in a few minutes*

Movements of Objects

H	I	Trembling of objects
H		'Earthquake effect'—seance room trembles as in earthquake
H	I	Objects move a short distance
H	I	Light objects move a long distance
H	I	Heavy objects move a short distance
H	I	Heavy objects move a long distance
H	I	Curtains pulled to and fro by request*
H	I	Light is turned off

Levitations of Objects

H   I   Tilts
H   Objects do not fall off a table that tilts
H   I   Light object levitates high
H   I   Heavy object levitates

Objects Moved Through the Air Without Support

H   I   Heavy and light objects move a short distance
H   I   Light object moves a long distance
     I   Heavy object moves a long distance
     I   Objects move as if they have been thrown powerfully
     I   An object moves between two places without being seen moving

Phenomena in Connection with Musical Instruments

H   I   Musical instruments play without anyone touching them
     I   Winding of a music box by itself*
H   I   Musical instruments played while being moved through the air

Movements and Levitations of People

H   Medium walks in darkness without bumping into furniture
     I   Medium is thrown or dragged along floor
H   I   Medium levitates
H   I   Others than medium levitate during a seance
H   I   Medium is 'transported' a long distance

Fixations (the opposite of movement)

H   I   Sitters cannot move medium's body or limbs
H   I   Sitters cannot move objects or stop them from moving
H   Object becomes light or heavy on request

Light Phenomena

H   I   Fire-flashes or fire-balls
H   Small lights, stars or 'phosphoric balls' in the air
H   I   Luminous clouds
     I   Small and large light-flashes on walls
     I   Light-spreads, as large as ten to twelve feet
H   Luminosity of objects, clothes, letters, etc.
H   Luminosity of medium's head, hands, etc.
H   I   Luminosity of materializations

Materializations

H   I   Only shadow/shape of apparently materialized fingers is seen*
H   I   Only a hand or foot is seen
H   I   Only shadow/shape of human figures is seen
H   I   Complete materialized human being is seen
H   I   Sitters touch materialized fingers
     I   Sitters touch materialized limbs/trunks that do not recede
     I   Monster-like 'animal' is seen*

Touches or Pulls by Apparently Materialized Beings

H	I	Sitters are touched
H	I	Objects are pulled
H	I	Sitters' clothes are pulled
H	I	Sitters are kissed
	I	Objects that have been firmly fastened are torn loose
	I	Sitters are violently pulled or punched

The 'Fire Test'

H	Medium handles something burning without hurting himself

Dematerialization

I	One of the medium's limbs becomes undetectable by touch

Changes in the Size of the Medium

H	Elongation
H	Medium becomes shorter/smaller

Phenomena in Connection with Essence

H		Medium 'withdraws' scent from a flower
H		Liquid is extracted from something, e.g., spirit from brandy
H		Liquid is 'moved' out of a glass/put back in a glass
	I	Medium produces apparently unknown substance

Sounds Heard Outside the Medium

H	I	Laughter
H	I	Clatter of hoof-beats
H	I	Footsteps
H		Music of ringing bells
H	I	Rustling noise of clothes or as if someone is moving
H		Whistle, whirr of wings, bird chirp/twitter
	I	Buzzing sound

Direct Voices

H	I	Whisper
H	I	A few words are spoken
	I	Voices speak through trumpets that are moved through the air
	I	Voices speak without the help of trumpets
	I	Singing of voices
	I	Two voices sing simultaneously

Phenomena in Connection with Writing

	I	Automatic writing
H	I	Medium writes while entranced, allegedly possessed by a discarnate
H	I	Direct writing, i.e., writing of a pen without human touch
H	I	Signature of a famous person is obtained with direct writing

Apports

	I	Transportation of objects through matter
	I	Transportation of medium through matter

Phenomena of the 'Mental' Type

H	I	Medium has visionary experiences*
	I	Medium describes event while it is occurring at distant location*
H		Medium 'reads' another person's mind
H	I	Medium describes the past*
H	I	Medium claims to see deceased people
	I	Medium recognizes from a photograph a deceased person whom he has not seen before
H	I	Medium speaks language which he apparently does not know
H	I	Medium provides knowledge from ostensible discarnate person

General

H	I	Two or more phenomena take place simultaneously in such a way that this is apparently impossible for one person to do
H		Phenomena often occur in full light
	I	Phenomena seldom** occur in full light
H		Small number of sitters allowed to attend sittings
	I	Large number of sitters allowed to attend sittings
H		Phenomena seldom occur spontaneously outside sittings
	I	Phenomena often occur spontaneously outside sittings

* These (and some other) incidents are not mentioned in the text due to space considerations.

** Many violent phenomena were reported to have taken place in full light in Indridason's presence during poltergeist outbreaks in the winter of 1907-1908.

Matylda

DR. ALEXANDER IMICH
NEW YORK, NEW YORK

he story of one of the strongest mediums of the Victorian era can be related only as a narrative, torn by blanks of memory: World War II has destroyed documents and reports connected with this remarkable psychic. Only the original paper about my first two seances published in the German *Zeitschrift für Parapsychologie*[1] was saved.

"I have discovered in Wloclawek, a small town in Western Poland, an exceptional medium," Alfons Gravier, president of one of the Polish parapsychological societies and a college professor, told me. "Extraordinary things happen in her presence. I have heard a whole orchestra of balalaikas playing in the basement under the room in which we were holding the seance, and when they finished, frantic applause was heard near the ceiling above us." "When are you going there, professor? I am certainly coming with you," I rejoined. At that time I knew paranormal phenomena from description only.

The professor was too busy and could not fix the date of our trip. For some time we exchanged letters; then the professor saw that his intentions exceeded his possibilities, and he decided that I should go ahead without him. I wrote to Matylda S., a widowed doctor's wife, herself a pianist, asking for permission to participate in a seance. She agreed quite willingly and invited me to come to Wloclawek from my home in the Polish town of Czestochowa.

My excitement grew exponentially as the train brought me closer to the so-much-desired moment. I went directly from the railway station to the indicated address where the other participants and Matylda herself were already gathered. The latter was a middle-aged woman, whose corpulence might have surprised those who would expect an intermediary between this world and the other to be more ethereal. Only one feature lived up to the most exacting phantasy: the medium's eyes which were large, green and resembled the eyes of a nocturnal bird.

Matylda's First Seance

After the introduction and the usual exchange of courtesies, I discovered that the seance had been organized in my honor. I could see that visits of people from out of town were by no means a frequent happening. I also felt the arrival of this expected "learned" man who had no beard or even spectacles was an anticlimax for those present. I reciprocated this disappointment, being far from delighted with the personalities of the gathered participants—mostly young people. It was obvious that the purpose of attending the seance was not only the study of paranormal phenomena. In such a gay group there was no possibility of applying necessary controls. Since I had no personal experience with mediums at that time, controls seemed so important to me that without them the seance seemed worthless. I did not know yet that there are phenomena which simply cannot be faked, and which make control, in its usual meaning, superfluous.

I knew, however, that most important is first to observe the phenomena and not to infringe on their natural setting. I also knew that not only the change of accepted routines but even visible lack of confidence of the participants can influence, in a negative sense, the performance of the medium. Thus, I accepted everything and did not protest even when the medium declared that she would operate the light switch, a procedure which violated every experimental code.

When the lights were turned off, the phenomena began nearly at once. They were so explicit and so violent, at first I had no doubt they were faked. I even admired the confidence—nay, the effrontery—of the person responsible for their production. They were exceptionally numerous, one could say crowded, and appeared simultaneously at different locations.

Very soon, however, I understood that they were authentic. Some were altogether inimitable. Others were such that, in order to fake them, it would have been necessary to transform the room into a technological marvel with hidden mechanical, optical and acoustical machinery and a team of operators to run it.

Thus, I suddenly found myself back in the true wonderland which I had left, with pride but also some regret, when I was seven or eight. I had left it, having discovered that the supernatural was but an invention of the grown-ups whose perfidy I got to know then. Now it appeared that people from my childhood were speaking the truth—though they did not know it. It appeared that all those negations of common sense—ghosts, phantoms, the supernatural—really did exist; it seemed that the power we were dreaming of was no fiction but truest reality. This thought made my eyes dilate with fear, my hair raise; a feeling of eeriness pervaded my whole being.

I am now giving a summation of the report of the first two seances, published in the German periodical.[2] The first one was held in a small room of a ground floor apartment with thirteen participants present. The shutters were closed, as was the door to the neighboring room. We sat down around a very large table—some three meters long—and formed a chain by linking small fingers. I was sitting on the right side of the medium. On her left sat Mr. K. whom of course I had not met previously. A few seconds after turning off the light, we heard sounds and felt vibrations of the table caused by strong blows coming from underneath. It was as if an extension board, often stored under a table top, was knocking strongly against this very top. (When the lights were turned on, I found there actually was such a board under the table top.)

Soon afterward, a light appeared behind one of the participants. It was of bluish color and lasted, maybe, a second. For a moment the silhouettes of the participants could be seen against the lighted walls. The knocks against the table continued, and half a minute later another light appeared in the corner of the room. This time of greenish tinge, it lasted for a second and vanished.

From that moment on, such a great number of phenomena began to happen that I was quite unable to memorize them and still less able to remember the order in which they appeared. Those which I do remember I shall list in groups.

Telekinesis

Chairs were torn from under the participants with great force and noise; they were "flying" to the walls. This was so violent the people frequently fell on the floor, and so rapid that within one or two seconds, six chairs had been extracted. Before the seance started, the medium put a piece of chalk on the table. When the light was turned on, we saw the letter "O" written on the table and another time three small crosses. In darkness we heard the chalk scribble with violence on the table. The chair on which I was sitting was strongly pushed and partly torn from under me. There was also movement and transportation of many objects. The following objects were found on the table: a wooden riding horse for children, a chair, a shaving blade, keys and a pocket knife from the pocket of our host and a loaf of bread from the cupboard. A cushion from the sofa was so strongly pressed against me that I was forced to defend myself with both hands. A sweater fell on my head, a cracker on my chest, then—on the request of the medium—another cracker; then a doll was put to my lips. In the red glow of my flashlight I saw a chair extracted from under one of the participants. The heavy table around which we were sitting rose first on two legs, then violently on all four, then softly descended to the floor. The height of this levitation did not exceed three inches.

Touches

Soon after the beginning of the seance, one of the participants exclaimed that something or somebody was pushing him. Matylda asked the spirits to show their strength. It was, however, fifteen minutes later that what I felt to be a warm, three-fingered hand lightly scratched my head. Then something pulled my hair, touching my eyelids quite strongly at the same time. During one of the heavy knocks against the table the end of my thumb was struck with great power; it continued hurting for a long while. I heard some noises of the medium being touched or struck and of her struggle with the invisible powers wanting to strip her of different articles of clothing. Time and time again one or another of the participants cried for help, beset by the invisible powers, so that it was frequently necessary to turn on the light. Illuminated by my flashlight, during a fraction of a second, I saw the tousled hair of the girl sitting next to me who was defending herself against something. Another girl had been dragged upon the table and was lying face down with her hands stretched out. Another one had been lifted from her chair and was found sitting on the table.

Acoustic phenomena

The sound of scratching the table as if by claws, a rhythmical drumming on the table, and blows against the table so strong, it seemed surprising the massive table could withstand them. Those sounds were sometimes heard in such rapid sequence that it took only a second to make a complete round of the table—a terrifying cannonade. In the corners of the room we heard boots stomping, then a fist knocking against the door, and unknown objects scratching and rapping the walls. Invisible lips whistled in the air above us, and there were sounds of blowing with the accompanying air currents. In addition to the croaking of a frog, were many other sounds difficult to describe or identify. When the light came on, the knocking of the board under the table continued; when I looked down, I could see the legs of all the participants—none of them involved in the movement of the extension board and the racket it was making.

Optical Phenomena

Ten or twelve times a light went on in different locations. Three times it appeared below the table, quite near to me. The source of the light was always hidden behind an object or person. When the medium asked that the light should present itself, an elliptically shaped light appeared for a fraction of a second at the other end of the table at the altitude of the head of a sitting person; then it went off with a metallic sound. The color of the lights was white, bluish or greenish.

Apports

The first apport was a pine-branch with a thick candle. It was shortly after Christmas and while a Christmas tree was standing in another room, I found that it was a fir. According to our host, there was no pine tree in the apartment; the candle, on the other hand, came from the Christmas tree in the next room. It was then an even more complicated, combined apport. Other objects brought from nearby rooms were: artificial flowers, one galosh, a strainer, a doll, a whip, and finally, a sheet of paper with greetings for the medium signed "Guzik."

On my request, Matylda got out of the chair. When she stood behind my chair, a deluge of events fell upon us so that the participants started screaming for light. During this short period of time a bunch of freshly cut alpine violets was brought; according to our host, there were no such flowers in the apartment. Towards the end of the seance, we heard a sound of coughing; more than a half ounce of clear fluid was later found on the table.

I shall describe separately the incident with the radio loudspeaker. At that time loudspeakers were still a separate part of the receiving set; thus, a loudspeaker, in the form of an elegantly curved trumpet, stood on the wardrobe, while the receiver was inside of it. In order to get to the receiver, it was necessary to open the wardrobe door which was not possible without moving the chair occupied by one of the participants. Somebody asked for spoken words to come from the loudspeaker. This request had been ignored and we soon forgot about it. After maybe ten or fifteen minutes, the loudspeaker started with music. I asked for another station and the tune actually changed. This happened at once and without the whistles that in the early radio receivers accompanied tuning in to a station. I made one more request, asking for German speech; I had in mind a man's voice. While German language did come out of the speaker, it was, however, feminine. The characteristic atmospheric noises of a distant radio transmitter accompanied this reception. Twice more the loudspeaker sounded. I found later that the receiver was a Marconi brand set with two tuning dials. It was practically impossible to manipulate the dials in the darkness to find a required station, not to mention the impossibility of getting to the set through the closed door of the wardrobe. Moreover, it would have been necessary to know the programs of the stations by heart to find a talking station at the late hour when most stations were broadcasting music.

Second Seance

The second seance took place in the ground floor apartment of Lieutenant L. The seance was being held in the middle room of three adjacent rooms, without doors in the doorways. Entrances to the two rooms were from the street and from the courtyard. Those two entrances and the shutters had been locked before the seance started. Ten participants included the medium and myself. This time I sat at the end of the table opposite Matylda. "There, the phenomena are the strongest; in order to prove their authenticity, things are happening as far as possible from my person," said the medium. When the light was turned off, raps against the table were heard at once. A vase with flowers was put into my lap; a crystal paperweight was thrown on the table with a grumble and a picture from the wall suddenly appeared on the table. When the girl sitting next to me cried for help, I stretched out my hand to encounter a warm and soft hand which vanished instantaneously. Then the "ghosts" began to annoy the young lieutenant who was attending a seance for the first time in his life. As a gallant officer, he had taken a bold attitude towards ghosts in whose existence he did not believe. Soon after the seance began, he seemed to become more and more excited. First we heard the keys in his pocket jingling, then the chain on which his sabre was suspended. Then he declared he was feeling the approach of a heavy mass and started to scream so loudly that we had to interrupt the seance and turn the light on. This did not quiet the warrior. His eyes were staring; he appeared to be in a trance. He fought with whoever tried to approach him, and when I attempted to calm him, he attacked me with raised fists. When he finally recovered consciousness, he left the seance, declaring he would never take part in any experiments with ghosts. I was told later that he did not feel well and stayed in bed for several days.

A direct voice was a new phenomenon. From the neighboring room a basso voice sounded near the floor. Approaching the doorway leading to our room, it introduced itself as the spirit of the well-known Polish medium, the deceased Jan Guzik. He spoke of my visit and bade me a friendly welcome. The voice was particularly low and pronounced words with difficulty. Suddenly, a bright light appeared on the chest of one of the participants, and I thought he was being dragged into the next room. Guzik's voice fell silent, and we heard from the next room a loud noise as if the door had been slammed violently. All that happened in just a few seconds. The light was turned on. From the next room our participant returned and declared that, in order to uncover a fake, he had suddenly lit his flashlight and run into the next room. There was nobody there; he found the entrance door locked, the key in the lock inside the apartment. In an agitated mood we returned to the seance. We heard the squeak of the door as if opening very slowly, and suddenly we heard a crash as loud as a pistol shot, followed by the noise of broken glass, as if a large glass vessel had been thrown on the floor. Terrified by this assault, we again interrupted the seance. There was no trace of glass in the next room, and the door leading outside was locked, key in the lock.

The tension mounted still higher, but we decided to continue the seance. In all three rooms undefined noises were heard simultaneously. Again the squeak of the opening door and, in the next room, the sound of steps of two or more persons. Then, some groaning and the sound of heavy breathing approached from the next room. The narrow strip of light penetrating the crack in the shutter disappeared for a moment, as if obscured by a moving body. The groans and heavy breathing now were near our table. Matylda exclaimed that something heavy was lying on her. In the darkness, through the change of acoustics, the presence of an additional body in the room could be sensed. The tension became unbearable and cries for light sounded. Imagine our terror when, in the full light of the chandelier, we saw on the floor a long body in a military trenchcoat. What powers did we rouse? What were we going to do now? Light, that until now had been saving us from the dread of the unknown, suddenly lost its power. As apprentices of the supernatural, we were now forced to face a great mystery. I quickly glanced at all present with the last faint hope that the body on the floor was one of them. My hope was futile; everybody was in his or her place. In the meantime, somebody recognized the prostrated form as the owner of the apartment. He had left town a few days ago. We lifted him up and seated him on a chair. He was unconscious but slowly recovering, looking with surprised eyes at the people assembled around him. He told us he had just returned from his trip, had gone directly from the railroad station to a cafe to say hello to his friends, had then gone out into the street in the direction of his home—and he remembered no more. He had no idea how he had entered the apartment. I checked the entrance door again; it was locked from the inside.

After a lengthy interruption, we once more returned to the seance. Of the many phenomena that followed, I will mention the apport of a letter. It was accompanied by a noise—as if a roll of paper many feet long was being unrolled. When the light was turned on, we found a small sheet of paper folded in four: "Matylda, your power is great" was written upon it. I snatched the paper as a precious item for future archives. Guzik's voice sounded again and made a false prediction that Gandhi would die in a prison. I asked Guzik to materialize, but he declared that he was tired from yesterday's seance. Some of those present said they could see a foggy person in a turban. I, personally, did not see it.

At a certain moment, the voice began to predict an erotic episode to the medium; I learned later that, in the past, this had happened many times. Matylda interrupted the voice, asking him to stop such prophecies. When this did not help, she reiterated her request more forcefully, trying to dumbfound the basso voice and telling him in not-complimentary epithets what she thought of such enunciations. The voice, however, was not to be persuaded or silenced; it was growing louder and faster every moment. The medium began to scream, and so did the voice. The whole incident resembled an ordinary quarrel between two mortals, yet extraordinary since it was taking place between a living person and an assumed spirit of a deceased being. It would be doubly interesting for Freud—not only for its erotic content, but because of this unique assignation of roles. Again light had to be turned on, and that's how the weird quarrel ended.

Some Reflections

When I recall the events of my life, I must say that those two seances belong to the strongest experiences of my adolescence. Although I had a book knowledge of paranormal phenomena, the fact of their existence did not really enter my mind. I felt that the same goes for other people: second hand knowledge is hardly convincing. Only actual contact with real "magic" can so strongly impact us that it can change one's basic philosophy.

Returning to the hotel, late after the first seance, my head was spinning from too many impressions and thoughts. Fear was the dominating feeling. You may not understand why I am using the term "magic," but that was precisely the impression the multitude of unexpected and seemingly senseless phenomena had made on me. A "rogue's ragout," as Ludwik Szczepanski, president of the Cracow psi society, used to call such wild and chaotic seances.

Though really tired, I could not sleep. Neither could I, nor did I want to. The shock was too strong; it was now necessary to bring new order to my world view, to find a place for the discovery of this extraordinary reality. So many conceptions of my early years would have to be changed! One idea returned over and over. How can it be that people who devote their life to the study of things miniscule, who are interested in the deeds of persons who maybe never existed at all and certainly ceased to exist a thousand years ago, people who inquire into the history of celestial bodies billions of years distant—how can it be that these people ignore the mystery of phenomena that exist here among us, that seem to be so infinitely more important? Be that as it may, it seemed to me that it shall become my duty to fight for the recognition of this important domain and point to the great blunder scientists commit by neglecting it. Later I discovered many times that it is a basic error to believe people are doing exactly what they should in this best of worlds. This attitude, this faith in the authority of grownups, was another left-over from my childhood years.

For the time being, I decided to inform the parapsychological community of the discovery of a subject producing physical-type phenomena. I sent a report of the two seances to the *Zeitschrift für Parapsychologie*.[3]

After the death of Julian Ochorowicz and Piotr Lebiedzinski, no serious research was being conducted in Poland at this time. Lack of interest in working with Matylda S.—whose existence was known in Warsaw and who was "languishing with the desire" for scientific research of her rare talent—was proof of the relative inactivity of Polish parapsychological societies.

More on Matylda's Mediumship

In many respects Matylda was a subject exceptionally suited for scientific study. When I visited her modest apartment, she was living in indigence. Her husband, a medical doctor, had died many years ago, leaving her with no means of subsistence. She had two sons to raise. A graduate of a piano class of the conservatory, she loved music and turned to giving music lessons.

Matylda was not interested in psychic phenomena and did not seem to possess any personal talents in this field. Once, a short time before his death, she was invited to a seance with Guzik. The wonders she saw, the existence of which she did not suspect, delighted her. "I liked it most when a beautiful little light moving under the ceiling drifted down, lifted a bunch of keys from the dresser and put them very, very softly in my hand. I was so delighted with the pranks played by the spirits that I simply began to like them and could not forget them." Though she had no more opportunities to participate in seances after Guzik's death, she did not forget. Then the phenomena themselves found her.

One evening as she was playing cards at home with a woman friend, the time was late when the bell at the entrance rang. "I got up and opened the door—nobody was there. Somebody must have mistaken the door, I thought." She returned to the game. A moment later, the bell rang again. "I opened the door—nobody was there. I looked into the staircase—nobody was there either. What a stupid joke!" And the bell rang insistently for the third time.

"Then, I suddenly understood," continued Matylda, "it was Jan (Guzik's first name) calling on me. His spirit has come to me and will appear during seances. At the first which I organized, something was already happening. During the next few, the phenomena grew stronger, richer and more beautiful. But what's the use if nobody is seriously interested in these miracles? This is my greatest sorrow. I would like to offer these miracles for the benefit of humanity. How much could humanity win if these miracles were investigated. Maybe you could do something about that rare gift of mine so that it should not be wasted. My dear spirits are always with me. And how intelligent, how sly they are. Oh, how cunning the spirits are and how beautiful the things they invent. What clever ways they have to tell us what they want. My greatest desire is to have seances every night; during the day I would like to play piano. I am modest and do not need much, as you see."

"And don't the seances tire you?"

"Oh no, after a seance I feel very good. If the participants were not in a hurry to get home, I could continue until morning."

"And you don't fall into a trance?"

"Never; then I could not see what is happening and would lose my whole pleasure."

Indeed, already at the first seance, I could not spot any sign of the medium in trance, even during the greatest intensity of the phenomena. This was very unusual. "The more seances, the stronger the phenomena are. I do not know what would happen if the seances were held day after day. And the more participants, the better," added Matylda.

"You are unique and a subject of great value for parapsychology. I will do everything in my power so that your exceptional talents should not be wasted."

Before the second seance, I talked with the participants. I had not been mistaken to conclude that many of them were treating the seances as a night's entertainment. Some did not even believe the phenomena were genuine. Without realizing the difficulties of such an idea, they thought the phenomena were faked by certain participants. "Oh no, Matylda is no fraud. She is really honest, but she is very naive and believes in spirits. We know very well there are no spirits. People amuse themselves at her cost." When I spoke to Matylda, I asked her how she chose the participants. She told me that young and gay people help generate and strengthen the phenomena. And when a military man is among them—then there must be war. Like human beings, spirits like to wage wars." That, I must admit, was quite a new idea—rather abominable for pacifists. "It seems to me that some of the participants do not believe the phenomena are genuine," I insisted. "I know it very well; I also know some of them try to fake them. That can be noticed immediately. However, how is it possible to fake those beautiful lights appearing everywhere and flying around the room? You know more about physics—tell me how that could be accomplished. It must be either very difficult or outright impossible. I will tell you that even my grown-up sons do not believe in spirits. Once, one of them declared, 'I will believe in spirits when they bring me 1000 zlotys.' And, just imagine! At the next seance we heard noise as if scores of bank notes were being counted by the fingers of an expert cashier. We turned the light on. On the table, before my son, lies a bank note—but one from the German occupation during World War I and without any value today. It's strange, but that's how it is. No great help can be expected from the spirits. They help with small things. They will bring an egg, a dinner roll, an apple or few tomatoes. They will gladly bring flowers, but money or other more valuable things—nothing doing. They know how difficult my life is, apparently they are not allowed to help too much. In the land of spirits there also must exist laws that cannot be broken."

I was to learn in the future how great was the power of such irrational beliefs and how destructive they can become for the performance of the psychic.

"If you want the world to know about the miracles performed by the spirits, we shall have to go abroad where people are more interested in parapsychology."

"I will go wherever needed," was Matylda's answer.

I could not stay in Wloclawek any longer. The third seance, in which I did not participate, was very successful according to Matylda's letter. An often-repeated phenomenon was a glowing orange globe, the size of a small apple, drifting in the air, rapping lightly against the walls, furniture or people, and vanishing to reappear in another place.

Matylda was a powerful medium, extremely valuable by her inde-
fatigability, but completely wild. The range of her production was so wide.
Visible materializations were rather rare, but one could hope that they will
become more frequent in the course of further experimentation.

A Visit to London

I informed the National Laboratory of Psychical Research of London of the existence of this little-known medium. I no longer remember
why I chose this institution. I described briefly what I had seen and in the
medium's name expressed her readiness to participate in a series of
experiments. I also was to take part in them. The medium, who had never
been abroad and knew no foreign language, did not want to go alone.
"There will be no question of remuneration, there can be no payment for
such things. They will have to cover only our expenses," wrote Matylda,
who was treating her affair with spirits in a non-materialistic way.

Harry Price replied immediately by sending a formal invitation and
a check for 300 pounds sterling.

Matylda, with whom I was exchanging letters, was ecstatic. At last
there appeared something serious. At last the moment of which she had
dreamt for such a long time was in sight. The world would learn of her
miracles. She was reporting that all her seances were very successful, and
I had asked her to have as many as possible so as to keep her powers in a
high gear.

Obtaining the documents for the journey (passports, visas, etc.) took
longer than we expected. In the meantime I made an excursion to
Wloclawek to see how things were going. The phenomena were strong and
numerous.

The day of our journey approached. I met Matylda in Warsaw, and
we began our railroad journey during which Matylda prayed frequently
and addressed short invocations to Mr. Jan, her leading spirit. When we
boarded the boat at Ostend, she confessed her fear that Mr. Jan would lose
track of her on the sea. She stood at the railing throwing small scraps of
paper overboard to mark the way for the spirits. Undoubtedly she had read
somewhere that the maidens carried off by Tartars after their attacks on
Poland had resorted to similar tactics. She drew a small horseshoe from her
bag and jingled it against a key to produce a melodious ring. That also was
a signal agreed upon with the spirits for marking her location. I did not yet
understand the danger hidden in these naive ideas.

At Dover, the customs officer checking our documents asked for the
purpose of our visit in the United Kingdom. When he heard that we were

invited by Harry Price's National Laboratory, he smiled friendly and told us that Rudi Schneider had been in this country just before us. It appeared that he knew something about parapsychology. We were pleasantly surprised. "Here they really love spirits," said Matylda, and added that English people would lose their heads when learning about her miracles. At last, we were in London where rooms for us were reserved in a boarding house in South Kensington.

A few hours after our arrival, I was called to the lounge where a reporter asked for an interview.

Price's only condition had been that, while we were in London, we should accept no invitation from psychical or spiritualistic organizations without his approval. I had not yet met Price and did not know whether contacts with the press, made without his knowledge, could be considered a breach of our agreement. Thus, I refused to be interviewed using as an excuse my insufficient knowledge of language.

The next day Price's secretary picked us up, and we went straight to the National Laboratory where the host and a group of invited guests were already assembled. We were greeted and Matylda conversed graciously by means of gestures and smiles, while I served as interpreter. Then the room was darkened by pulling down heavy blinds and we started the seance. There was no control of the medium. Price had enough experience to be initially content just with observing. It was rather a short sitting which proceeded in complete silence. Somebody asked whether the medium was accustomed to day-time seances, and as Matylda always held the seances at night, we agreed at once to meet on the evening of the next day.

Before the second seance, Matylda confessed her fears to me. Mr. Jan had probably left Poland after our arrival in London, consequently he could not have been present yesterday. Maybe he will come today? It appeared, unfortunately, that he was still absent. For the third seance, the medium prepared herself intensively. She prayed, uttered incantations, rang the horseshoe. She also timidly confessed new doubts that were assailing her. How was Mr. Jan to come here? Are there trains in the land of spirits? If not, if he must walk, then this is a long way and it may take a long time before he is here. What do we know about the organization of the other world? I really did not have the proper answer to counter her gloomy suppositions. I expressed my belief that spirits were much freer than those of us burdened with the body, and surely move with greater ease. Unfortunately, my lack of more specific information did not have the beneficial effect. During the third seance, the same silence reigned, terrifying the medium accustomed to tumultuous happenings. Our host and the participants, seeing Matylda's sorrow, comforted us by stating that the phenomena would certainly appear and that they were accustomed to much longer waits.

Matylda's imagination was in full swing. During the day, I was apprised of new and more threatening fantasies. If Mr. Jan was actually compelled to walk, it may be that he had no shoes and it must be very painful to walk barefoot over such a long stretch. Then, how was he to cross the channel? This time I countered her by stating that, according to all we knew, spirits do not need to walk because they can fly, and Mr. Jan would have no difficulty flying over the channel. Yes, but did he know the way sufficiently well; it was so easy to lose track over the water.

I told Price and the other members of the group about Matylda's imaginary doubts. All of them were very polite, hiding their smiles and comforting Matylda. At the seances, however, silence—the most depressing silence—continued. I do not remember how many were held till during one there was a knock at the door. Though zealously expecting something to happen, we were taken by surprise. But a knock at the door need not be necessarily a paranormal phenomenon. One of us got up from the table and opened the door. There was nobody on the other side. The medium exclaimed with joy, "Mr. Jan, Mr. Jan has come at last. Welcome my dear, and thanks for following me. I knew that you wouldn't let me suffer any longer. I am sorry for all the trouble I have caused you." But Mr. Jan did no more than notify us of his arrival. "The long journey has certainly tired him. He must rest and tomorrow we shall see what he can do," said Matylda. We ended this sitting, the first one that had brought a ray of hope.

It turned out that it was a false ray. The chauffeur of one of the lady participants had wanted to speak to her. When the door had not been opened immediately, he had understood that he may be disturbing the meeting and had returned to the car. Obviously, we did not tell this to Matylda. When at the next sitting Mr. Jan still was not with us, Price suggested that somebody will rap against the table to start things rolling. Matylda, terrified and desperate, revived instantly. "Ah, it begins." However, this artificial start was not followed with real events. At home, Matylda told me: "That was one of the participants who must have knocked at the table. And Mr. Jan is still not with us. What do we know about the land of spirits? Maybe they also need passports to go abroad? Maybe Mr. Jan has had some trouble in getting one? They may not let him out. What are we to do then?"

What were we going to do then—I asked myself the same question. I understood the danger of working with untrained and undisciplined subjects whose performance is contingent upon wild ideas acting as negative autosuggestion. Matylda categorically opposed any efforts to help her performance by hypnotic induction.

She was really suffering. She did not like London or English food; no entertainments attracted her. Her only consolation was to play the piano, but she could not play frequently as our boarding house had no instrument. At a party given by one of the ladies from the circle, she could prove her mastery in at least that domain.

She tried to contact the spirits using sophisticated procedures. She complained that the spirits had let her down mercilessly, that she had exposed herself to the greatest shame of her life. She explained that this was an exceptional opportunity to do what the spirits had always wanted—to let them be known by the entire world. The actual opportunity might be the only one forever. She implored, encouraged and threatened the spirits. All in vain; the spirits had a deaf ear.

I was the initiator of the London venture and my situation was not enviable either. Somebody else might have felt even worse, but my conscience was clear. When I accepted Price's invitation, I was sure of one thing only: I was not presenting a fraudulent psychic. My reason for feeling safe in this respect was my knowledge of Matylda's convictions: she considered any kind of trick as a sort of sacrilege. I was also not concerned with unconscious fraud because Matylda never fell in trance. Price and the others, seeing the medium's grief, kept repeating that unsuccessful sittings are more a rule than an exception and that their patience was far from exhausted. We tried many ways of stimulating the start of the phenomena during the seances. Certain people were excluded; new ones were invited. Sometimes we concentrated and kept complete silence; other times a record player was turned on, or again, we were talking in a light and desultory manner. All in vain. It was clear to me that our host's and the participants' zeal was gradually melting down and their patience getting short. Matylda no longer knew which was the greater torture—the seances or the hours in-between when she was more and more doubtful whether the phenomena would ever appear in London.

Thus, three weeks passed with about seventeen sittings. We might have continued the fruitless attempts but the time of summer vacations was approaching, and some of the participants were preparing to leave the city. Thus it was mutually agreed to end the unsuccessful series.

Back to Poland and More Phenomena

Matylda was leaving London in a state of prostration. We invited Price to come to Warsaw. He promised, but never did. Paul Tabori in his book, *Harry Price: The Biography of a Ghost Hunter*,[4] writes that after we left London, Price exclaimed: "How we wished to be floated around the room, or to witness a materialization!" He does not mention that in order to witness a materialization, Price promised to come to Poland but never did.

Assailed by doubts that the spirits had deserted her forever, as soon as she was back home, Matylda organized a seance. With only a few participants present, the phenomena appeared in all their splendor as soon as the lights were off. What an irony of fate!

Soon I visited her and took with me a couple of friends as witnesses. The phenomena were as strong and as numerous as in the before-London time. A large dining table, some 50 x 70 inches, rose a few times pretty high. I wanted to photograph the levitation, so I mounted my camera on a tripod and turned the light off, asking to signal when the table rose. After two or three minutes, it happened. I turned the light on; the table was suspended in mid-air some three feet from the floor and the participants were touching its top with raised hands. The table hung immobile as if it had no intention of coming down. When I adjusted the camera in order to have the table in the center of the picture, a small sweeping brush flew out of the corner of the room and fell on my arm, quite near the camera. I had hardly recovered from the attack when, in another corner of the room, another brush—now one for cleaning clothes—rose and directed itself towards the camera. In the very last moment, I was able to shield the camera with my arm and, without further delay, opened the shutter for a several-second exposure. The table hung immobile in the air and when I closed the shutter, it began to descend slowly and, in full light, landed gently on the floor. The picture was perfect. It was lost together with many other documents during World War II.

I remember another remarkable phenomenon from the same seance. Matylda did not prepare any reception for the guests. During a pause in the seance, with lights on, suddenly from the center of the table small objects began to jump up. The objects were spurting in parabolic arcs some 20 to 30 inches high and falling to all sides, on the table, on the floor. They were grasped by the astounded participants, eager to find out what sort of things were coming from the other side. It turned out that only the arrival of this mass apport was mysterious, while it was not, itself, a product of the spirits. Quite to the contrary, it was a product of the well-known factory of sweets, "Plutos." We all were familiar with this particular chocolate candy; on the market for some time, they contained more cocoa butter, the melting of which required heat, and therefore produced a feeling of coolness in the mouth. This brand of candy was sold under the name of "Iced Chocolates." The candies, wrapped in aluminum foil and waxed paper, tasted delicious. Matylda was most pleased with the smart spirits, who rescued her from embarrassment by delivering some edibles. The local guests and Matylda did not demonstrate any pietism for the chocolate apport; it was consumed on the spot. Only the visiting party felt the eeriness of the event and did not eat the sweets. For them, the candies were of very special value, almost museum pieces.

This was a very successful seance. The spirits were frolicking. The acoustic phenomena were particularly numerous. In the darkness several mouths were emitting separate whistles or whistling fragments of a tune. Toothless mouths were muttering words or broken sentences, sighs, groans; smacks were heard; dumb beings were trying to utter a word, dashing ineptly to do it and repeating, like with swollen lips, the same syllable, finding it difficult to pronounce, so that the sound receded and vanished. From corners of the room came meowing of cats, croaking of frogs, obscene sounds which, at times, were terribly natural; there were sounds of panting and blowing, accompanied by cool breezes on our faces or hands. With one finger, then with the whole hand, something struck the keyboard of a piano, the lid of which I was holding down. Several voices were heard at the same time in different points of the room accompanied by a large number of kinetic phenomena, transports, apports, touches, raps, jerks. Big hands and small hands—that is, either greater than the average person's or smaller than the hand of a child, either soft or hard as if wooden, warm or cold—were finding in the darkness our lips, noses, ears, cheeks, reaching them at once, infallibly and without searching. These hands were sometimes brushing us lightly, caressing us gently; more often, however, they were rapping us, pinching, pulling and dragging our hair. All of this was done suddenly, unexpectedly. Sometimes the hands penetrated the outer clothing to the very skin in various areas of our bodies. They turned up equally as easily on the decolletage of a lady as between the chair and the posterior of a man, or in his pocket, jingling coins or keys. Rings vanished from the finger of one person and turned up on the finger of another; beads and other jewelry were taken from the necks of their owners, flying around the room with the characteristic clatter of one bead striking another, and were put on the neck of another person, or found, when the light was on, in the pocket of somebody's overcoat. Chairs were violently pulled from under people who, either fell on the floor or were pushed by invisible but strong bodies or thrown on their neighbors. Every few moments tumults arose, cries of fear, clamors for light—the only refuge from the powers let loose. And even this was not always effective; at the end of this seance, when the guests were leaving, in full light, there came from under the ceiling of the hall a loud and terrifying scream. Matylda told me the next day that long after our departure, she still heard sudden rappings and noises, objects went jumping or flying through the air from one place to another.

It was really difficult to understand Matylda's complete London failure. "English people would have gone mad with admiration if they had seen what was happening here. What extraordinary bad luck," Matylda kept repeating, still unhappy when recalling the past but comforted that the phenomena had not abandoned her. She did not lose hope that she would still be able to display the miracles to those really interested in them.

In order to ascertain whether it was only the complete change of mode of life or the change of location that influenced her performance so badly, I invited Matylda to my parents' house in Czestochowa. As I was fully prepared for a failure, I made it a condition for the participants of the seances to attend all 20 sittings, whatever would be their outcome.

The hopeless sittings began. During twenty evenings, there was the same "unbearable silence," as Matylda called it. She did not, obviously, omit any of her attempts at telecommunication with the spirits by means of a horseshoe, needles and other gizmos that she hid even from me, keeping them in a special box. The participants sat for 20 evenings waiting in vain for miracles that most of them believed were nonexistent. As Matylda was leaving, she expressed for the first time her conviction that she would have to stay two or three months in a new place to give the spirits time to learn her location. I took notice of this new revelation.

One of my friends was a personal secretary to an industrial magnate. When she told her boss of the extraordinary phenomena she had witnessed, he was so intrigued that he expressed his desire to participate in a seance. A pioneer of the artificial silk industry, a man of shrewd intelligence, Mr. W. said, "If such phenomena really exist, I will provide means for their investigation." Such a declaration could not be taken lightly. Without delay, we agreed upon the date of the seance. But this busy man could not tear himself away from the duties of his own creation. He was suddenly obliged to fly to a conference abroad and could not keep the date. When he returned from the trip, other unforeseen duties kept him inside the circle of his industrial magic. In the meantime, first impressions made by the weird tales faded. After lengthy delay, he was reminded of his desire to witness the unbelievable; he declared that he was so tied up with practical matters, he doubted he would be able to undertake an excursion into the fantasy world.

Still More Phenomena

Soon afterward, I moved to Warsaw from Czestochowa and succeeded in inducing Matylda to visit her sister there for a longer stay. No seances were attempted for the time being. After many weeks only, I suggested a trial which had to take place in the apartment where Matylda was staying. In this first trial things appeared in their full splendor. "The spirits know already where I am," declared the medium. The next seance took place in the one-family house of our friends, situated in a new quarter of Warsaw. It was most successful and, as usual, equally wild. I shall describe by groups the events I remember.

The kinetic phenomena were numerous. Nearly all objects in the room moved at one time or another. From the many seances at this location I assembled an entire collection of apports, among them: a dozen hemorrhoidal suppositories thrown one evening on the table, a tablet from a linotype, steel balls of about one centimeter diameter, a large key to a gate and various latchkeys, bear's teeth, boar's tusks, bird feathers, many flowers, flower petals, letters scribbled on scraps of paper, a hare's paw, and many others I no longer remember. Apports of fresh flowers and flower petals were frequent. Upon them were written—by means of some sharp instrument and in a variety of handwritings—short messages, invocations, greetings for the medium or other participants. Less often the messages were written on blank pieces of paper. Matylda usually furnished a piece of chalk, and writing on the table appeared frequently; but it happened also when no chalk was provided. In an attempt to copy the classic experiment, two slate tablets were bound together and sealed by myself, with a crayon in-between. They were completely ignored. Having placed them on the table in front of Matylda, I found them, later, pushed away; the spirits did not like sophisticated assignments.

Hands touched us quite often. When I grew to like their touch and did not try to grasp them, they remained with me long minutes. They also ceased small malices, such as pinching the nose, pulling hair, and blows. When I tried to move my own hand higher, toward the elbow of the materialized hand resting on my thigh, the hand vanished. At one of the seances, when we formed a chain by joining hands, there quickly appeared out of my arm, in the full light of the chandelier, another long, grey and incompletely formed arm with a somewhat transparent hand. It touched either my face or the face of my neighbor to the right—I no longer remember which. This phenomenon was in agreement with Matylda's oft-repeated hypothesis that spirits for their productions used organisms of the participants, splitting parts of their entire bodies.

I will never forget a kiss of a phantom. I had asked for it when something had floated in the air over us. An invisible face, whose breath I could distinctly hear and feel on my face, drifted vertically toward me from under the ceiling, and thick, warm lips touched and kissed mine. It was a strong but pleasant sensation. By now the dread and terror I had felt during the first seances and which had been in such a contrast with my interest and desire to be close with the phenomena, had completely passed—to be replaced by a love of the mysterious. The spirits—I should be using quotation marks, because I did not feel that what was happening during seances was a work of spirits—were reciprocating my friendly feelings. The basso voice of Mr. Jan, pompously drawling words somewhere near the floor, expressed that many times. When the medium declared "Spirits, Dr. Imich loves you very much!" the basso voice replied, "And we love him too." Direct voices, incidentally, were rather seldom heard in Warsaw. Instead, a visible phantom started to materialize. It always appeared in the seance room in the same violent manner. That room was one of four which were entered directly from the hall. Before the seance other rooms were checked. I always bolted the entrance door and locked all the doors to the rooms, leaving the keys in the locks on the passage side. In these conditions the door to the sitting room, locked from the inside, would crash open as if a heavy person was throwing himself against the door, almost tearing it from the bay. The room was shaken by this blow. The door was ajar and on the background of some mysterious shine appeared a black human silhouette with two luminous points in place of eyes. This phantom, after having thrown an object in our direction, slammed the door, somewhat less loudly than at its appearance. Then, for a moment, a tremendous uproar was heard in the hall. We turned on the light and ran into the hall. The door, having burst open a moment ago, was now locked and the hall presented an extraordinary sight. The settee, chairs and carpet, all the overcoats of the guests, hats, mufflers, wraps and umbrellas that had been placed on the rack were now lying in a heap on the floor mixed together in the greatest possible confusion, as if a whirlwind had passed through the hall. All the doors to the rooms, as well as the entrance door, were locked—keys in the locks, the bolt and chain as we had left them. An immediate and meticulous search of the apartment, including closets and beds, did not reveal the presence of anybody but the participants of the seance. Some of the objects thrown by the apparition during several subsequent seances were: a metal tray from the kitchen which, if it had struck somebody, might have caused considerable pain; pieces of sheepskin, which according to our host were not present in his apartment; a dozen suppositories for hemorrhoids, already mentioned; a paper bag full of large ants—alive but moving slowly, as if stunned. Another time a heavy bunch of wild flowers, moist as with evening dew, was thrown at us.

Speaking of apports, I have to mention some extraordinary ones that I did not witness myself but was told about by Matylda or other participants of the circle. Matylda was once walking in a forest and noticed a colony of mushrooms under a pine tree. What pretty mushrooms, she thought. At the next seance there was an apport of mushrooms growing in moss.

Another time, she was crossing the bridge over the Vistula River. Overhead a gull was steering against the wind; she was looking at the bird with interest and wonder. During the next session a living gull appeared on the dresser. Still on another occasion, when the seance was held on the ground floor of an apartment, a tall oleander plant in a wooden pot, weighing possibly a hundred pounds, was brought to the room, all windows closed. Once a great dog, also from the courtyard, suddenly appeared among the assembled guests. I was also told about an almost incredible (can apports in general be called credible?) apport. At one of the seances in Wloclawek the spirits were more than usually militant toward the participants. One of them, a senior army officer threatened to "deal" with them if they would not quieten at once. After that declaration, a tumultous riot started in the room. The light was turned on. Matylda and two of the participants found that they were alone in the room; the seven others had vanished. There was a knock against the closed shutter and a conversation started with the disappeared ones. They told that after the tumult ceased, they found themselves in the courtyard. Apports of living persons are extremely rare; I have never heard of a similar deportation. When I had the opportunity to talk with two of the "deportees," what they told me concurred with Matylda's account. (As I already mentioned, Matylda has never given me reason for doubting her veracity.)

Another apparition I did not witness personally was the chimney-sweep's brush with the iron ball and cord which flew into and out of the seance room. Matylda liked to mention that case, calling the appliance by the name used in the vernacular. The window had opened suddenly and on the background of the town's lights, the whole chimney-sweep's contrivance flew into the room, cruised for a moment over the heads of the assembled and flew out into the street.

Still another seance took place in a house situated next to a paper factory where there were stores of cut-to-size wood logs. One pane was missing in the window of the seance room. Several times a log appeared, in that opening, through which previously had come the apport of a bunch of plants, as if it were trying to get inside. According to Matylda, "It was forcing its way into the room." Another time half a brick cruised above the heads of the participants, and one learned of it when somebody turned the light on without having arranged it with the medium. At that moment the half brick fell down on the knee of one of the ladies hurting her rather painfully. At still another seance, the medium and the participants went into the courtyard and formed a circle holding hands. In the darkness of the night they saw light sparks creeping over the roof of the bungalow in which the seance had taken place.

It was a desire of Matylda to hold seances outdoors, in nature. "Who knows what beautiful phenomena we may get when holding seances outside," the medium kept saying. Today, I ask myself why did I not fulfill Matylda's wish.

At seances held in Warsaw, lights were less frequent. They might appear at different locations—usually hiding behind various objects so their source was not visible. They were white, yellow, reddish, green and blue. Some lights changed color while the phenomenon was occurring. Their average intensity could be compared to the light of a 40-watt bulb, but the light source was more concentrated: shadows of the objects had sharp contours. No sound accompanied the light. There were also other light phenomena. Through the keyhole, bundles of rays might spurt in one or two directions, as if one or two flashlights were shining through the keyhole; there was nobody on the other side of the door. Once a band of weak light appeared on the wall, about three feet long and one and a half feet wide, as if from an invisible projector. A moment later, there appeared on this lit rectangle a pair of green eyes and a red line, a primitive outline of a mouth without any graphic details. Several times we observed a dancing light we called the flying butterfly. Behind a pane of corrugated glass in the door, a yellow dancing flame continuously changed its shape. It was soaring in the air a few inches from the glass, its movement, even more than its shape, suggesting a flying butterfly. This phenomenon pleased both the medium and the participants who noisily expressed their delight.

Among mixed kinetic phenomena occurred the lighting and turning out of the flashlight I was holding in my hand or had put on the table. In the latter case, it changed its position by small jumps accompanied with appropriate noise. Raps were never absent. Scraping, as if a mouse were gnawing at a piece of dry bread; a sound produced by a pea jumping and rolling on a wooden floor; the soft rapping of a knuckle against different objects; the rustle of rumpled paper; the sound of a small sweeping brush touching the walls; and scores of other sounds difficult to describe and which I no longer remember—all these are examples of the more subdued sounds we heard. Frequently and without any gradation, they might change into loud and violent noises—the jarring of talons against the window; raps on the window pane threatening to break it; a rabid rolling and rubbing of the chalk Matylda liked to have on the table during seances; the stomping of heavy boots on the floor; a fist battering the door, the walls or the furniture; and, finally, powerful blows on the table or floor, as if by a heavy wooden hammer, producing a deafening noise and shaking the room.

Conclusion

Matylda never showed any signs of trance, fatigue or weariness. Her constant anxiety was the fact that men of science were not interested in her; her constant desire was to have seances every day. She maintained that seances made her feel stronger and better. Actually she was enjoying good health. It is well known that seances tire mediums and sometimes make them ill—serious obstacles in work with psychokinetic mediums. For the king-of-materialization medium, Kluski, seances so much harmed his health, he had to stop seancing completely. A unique exception to this rule, Matylda was an ideal research subject. The negative attitude of the scientific establishment toward parapsychology—possibly the most important scientific discipline of our times—was at that time and still is an unpardonable blunder.

After the events in Wloclawek, in London, at my place in Czestochowa and in Warsaw, the overwhelming power of the autosuggestive mechanism of Matylda became clear. Warsaw parapsychological societies were still not ready for an extended and methodical study of a psychokinetic subject. I reiterated my invitation to Harry Price—he did not avail himself of it. When I corresponded with Hans Driesch and Fritz Quade in Germany, the latter took an active interest in my proposal. But he also was suffering from a chronic illness—a lack of funds. He suggested our meeting in Berlin, offering to arrange paid seances in order to create financial means for further research. Matylda would not hear of such a proposal. For her it was a sort of sacrilege to take money for her performance. I had decided to accept any invitation only after the inviting party first had the chance to witness the phenomena in Warsaw or Wloclawek. I had been in touch with the societies in Czechoslovakia and France. Professor Fisher from Prague planned to come but was unable to realize his plan. My efforts to obtain funds for research in Poland were unsuccessful; I could rely only on myself.

Unable to support herself in Warsaw, Matylda had to return to Wloclawek, and I could visit her only infrequently. Participating in the constantly successful seances was always for me an awe inspiring experience, but that was not my real aim.

I was at the beginning of my professional career, I had to establish my position, gain experience in my industrial specialty, and start saving money for an extended series of future experiments. This took longer than I expected; it usually does. I did not, however, foresee the last obstacle. September 1, 1939 was the beginning of WWII. It destroyed millions of human lives. Do I have to mention that it also ruined my project? When the disastrous times were over, I could not find Matylda anymore. I am sure she has never ceased to regret that the world did not want to use the unique gifts she so eagerly and generously offered to society.

Teofil Modrzejewski

DR. ROMAN BUGAJ
WARSAW, POLAND

*J*n the years 1875-1925 various mediums gained renown, among them: Daniel Dunglas Home, Florence Cook, Eusapia Palladino, Elisabeth d'Esperance, William Eglinton, Linda Gazerra, Henry Slade, Marthe Beraud (pseudonym Eva Carriere), Kathleen Goligher, Carlos Mirabelli, Stanislawa Tomczyk, Stanislawa Popielska, and Jan Guzik. But surely the greatest of them, producing a great variety of paranormal phenomena, was Teofil Modrzejewski, the famous materialization medium who used the pseudonym of Franek Kluski.[1]

Literature regarding Modrzejewski's mediumistic phenomena is not extensive, but does contain a number of interesting items. His name became known worldwide in the paranormal circles in 1921 when Dr. Gustave Geley, director of the Institut Metapsychique International of Paris, presented a report on the successfully completed materialization seances conducted with Modrzejewski in 1920 and 1921 at the institute (additional ones were held later in Warsaw). Articles written by Geley, published in the institute's *Revue Metapsychique*[2] and later translated into German,[3] were reported with extensive commentary by the European and American press. Dr. Geley's full account, representing the results of studies on Modrzejewski's mediumship, was published in Paris in a book titled *L'Ectoplasmie et la Clairvoyance*.[4] In attendance at the seances with Modrzejewski were, among others, the distinguished scientists: Prof. Charles Richet, Prof. Camille Flammarion, the physicist Arnaud Gramont, Prof. Tadeusz Urbanski, and Count Julius Potocki, a Pole permanently settled in France.

The fundamental work pertaining to the mediumistic productions of this famous medium is to be found in a book by Col. Norbert Okolowicz, published in 1926 in Warsaw by Ksiaznica Atlas.[5] Several interesting details pertaining to this book were announced by Andrzej Niemojewski,[6] a participant in seances with Modrzejewski, and by Ludwik Szczepanski.[7] A concise biographical sketch of Modrzejewski appeared in the *Polish Biographical Dictionary*.[8] In addition some more or less detailed accounts of this medium's activity, along with commentary, are found in many books dealing with parapsychology.[9]

Teofil Modrzejewski was born on February 13, 1873 in Warsaw, where he completed high school. He was a poet, newspaperman, and a bank employee. His main income derived from working for Warsaw banks. From 1897 he became connected with newspapers, with *Kurier Polski*, and later with *Kurier Poranny* where initially he worked as a reporter for the economics section. In the latter, from 1911-1914 and 1920-1932, he published some rhyming gossip which was full of lyrical charm, and from 1926 he ran a column titled "Z dymem papierosa" (With the smoke of a cigarette).

Modrzejewski travelled a lot. He knew the Italian and Russian languages perfectly, however did not do well with German and French. He had several books published; a collection *Z repertuaru "Momusa," Piosenki i satyry* (Songs and Satires; Warsaw, 1910), from his repertoire as a satirist at the Momus cabaret; *Poezje* (Poetry; Warsaw, 1912), *Strzepy zycia. Poezje* (Shreds of Life, Poetry; Warsaw, 1913) in two volumes, and a translation from the Italian of Giovanni Pazzi's historical novel *Hugo i Parisina* (Hugo and Parisienne; Warsaw, 1921). Modrzejewski died in Warsaw on January 21, 1943.[10]

I will now present a brief characterization of Modrzejewski, the medium. Unfortunately, there is no photograph of him, except for some group pictures. He was slender, short in stature. He had poor vision and a weak voice, so he spoke softly and not clearly. However, in writing he expressed himself concisely and to the point and had at his disposal a vast number of expressions.

Dr. Gustave Geley at the Institut Metapsychique International in Paris conducted a series of very thorough medical examinations on Modrzejewski. He did not find anything organically wrong, however "examination of the nervous system showed great supersensitivity in the psychic system rather than in the physical."[11]

And here is additional information provided by Okolowicz:

> Being able to look at Modrzejewski's life at close range I knew that it differs greatly from an average one. Enormous sensitivity and frequent changes in his mental state; one time bewilderment, then again clearheadedness. Even those close to him were unable to properly orient themselves as to his mental state.

> In general, Modrzejewski did not "live" until evening; he spent daytime as if in a state of slight apathy, performing his functions mechanically. His entire creativity, whether as a medium, poet, or newsman, came through only at night.

> He led a night life from his earliest days, exacted by the need to make a living independent from his daytime responsibilities. Here the peculiar property of his organism is shown. It allowed him to sleep an average of three hours per night, following which he was completely rested, as would be those who slept a full night.

> The exceptional properties of his organism would be expressed in a great number of serious illnesses throughout his life. He would fall ill suddenly, the illness reaching its culminating point within hours. In a short time the fever would drop rapidly, Modrzejewski would be up, and to the astonishment of doctors he would return to his daily tasks. There were instances where within hours he would be back at peak health, only to again fall ill with some other illness, without the usual initial symptoms.[12]

It is worth mentioning an unusual occurrence in Modrzejewski's life: around 1900, at the age of 27 he fought a duel, in which he was shot through the heart. From that time on he suffered from heart trouble due to the bullet remaining lodged in his chest.

Modrzejewski's mediumistic abilities appeared relatively late—not until 1918, when he was 45 years old. It is true that in childhood he had various visions, the ability to foresee various events and was subject to exosomatic states, but these facts did not play a significant role in his life. It was only in 1918 that the situation took a dramatic turn. At the end of winter Modrzejewski was invited to participate in a seance with a medium, whose name is unknown, the seance being conducted by the president of the Polish Society for Psychical Research, Thaddeus Sokolowski, M.D. Shortly after the lights were turned off, phenomena such as knocking, rustling and touches by unseen hands occurred not in the vicinity of the medium but near Modrzejewski. During seances that followed, but without the unnamed medium, the aforementioned manifestations along with light phenomena occurred with greater intensity and were grouped mainly around the newly discovered medium. It is thus, thanks to Dr. Sokolowski, that Modrzejewski's great mediumistic career was launched.

Thus began systematic seances with Modrzejewski, to which he consented. They lasted for six years, from December 1918 until March 1925. Modrzejewski's friend, Col. Norbert Okolowicz, conducted the sessions. Both he, and Dr. Gustave Geley, prepared a systematic documentation—about fifty detailed accounts.

Whoever had the chance to know Kluski (Modrzejewski) became convinced that the moral makeup of this man in itself precluded any conscious fraud. Kluski had rejected lucrative offers from the USA to perform publicly as a medium; nor did he ever accept material rewards from friends, acquaintances, or total strangers who participated in his seances. It was evident to all who knew him well that his financial status excluded the possibility of paying hired helpers (animal trainers included) or procuring special, expensive equipment capable of generating the literally thousands of phenomena, each containing a variety of components. And it should not be forgotten that the name Kluski is a pseudonym. Mr. Modrzejewski felt that public opinion considered the paranormal to be in bad taste—something disgraceful for his stock. When he discovered his capacities by accident, he was convinced for weeks that he was sick and thought he should seek medical help to rid himself of this abnormality, but he was too ashamed to tell a doctor about it. Later, he had to see doctors when his health, possibly in connection with the medium activity, started to suffer seriously.

Physiological correlates of psi performance are characteristic of some subjects producing paraphysical phenomena and were in evidence with Kluski. He would empty the pockets of his garment before the sitting. Once, when he did not do so, a red sign like a burn in the form of a watch and chain appeared on his body. Sometimes, the next day after the seance, bleeding and suppurative wounds appeared and, upon disappearing in one or two days, left no visible traces on the body. At times, his body emanated the scent of ozone for one or two days after the seance. Tachycardia, palpitations, extreme physical fatigue, fainting fits, catalepsy, internal and external hemorrhages, vomiting, intestinal troubles, sudden loss or gain (!)

of weight, strong thirst or unsatiable hunger, complete insomnia—such were often the aftereffects of seances. Sometimes, after seances rich in happenings, the participants felt exhausted and depressed.

Let me mention the phenomena which cannot be explained by conscious, unconscious or simply any kind of fraud. During the seances Kluski's double appeared. Visible simultaneously with the controlled medium, one phantom had Kluski's face, the other, Kluski's immobile shape. At other times, one of the participants was visited by Kluski at his home after seances. Upon telephoning Kluski, however, he would find the medium still at his apartment. Dr. Geley reports seeing Kluski walking the street near his home in Paris. Yet by checking the dates of the visas in Kluski's foreign travel passport, it was established that Kluski was in Warsaw at that time.

Sometimes, before Kluski had arrived at a seance (or after he had left), raps were heard or ozone scented in the apartment where the sitting was to be held.

Okolowicz divided all the evidential material into three periods. December 1918 through November 1920, accounted for the material gathered during the first investigative period of Modrzejewski's mediumship, prior to his going abroad. The second period involves evidential material prepared by foreign investigators about seances with Modrzejewski (who never requested compensation) held at the Institut Metapsychique International in Paris between November 1920 and February 1921. The third covers material gathered from February 1921 to the end of March 1925.

Prof. Charles Richet, Dr. Gustave Geley, Mr. Arnaud Gramont and others enforced strict control in the experiments conducted with Modrzejewski at the Paris institute. The seances took place in a laboratory, with windows having curtains that totally kept out light. The room was illuminated by a 50-watt bulb, whose intensity could be varied by a rheostat. In addition, the experimenters used large phosphorescent screens coated with a layer of zinc sulphide; sometimes they used flasks with phosphorescent bacteria.

"The luminosity of the screens has a valuable feature, in that the materializations bear it immeasurably better than the red light. Phosphorescence resembles greatly the light which the phantoms emanate themselves," states Dr. Gustave Geley.[13]

> The medium sat on an ordinary chair, in front of the so-called black cabinet, the curtains of which were generally open. This meant that the cabinet was unneccesary in experiments with Modrzejewski. Control under those conditions was very

simple. Two controllers sat on the left and right side of the medium, each holding one of his hands. Thus, their contact with the medium was so close, the medium could not make a move that would not be detected by the controllers. Throughout the seance the medium was completely immobile, except that occasionally he would place his head on the table top or rest it on the arm of one of the controllers. However, the medium's hands remained immobile. Never did I detect anything suspicious. Since Modrzejewski was in the habit of emptying his pockets before a seance in order to feel more comfortable, his suit would closely adhere to his body, without any suspicious bulges. During the seances, we always held hands, making a chain, so no participant was outside the circle.[14]

The medium was controlled in an identical manner at all sessions in Warsaw conducted by Norbert Okolowicz.

Two facts must be underscored:

1. Modrzejewski—in contrast with many mediums—never accepted any remuneration for his mediumistic manifestations.

2. No investigator has ever caught him in a fraudulent act.

The French journalist Paul Heuze in his book[15] accused Modrzejewski of not agreeing to participate in a seance conducted by the illusionist Dickson or any other prestidigitator. This was not true, for Dickson never approached Modrzejewski; however, three of Modrzejewski's seances were attended by the French magician Geo Lange who came to Warsaw in April 1921 with Prof. Charles Richet and Dr. Geley. His role as an expert prestidigitator was not revealed until the investigators were ready to return to Paris, when Mr. Geo Lange stated authoritatively that, in the three seances with Modrzejewski, he observed nothing that could be done with prestidigitator tricks.

I will now address Modrzejewski's mediumistic performances. The general sequence of steps taken during the sessions was as follows. As I already mentioned, following a thorough search of the seance room and darkening the room, the doors were locked with a key and a red lamp was turned on. The phosphorescent screens were placed on the table where the medium and participants would sit down and join hands. Persons sitting on both sides of the medium served as controllers. Paranormal phenomena would generally start to occur from several to fifteen minutes following formation of the chain. Lights would appear first, then fragrances along with the lights, accompanied by rustling and noises, sometimes human or animal voices. The final stage of manifestation was materializations of human or animal phantoms, partial or complete, which generally lasted until the end of the seance.

Light Phenomena

Light phenomena appeared at virtually all seances with Modrzejewski. Okolowicz, who observed these phenomena many times, placed them in certain characteristic groups.

I also had the occasion to meet Mr. Okolowicz's wife Sophie, who attended all sessions, and confirmed all the light phenomena and materializations described below.

Within the first category must be included light phenomena in the shape of a greenish globe, not greater than one centimeter in diameter. Generally, this type of light appeared at the beginning of a seance conducted in the dark and in the vicinity of the medium. They resembled lit soap bubbles floating lightly on the air. At times they would stop in one place, providing a start for the materialization process itself. They would appear suddenly, at first weak and diffused; then the center of each would brighten. Each globe was surrounded by a radiant aura. It was very strange that light phenomena of this type appeared in the vicinity of the medium after the seance; at times they would even appear in the medium's open mouth.

The second group of light phenomena consisted of larger lights, triangular or elliptical in shape. The triangle would rest on one of its sides, and the elongated axis of the ellipse was horizontal. Here, the color was also greenish and the center was surrounded by a misty cloud thrice its size and of the same color. This phenomenon appeared and disappeared suddenly, only to reappear in a different place. Movement of this type of light was swifter than that of the first group.

The above-mentioned lights would at times touch the exposed body parts of those present, leaving a trace of light which would linger for a fairly long period of time. These lights would on occasion pass easily through the medium or participants, as well as the table, chairs, etc. Those experiencing it would report a light touch at the points of entry and exit.

In the third group, Norbert Okolowicz included manifestations of strong phosphorescence which left behind the bracing smell of ozone. This smell, which frequently manifested during Modrzejewski's seances, was first identified in 1919 by the chemist Dr. Casimir Nencki, and then confirmed in November 1920 by Prof. Charles Richet, Dr. Gustave Geley, Arnaud Gramont, and others. It is worth mentioning that conversion of oxygen to ozone occurs under the influence of electrical discharges or shortwave radiation, also during many chemical reactions. Thus far, the factor involved in Modrzejewski's mediumistic manifestations has not been determined.

Light phenomena of the third type generally augured the start of further manifestations, namely the materialization of specific members or the entire figure of a phantom. Participants of the seance would then experience the touch of often invisible fluidic hands. These manifestations would give the impression of an extension or separation of the medium's hand, although usually they did not resemble the medium's hand.[16]

The light phenomena manifested themselves, "as if they were attached to ends of fingers or to human faces. Movements of these lights resembled human movements and usually took place near the medium. The light phenomena would at times be composed of a greater number of sparkles which would come together and separate, sometimes with the sound of friction, light claps or knocks."[17]

Similar light phenomena were observed by psychologist Dr. Julian Ochorowicz, who from 1907 was co-director of Institut General Psychologique of Paris. His studies on fluidic hands were reported in his book, *Mediumistic Phenomena,*[18] as yet not translated into English. Sklodowska-Curie showed a lively interest in studies by Ochorowicz, and took an active part in seances involving the famous Neapolitan medium, Eusapia Palladino, who frequently manifested light phenomena. Curie was well acquainted with light radiation in the dark, of radium and other radioactive elements, and was fascinated by the phosphorescence of fluidic hands, which manifested around Eusapia and seance participants. Most likely, she was intrigued by the possibility of a connection between these two groups of unusual phenomena. Participation by Sklodowska-Curie in these experiments is generally unknown.[19]

Production of light phenomena always badly exhausted the medium. Following a seance, he would exhibit a mental idleness and was unable to concentrate. Sometimes during a deep trance, phosphorescent spots appeared on Modrzejewski's body. The size of a human hand, the spots gave the impression of a luminous fluid in movement. This possibly was connected with the formation of ectoplasm and was always accompanied by a strong smell of ozone.

In the fourth group, Okolowicz included light manifestations which served to illuminate the phantoms. They gave the impression of small electrical bulbs covered by something like muslin or gauze. They would light up faces of the phantoms, most often from the side, less frequently from the top or bottom.

Another phenomenon was a light emanating from the fingertips of a hand in motion. The phantom, in moving its hands, emitted phosphorescent smoke which gave off a strong odor of ozone. At times it held in its hand an object similar to a luminous precious stone. The light was milky, sky-blue in color, and greenish-yellow in the case of phosphorescent smoke. Here Okolowicz observes that the fingers of a phantom holding a luminous crystal, although they gave the impression of belonging to a living person, did not appear red, as it would be in the case of a living hand back-lit by electric light.

Okolowicz also describes light effects in the form of luminous globes, trails, columns, triangles, and miniature lightning. Worth mentioning are light phenomena in the shape of a small cross or a moon, about ten centimeters in diameter. There had also been a manifestation in the form of a miniature volcanic eruption, disgorging not only phosphorescent smoke, but also tiny lights which gave the impression of glowing stones.

A characteristic feature of the above-described light phenomena is that at times they would result in lowering the temperature of the seance room by as much as 10°C. The author also emphasized that with the development of light phenomena all motion manifestations ceased. This is completely in accord with previous observations by Ochorowicz, who brought attention to the fact that mechanical energy would transform into light energy.

Okolowicz says that light phenomena belong to the most beautiful, most spectacular and, if one could say, most noble phenomena that appeared during seances with Modrzejewski.

Materializations

The most striking manifestation of Modrzejewski's mediumistic abilities were materializations. As we know, this unusual and puzzling phenomenon was observed and confirmed by many outstanding researchers. Considerable difficulty exists in describing these manifestations, due to their wealth and variety. Complete phantoms of human figures dominate here.

First and foremost, the constantly changing stages of materialization make their description more difficult. During seances with Modrzejewski, the greatest variety of personalities manifested themselves, sometimes of outstanding individuality and exhibiting complete psychic and intellectual autonomy.

Ethereal and foggy materializations, as well as those formed completely and looking like normal living persons, have been observed. Disjointed and incomplete materializations of human heads, faces, arms and legs, as well as parts of clothing or other accessories, have also been seen. Certain phantoms did not seem to agree with others, and displayed some discord which seemed to be connected with their appearance out of the sequence they themselves established.

In the first period of Modrzejewski's mediumistic evolution, he was completely conscious during the seance and was very active both before and during sessions. The second period was characterized by a uniformity of manifestations with a simultaneous cessation of the medium's activity. In the third period, the variety of materializations encountered in the first period reappeared. Phantoms manifested themselves longer and sharper; however, the medium almost always lost consciousness and would enter a deep trance. The closed circle, with all participants holding hands, was the usual arrangement. This made observations considerably easier and to a degree assured protection against fraud, if it were intended.

Some of the most typical manifestations preceding the materializations proper were: touching participants by unseen hands, tapping at indicated objects, or turning the red lamp on or off. On the basis of observations and analyses made, one may assume that the initial touching of participants may have as its aim the collection and condensation, by an unknown and unseen intelligence, of energy and matter indispensable for the production of materialized forms. It is characteristic that the first touches gave the impression as if performed by the medium's extended fluidic hand. Minutes later, the touches were as if by children's or women's hands, not resembling the medium's hands. Other participants would report cold and stiff hands, some as incomplete, wooden or artificial. These phenomena appeared to be the first sensory contacts between phantoms and participants.

During one of the seances, an interesting occurrence was noted. The medium, in deep trance, his hands held by two controllers, was asked to turn off the red light.

> Almost immediately the medium moved, attempting to get up, and in the light of the red light bulb we saw a third arm, as if growing out of the medium's right shoulder and rapidly moving toward the lamp. From the fingers to the elbow, the hand looked completely materialized, but further up it would dissolve into a fog-like trail, disappearing close to the medium. The hand turned off the lamp by turning the switch and was clearly visible.[20]

This experiment was repeated, the lamp was turned off, but this time the participants did not see the fluidic hand.

A regular type of materialization during seances with Modrzejewski were the so-called "dark figures." They exhibited complete signs of life: breathed, possessed a beating heart and warm extremities. At times they gave the impression of the medium's "double." The more active they were, the greater the medium's torpor. Here I will quote Dr. Julian Ochorowicz, who stated: "The stronger the manifestations, the more inert the medium's body. In a complete materialization, the medium is lifeless."[21]

This type of manifestation is characterized by exceptional properties: one dark figure may split into two, three or more forms of varying stages of materialization. The figures different activities: walk around the room, touch the participants, type on a typewriter or make penciled notes on sheets of paper. These phenomena which occur in total darkness betray their presence by muffled noises, by moving around the furniture, touching the participants, etc. Some of these phantoms show interest in the events of the seance, while others are totally disinterested. One of the phantoms, a small boy the participants named "Tazio," continuously amused himself by tapping at the lamp shade of an old lamp; he ignored admonitions of the participants, whose observation of other phenomena was being interfered with.

According to Okolowicz, the majority of dark figures represent an intermediate phase of transformation into other phantoms, i.e., into those which illuminate themselves with their own source of light or are illuminated by a phosphorescent screen. The process of this transformation is, of course, a total mystery; however, the author noted, the process of phantom's materialization takes more time than its dematerialization, which is almost always instantaneous.

Observations were made with the aid of a large (80 x 100 cm) phosphorescent screen, which illuminated almost two cubic meters of space in front of the medium; another screen illuminated another portion of the room, in addition to the red lamp behind the medium.

Under these circumstances Okolowicz noted the creation of a phantom of the "Primitive Man," as it was called. Upon the medium's head "appeared a large mop of hair, below the lower jaw a long beard, the entire body was clothed in a fog. After a short time, a grey, misty human form separated from the medium, floated through the light emanating from the large screen, and disappeared in a dark area near the window, directing itself seemingly toward the floor."[22] Knocks, rustling, and smacking sounds manifested the continuous presence of the "Primitive Man," although he remained invisible. In trying to duplicate this experiment, the author was unable to observe the previously described phases of materialization, which led him to the conclusion that "materialization processes do not follow specific rules."[23]

Another phenomenon emanating from the medium were cool breezes. This has been observed with other materializing mediums and described in parapsychological literature many times. In the case of Modrzejewski, the cool breezes, appearing in waves, could be felt even before the first light and rustling manifestations. They always emanated from the medium, moved along the chain of hands, and were felt most strongly where the materialization would take place. The smell of ozone would accompany it. The medium would begin to twitch; tightening of muscles and heavy breathing revealed his efforts.

The next materialization phase was the appearance of luminous nebuli, visible in total darkness. Usually they would separate from the medium and constantly change their shape and location. They were of various colors: grey-green, less often yellow, and very seldom bluish.

At one of the seances, in the light of the red lamp standing in the corner of the room, a misty human shape was observed. It was ethereal, and it easily flowed through the furniture without jostling them. It stopped by one of the participants who felt the touch of a warm hand giving him a piece of paper. It then disappeared.

Not all materializations were complete. Often it happened that only a fragment of the human body would appear, i.e. the head with a torso and one hand, head and a hand, etc. Often the incompleteness of a phantom could be observed in the light of the phosphorescent screen. Part of the figure was transparent. Such incomplete and fragmentary materializations occurred primarily in the first phase of Modrzejewski's mediumistic evolution, and occasionally also in the later stages. Once, an accurately materialized bust of a man appeared several times in the center of the table, giving the impression that the phantom had no legs.[24]

Some phantoms, appearing as if made of cardboard or rags, nevertheless exhibited traits of life and "perfected" the shape of their limbs in full view of the participants. This type of phantom was also observed by the German researcher, Dr. von Schrenck-Notzing, who experimented, among others, with the famous medium Martha Beraud (Eve Carriere). The photographs he published brought accusations that he fell victim to a hoax.[25]

The materialization of human phantoms smaller than the normal human being was distinctive and unusual in some of Modrzejewski's seances. They manifested all living traits and had normal proportions. A number of paraffin wax impressions were made, which resembled miniatures of the medium's hand, as well as one which was a third longer than Modrzejewski's hand. "The ratio of the miniature faces to normal ones, and of paraffin wax impressions of hands to the medium's hand, was 1:2 or 2:3."[26]

Materialized Accessories

Phantoms appearing during seances with Modrzejewski were always clothed, and operated with various material accessories. They easily created for themselves clothes, ornaments, and other objects. We say "created" because seance participants frequently noted that in the initial phases of materialization the majority of phantoms wore clothing similar to the medium's suit, only to have it transform into some other design. For instance, "the only military item of clothing the phantom of an officer had was a cap. Instead of a uniform, something like the suit that the medium had on that day was visible."[27] At times the uniform was a combination of civilian clothing and uniform. The phantom of an Italian officer, Cesare Battisti, "created" with its finger a metal star, and kept tapping it to demonstrate that it was of real matter. This star would disappear, only to show up a moment later. At times, the phantoms made use, in an obvious manner, of cloth available in the seance room, as well as clothing of the participants, to produce their own attire and their own ornaments. Utilization of these "raw materials" took place in a singular manner. Participants would feel that some dark, non-illuminated figures would, one after another, approach them and quickly rub their clothes, buttons, etc., with their hands, and then, in the light of the phosphorescent screen, appear in complete attire. When once a participant loudly stated that one of the military phantom's metal buttons was not sufficiently polished, the phantom put aside the luminescent screen he was holding, and the military participants present at the session felt that hands were rubbing their silver epaulettes and buttons. A few moments later, the phantom turned up again in the light of the screen, but this time his epaulettes and buttons shone more brightly.

During another seance, an exotic looking woman phantom was rubbing a pearl necklace worn by one of the participants. After a while the phantom reappeared illuminated by her own light, wearing a long string of pearls. It is interesting that the string of pearls was twice as long as the participant's and the phantom also wore it the following day when the participant was not present. This type of manifestation was noted frequently during Modrzejewski's seances. What is astounding in this dividing and duplication of material accessories is the speed with which it is accomplished. Who created the plan and structure of the object? Who filled it with the specified matter?

Okolowicz reports: "The participants' and especially the medium's clothing wears out during the sessions. I have noted it with my own suits. It looks as though someone subjected it to cleaning with a rough brush. The fabric becomes more and more transparent, as if worn."[28]

At times, the phantoms utilized for their purposes various items to be found in the room. Once, one of the phantoms put on the medium's glasses and kept them on through the entire appearance. "On another occasion, one phantom placed a military cap, which happened to be in the seance room, on top of another phantom. The phantom kept doing this a number of times, when finally the phantom on whose head the cap was being placed (it seems against his will) grabbed it and threw it into a corner of the room."[29]

Another time, a phantom "possessing luxuriant braids, took the medium's comb from a dressing table and started to brush out the braids. This happened after a participant remarked that the hair looked matted and artificial."[30]

During the seances cases of apports were observed. Once a bouquet of flowers was brought to the seance room and later returned to the water-filled vases in other rooms. Lost petals and drops of water marked their path. At another time, an apple hanging on a branch was apported; there were no apples in the building.

The only instance of the medium disappearing from the seance room occurred in August 1919. It was noticed during the seance when the manifestation began to be weaker. The medium was sitting on a chair in the middle of the group which formed a chain by holding hands. As the manifestations weakened, the participants noted that the medium's chair was empty. The light was turned on, but the medium was nowhere in the room. The anxious participants left the room and only in the third dimly lit room found the medium asleep on a couch. When awakened, the medium was totally disoriented as to his location, and after coming back to consciousness, remembered the events of the seance and falling in trance but not his disappearance from the room. While leaving the room in search of the medium, the participants noted that the door had been locked and the key was in the lock—on the inside.[31]

Okolowicz described another very interesting manifestation, namely "phantoms which illuminated themselves by their own light and (occasionally) used small empty bottles (from the medium's wardrobes) to temporarily store the "light" substance, which they created by rubbing their hands."[32] After the seance, the author noted that there was no substance in those bottles except the scent which was felt during that particular session.

Phantoms of Animals

While human forms prevailed, many animal forms had also been observed with Kluski. Some manifested themselves only once. Their presence was detected by voices or noises they produced, sometimes by the touches of their hairy bodies. At other times their shapes were vaguely perceived in the paltry light of the red lamp illuminating the sitting room. Was it due to poor observation or the vague shapes of the animals created by the imperfect memory images of the medium that their taxonomical position could not have been properly established?

A few animal forms appeared many times and were seen more clearly, even photographed. While some completely materialized human phantoms (resembling in every detail a real human being) were visible due to the light emanating from their interiors, animal forms, with one exception, were dark and visible only in the red light of the lamp or the light of the phosphorescent screens. In the protocols of the sittings, there is only one note, from September 1919, concerning the appearance of a large bird of prey which was self-illuminated by the light radiating from inside. The same bird appeared in the regular dark form many times. Its first appearance was preceded by a sound of whirring wings and gusts of air. A fairly good photo of this materialization was taken.

Some animal phantoms appeared simultaneously with human ones that behaved like their owners or handlers. Usually, only one human-animal pair was active. When the animal would come into contact with the participants, its companion would merely stand by and vice versa.

A phantom calling himself Hirkill from Afghanistan appeared for the first time in September of 1919. His behavior was unruly. He threw objects and struck the floor with a long, heavy bar. An animal the size of a very large dog accompanied Hirkill. The animal was a fallow color with a slender neck, large teeth and eyes that glimmered in the darkness as if they were provided with tapetum lucidum. The form resembled a lion without a mane. Its behavior, especially toward people who were afraid, was also threatening. It exuded a pungent odor characteristic of wild cats. After the sitting, the clothing of the participants and especially of the medium were saturated with this strong odor. The animal would lick the participants intrusively with its spiny tongue. Somewhat humorous and unexpected was the fact that not only the participants but other phantoms were unhappy with this wildish couple. The phantoms would disappear when Hirkill and his companion visited the seance room. Despite their negative appeal, the two phantoms would appear at almost every sitting in the summer of 1919. They disappeared thereafter and were never seen again.

Most famous of Kluski's phantoms was the one likened by Dr. Geley to the Pithecanthropus (ape-man). It first appeared in July of 1919 as a bundle of tangled hair, a sound of smacking coming from its midsection.

The participants' lively interest probably aided this phantom to become better materialized. It was covered with long, coarse brown hair with some greyish spots and was quite curly on the head. With hair growing on its forehead down to the eyebrows, it resembled a large anthropoid ape. It was endowed with such physical strength that it moved a bookcase full of books with ease, carried a sofa, or lifted people in their chairs over the heads of other participants. However, its behavior was usually gentle, and it was rather eager to obey the wishes of those present. Its overzealousness created sometimes funny but uneasy situations. Pithecanthropus considered the imitation of other phentoms its duty, especially when these phantoms were asked for a particular performance. When other phantoms were requested to bring a small object, Pithecanthropus, or Primordial Man, as some called him, would grab the closest object, regardless of its size or weight, and bring it to the bidder. The seances had to be interrupted a few times: once when Pithecanthropus brought a leather-covered sofa and deposited it on the knees of the requesting participant, another time when it brought a heavy desk and placed it in the middle of the participants' circle, and still another time when it tried to lift two participants in their chairs. In the last case, the chain of joined hands was broken, and the medium awakened from his trance. When other phantoms were asked to step in front of the phosphorescent screen, Pithecanthropus eagerly used the invitation to let everyone admire his shaggy head or hairy hand in the greenish phosphorescence. When rebuked, Pithecanthropus would hide under the table and manifest his presence by lightly scratching the legs of the participants. Pithecanthropus also liked to lick the faces of the participants and the medium with his salivating tongue. This always evoked loud protests, and the participants would demand that he either stop this bad-tasting performance or leave. Pithecanthropus eventually refrained from his habit. After his long sojourn, the room was full of animal odor, which Dr. Geley likened to that of a "wet dog."

Unfortunately, none of the three photos of Pithecanthropus belong to the best of Kluski's phantom pictures. Sudden, unannounced interruptions of Kluski's trance (similar to many mediums) caused headaches, accelerated heartbeat, and other undesirable physiological reactions— sometimes even hemorrhages. Pictures were therefore taken with the consent of the phantoms, speaking in the name of the medium. Such consent was usually expressed by a previously agreed number of raps. In all three photos, the time interval between the end of the rapping and the flash was too long; the phantom of Pithecanthropus was in the meantime disintegrating—melting into the body of the medium—so that the camera caught only the curly crop of hair on or near the medium's baldish head. Let us not forget that at that time flash photography was not the simple pushbutton operation of today. There were no electrically ignited flash-bulbs triggered simultaneously with the camera shutter; the camera shutter had to be opened in advance for time exposure and an igniter used to fire the heap of magnesium powder strewn on a separate tray.

Pithecanthropus and other phantoms seemed to appear by emerging from the body of the medium. Colonel Okolowicz decided to check this theory. To secure as much visibility as possible during the seance, the large 80 x 100 cm phosphorescent screen was placed on the left side of the medium. He and another controller held a smaller screen, one in front and the other in back of the medium. Both controllers sat quite close to the medium, each holding one of his hands. At a certain moment, the medium in trance took a deep breath, and a large crop of hair appeared on the top of his head—long hair below his jaw. The entire body of the medium became cloaked in fog. The grey cloud of a human shape detached itself from the body of the medium and moved across the streak of light projected by the large screen toward the dark corner of the room, where it became invisible due to the darkness of the place. The medium came out of the trance, and from the area where the cloud disappeared all participants heard raps, noises, and sounds of smacking—the calling card of Pithecanthropus. The experiment brilliantly confirmed Okolowicz's theory of the materialization locus. However he, like many other experimenters before and after him, did not realize that his state of mind, his theory, or conviction could have a decisive influence on the phenomenon directly or through the personality of the medium. The Polish experimenter soon had the chance to learn about his error. He had observed many materializations, some in full light and appearing far away from Kluski, and he was not ashamed to recognize the error of his judgment. During one of the consecutive seances, the medium's fur coat was resting on a sofa, when the coat began moving. Initially slow, the movements became faster and faster, their amplitude also growing. Finally the fur coat was literally jumping. The phantom of Pithecanthropus emerged from the fur coat and went running about the room while the coat was again motionless resting on the sofa.

Toward the end of 1919, the phantom of Pithecanthropus grew weaker. It appeared in November in a curiously fragmented form but at three locations simultaneously: a weak smacking sound came from one corner of the room, a light scratching of the floor from another, and one of the participants felt the rubbing of a hairy body against his legs. After this seance, Pithecanthropus was not seen for the entire year. When all hope was lost, he appeared suddenly on November 20 at the laboratory of the I.M.I. in Paris, where Kluski went for several months of study with Charles Richet, Gustave Geley, Camille Flammarion and other investigators.

French researchers were extremely interested in the half man-half ape creature—the product of Kluski's inner personality—immaterial and yet endowed with physical strength, all in all a crazy affair. However, the Paris appearances were not as strong as the previous ones in Warsaw. The best appearance was the first one on November 20, when several people saw him. In his book, Geley describes this seance:

> One of us felt his large head leaning heavily on the right shoulder against the cheek. The head was covered with long, coarse hair. One of the assistants stretched his hand toward the phantom, who seized it and gave it three series of lickings. Pithecanthropus' tongue was large and soft.[33]

After Paris, the phantom disappeared for a long time, then suddenly emerged during a May 1922 seance in Warsaw while Dr. Geley was present as a guest. Man-ape was then full of energy. The sitting had to be interrupted because of his uncontrollable behavior. On November 13 of the same year, he appeared toward the end of the sitting, making violent jumps and striking the floor with his feet and hands. Later he rubbed against peoples' legs, and a continued smacking accompanied all performances. Pithecanthropus' next appearance was on December 25 when he started lifting heavy furniture, as well as one of the participants, and was brought under control with difficulty. The next day he appeared in the abortive form in which he had first manifested itself. He was perceptible only through dispersed acoustic phenomena, such as scratching and smacking.

Among other mediums, one notable animal phantom was that produced by Jan Guzik (Gouzhyk), also a Polish medium. This phantom resembled a weasel (some participants likened it to the Indian Ichneumon). Its appearance was preceded by touches of its hairy fingers on some of the participants. The animal was always accompanied by a human phantom of Oriental type with a very serious facial expression and dignified manner. The animal was lovely and so pleasant in its behavior, the participants tried very hard to prolong its appearance, but with little success. The pair seemed inseparable; whenever the noble companion disappeared, the lively animal vanished. It was seen many times. The animal would run quickly atop the table or over the arms and shoulders of the participants, stopping often to sniff their hands and faces or to rub its cold nose against their skin. Sometimes, as if frightened, it would jump from the table and run about the room overturning small objects, displacing papers on the desk, etc.

The behavior of real animals during, after, or even before the seance was surprising for the people who had the rare chance to enter Kluski's land of wonders. The reactions of these real creatures was a reinforcement of the reality of the miraculous events the participants had been witnessing. Kluski's own pets exhibited a wide range of responses, from excitement through fear, panic, aggression or rage to vivid interest and attraction toward a particular phantom. A dog examining the floor of the room would appear to search for something or someone and would become excited when losing the track. Then he might bark as if hostile to the phantom or whine as if friendly. The object of the search, mostly human phantoms, was usually slightly visible, though at other times people saw nothing and the entity was perceptible only to the animal. Occasionally, after the sitting was over, a dog would be let into the seance room. It became animated, sniffing at the places where phantoms had previously appeared or at the wet, gradually vanishing spots of some unknown substance, which exuded fragrances or smelled of ozone.

Phantoms Illuminated by Phosphorescent Screens

The largest group of human-like phantoms making their appearance, already in the early stages of Modrzejewski's mediumistic career, were those illuminated by the light of a phosphorescent screen. They did not resemble one another and frequently represented themselves as persons who had died in the fairly recent past. They appeared either singly or simultaneously in groups of two, three or more. Okolowicz identified over fifty widely varying types. Some of the phantoms would write, but very seldom would they speak.

The emotional attitude of participants toward the phantoms varied. Some phantoms found a sympathetic audience, while others would elicit expressions of disgust or repugnance due to their appearance or behavior. For example, the phantom of an Afghan named "Hirkill" who appeared together with a predatory animal which looked somewhat like a lioness caused agitation and fear, because of the brutal and aggressive behavior of the person and the animal. Other phantoms gave the impression that they did not come to contact anyone, but rather out of their own curiosity. Still others showed anxiety and disappeared shortly after unsuccessful tries at contacting those present. There were also cases of fights between phantoms, as was the case of a "Russian gendarme" and a "revolutionary worker" who in 1905 died in a mortal battle, fighting each other in the streets of Warsaw. These phantoms later and independently provided this explanation.

Okolowicz states that the longer the phantoms lasted, the more they assumed human traits, becoming at times indistinguishable from living persons.[34] This was confirmed by Okolowicz's widow in a personal conversation with the author.

Out of about 650 phantom manifestations, nearly 200 were illuminated by a screen. The "Primitive Man" phantom was regarded by other phantoms as an oddity, a freak not encountered "there."

Phantoms claiming they represented persons who had passed over, generated interest. "The behavior of these phantoms is striking, as they manifest themselves in a characteristic manner that allows them to be easily recognized," says Okolowicz. "They create the impression of more or less intelligent, educated persons, more or less aware of why they came."[35]

Phantoms appearing for the first time always exhibited some clumsiness and lack of orientation; however during manifestations that followed, they behaved quite naturally and at ease, even if the make-up of the participating group was different. Some phantoms "frequently gave the impression that not only did they not know what they wanted or why they came, but they did not seem aware of their existence."[36] Still others manifested a variety of temperaments, expressing grievances, resentment, crying, at other times joy, good humor, and joviality. As an example, I quote here a fragment of the minutes of a seance of June 30, 1924, as reported by Dr. Gustave Geley:

> A new being appears, as perfectly formed as those who had come before. It goes first to Mr. Sabin Przybylski, who feels he is kissed and hugged by unseen hands. He states that in the light of a screen he recognizes his son, who died in 1920 during the war. The phantom kisses his forehead, his cheeks and hands. He appears once more and goes to Mrs. Przybylski, who screams and displays such strong emotion that the phantom disappears momentarily. It then materializes anew, and I see the fully alive face of a beardless young man. The phantom returns to Mr. Przybylski and remains there for quite some time. I hear a muffled whisper. The screen is then put on the table.[37]

When this phantom reappeared during a July 11, 1924, seance, it immediately went to the seat his father had occupied during the previous seance. However, his father was not present. It kissed Dr. Gustave Geley's hand, as he sat in Mr. Przybylski's seat. Realizing its error, it said in a loud whisper and a disappointed tone, "Father is not here".

Okolowicz states that while the phantoms' senses allow them to move easily in darkness, to sense the mood of the participants, and even to read their thoughts, nonetheless, mistakes occurred, as described above.

Andrew Niemojewski speaks of this matter in even greater detail:

> When we conducted seances at the home of a certain famous dramatic actor, where we always had the greatest number of vocal manifestations, I at times conducted conversations with the phantoms lasting up to half an hour. One phantom gave the host a formal lecture on the topic of permeation of objects through other objects, illustrating it by passing its luminous finger back and forth through the table. Then it teleported to him—from another room through a closed door—something "readily soluble": two lumps of sugar.
>
> In order to assure myself that there was no deception, I sometimes selected sophisticated topics from my studies of astral, gnostic, Greek astrology, stylization of astral texts and frescoes in other words matters about which no one in Warsaw would have the faintest idea, especially since these matters required a specialized vocabulary, completely unknown to the layman. However, the phantom answered as if this was its specialty. I had the impression I was conversing with myself, albeit a different self. In other words, that my consciousness was conversing with my subconscious.[38]

Reactions of participants to the phantom's touch were significant. The first touch would evoke a certain degree of fear, send shivers through the body and an impression of an electrical shock. Other and very strange manifestations would also occur. This is what Okolowicz wrote on the topic:

> At the beginning of the third period of experimentation, it was noted three times that a phantom appeared who gave the impression of one form being filled by several beings. It was an uncanny, nightmarish impression. The phantom's movement was ponderous as it illuminated itself with the phosphorescent screen. Special attention was paid to its facial features which became feminine, only to change to masculine, but never losing its double character. It was as if two, and at times three faces slid over one another— clear as glass, despite their seeming to be flesh-like.... This personality had a disquieting and unpleasant effect on the participants.[39]

Okolowicz wrote further:

> In describing seance conditions, I mentioned the detrimental
> effects, both for the medium and for the course of the seance,
> when the chain of hands near the medium is broken.... It had
> happened a number of times that some of the phantoms
> themselves broke the chain of hands and joined in for a time
> as participants.[40]

Phantoms of the Deceased

Many of the phantoms appearing during seances with Modrzejewski
were identified by participants as persons known to them during their
lifetime. This was true both for phantoms illuminating themselves with the
phosphorescent screen and for those illuminated by their own light. The
question of survival is intriguing and important, and at the same time very
controversial, not only from a parapsychological but also a philosophical
point of view. Of necessity, the question of accuracy, credibility, and
truthfulness of observation by participants must remain open due to the
impossibility to repeat and to study past events.

Although Okolowicz had at his disposal reports of many sessions
signed by persons who claimed to have recognized some of the departed,
with remarks stating that they "without doubt recognized phantoms of
persons known to them in life," unfortunately no photographs were taken.
These would have been priceless in corroborating such statements. Phantoms recognized by participants almost always gained in clarity, and their
form became more perfect. They generally appeared close to the person
who claimed to recognize them. Some of the recognized phantoms
reappeared in subsequent sessions with a different set of participants. The
phantom of the Italian military, Cesare Battisti, who appeared eighty-eight
times, was typical.

Okolowicz noted:

> Over the course of the three periods of seances eighty-four
> persons who recognized a deceased one, identified a total of
> eighty-eight persons. In many cases several participants iden-
> tified the same person. Only the appearance of specific phan-
> toms has been accounted for here and not the total number of
> times the phantoms made a repeat appearance, which totalled
> about 260 manifestations—over one quarter of the total num-
> ber of manifestations ascertained in the course of

Modrzejewski's seances from December 1918 to the end of March 1925.[41]

Okolowicz had a number of difficulties when describing phantoms of the deceased. A certain number of participants who recognized their relatives and dear ones in the phantoms did not want their names or those of the phantoms publicized. Although they represent a quarter of the persons who claimed recognition, their refusal makes a detailed description and analysis of facts more difficult. Frequently phantoms showed a clear attraction toward certain persons and a complete indifference or even antipathy toward others. Similar attitudes toward the phantoms were seen in the participants. Some participants could not control the psychic stress, and their nerves would buckle. This, of course, caused a break in the seance and an end to the manifestation. Most frequently the phantoms would appear as they were known in life. Sometimes, however, they looked much younger. They seldom spoke; most often communication was achieved with the aid of an alphabet read aloud. At the appropriate letter the phantom would knock with an object on the table or some other piece of furniture.

Communications obtained in this manner were of varying content— generally containing personal notes or short items of information. If the phantoms wrote, the notes were more detailed. Okolowicz quoted only notes of a general nature, skipping those with a personal content. One of the phantoms penciled on the paper: "A child reaching for the moon is closer to the goal than you are." Another one pecked out on the typewriter: "Animal instinct senses truth better than the human." Yet another enigmatically announced: "I am the smile of balance, my poem of love and life survived aeons of time."

It needs to be underscored that many persons came to Modrzejewski's solely for the purpose of seeing dear ones who passed away in the recent past. Modrzejewski never refused to help people, although frequent seances disorganized his personal life and even ruined his health. This last statement I shall illustrate with a few examples.

As a rule, materialization seances exhausted the medium, who recovered quickly. There were nevertheless exceptions. On the October 10, 1921, an improperly conducted seance brought the medium into a desperate psychic state bordering on insanity. On the June 23, 1922, after completion of the seance, the housemaid suddenly walked into the room and turned on the light. The half-conscious medium fell from the couch and suffered a mild heart attack.[42] Following the July 3, 1924, seance the medium had several nosebleeds.

The medium paid with his health for his practice. After several years of intensive involvement in seances, Modrzejewski withdrew totally from these experiments upon the order of his doctor.

Similarity to and Attitudes of Phantoms Toward the Medium

It was Alexander Aksakov who at the beginning of this century noticed that phantoms in the first phase of manifestation show great similarity to the medium. It is only in the course of development of the medium's psychic capacities that the similarity disappears completely and totally different personalities appear. As we already know, in the early phases of manifestation the Katie King phantom was so similar to medium Florence Cook that Prof. William Crookes came to believe they were two different entities and proved this scientifically only when he photographed the medium and the phantom simultaneously.

Similarities between the medium and the phantom occurred also in Modrzejewski's case. Physical interdependence manifested itself most frequently in movements and timbre of voice, and at times in a certain similarity of silhouette and facial traits. Not all phantoms exhibited such similarities. Most frequently they were discernable in the first stage of manifestation and later disappeared completely. Any "bodily" injuries to the phantom were immediately transferred to the medium. This proved the close connection between them, although this connection was not always obvious. I quote the following example:

> At the May 27, 1923, seance, the following incident took place. Intrigued by the distinctness of the phantom's figure, two seance participants decided to discover whether the manifestations were real and not merely a hallucination. At the moment when the phantom of a young, tiny self-illuminating woman was about two meters away from the medium, the two quickly extended their hands to touch or grasp the phantom. Unexpectedly, their hands met a resistance, striking a blow to the phantom's chest. Simultaneously the medium gave off a deep groan and for a moment convulsively squeezed the controllers' hands. The two persons having verified the phantom's reality did not try to repeat their test. The figure of the woman stayed in place for a while, wagging her finger disapprovingly in the light of the phosphorescent screen. She reappeared a few more times very clearly—then vanished.

> The day after the seance, a mark of a blow on the medium's chest was visible.[43]

Light also had a negative effect on the medium. A sudden shining of the light of the phosphorescent screen into the phantom's eyes caused restless movements of the medium. However, if the phantoms themselves manipulated the screen, it was clear they were doing it to prevent the light shining into the medium's eyes. If a phantom, illuminating itself with its own strong light, appeared in front of the medium, then other phantoms present would solicitously shield his head with a nearby curtain, or some other cloth. If there was none, they would bow the medium's head onto the table.

The following very interesting fact was often noted by the participants. The medium's body never presented a material barrier to the phantom though, while moving freely about the room they avoided contact with the participants, they would pass through the medium with no difficulty. At times they would grow into it, becoming somewhat like his extension.

Phantoms which resembled the medium appeared most often and seemed to be subject to his will, especially when the medium remained conscious and was interested in the proceedings. Sometimes Modrzejewski would angrily and arbitrarily shout at the phantoms, giving them various instructions and orders. They reacted by manifesting demands, feelings of hurt, or tenderness and submission.

Phantoms Illuminated by Their Own Light

The self-illuminating phantoms, therefore fully visible, were the most interesting during Modrzejewski's seances. Their precise characteristics were given in minutes of sessions, quoted both in Geley's and Okolowicz's books.[44]

All in all, forty-five phantoms illuminated themselves by their own light. Some would also use the light of phosphorescent screens. Following such strong light manifestations, Modrzejewski was always exhausted both physically and psychologically.

Of forty-five phantoms, thirty-six were exotic, the rest European types. The participants gave different names to each self-illuminating phantom. Among them, four were recognized as deceased friends or relatives of participants. The self-illuminating phantoms appeared 182 times. To illustrate, I will quote examples noted by Okolowicz:

Several very clear and beautiful phantoms appeared at the October 26, 1924 seance. One was the figure of a woman of exceptional beauty and was seen down to the waist. This phantom illuminated herself with a quasi-precious stone held above her head in her left hand. The light was moon-like in quality, and it made an impression as if she held in her hand a piece of the moon. Her arm was bare and, like the rest of her body, beautifully draped in muslin."[45]

The face of a young man appeared during the May 9, 1924 seance. It was illuminated by an intense azure source of light, heretofore never seen, which the phantom held in his fingers. It looked like a large sapphire emitting strong and twinkling rays. Before disappearing, this phantom whispered to the nearest participants its name: Nino Bixio. As is known, Nino Bixio was Giuseppe Garibaldi's adjutant.[46]

Phenomena of this type became the unusual attraction in Modrzejewski's seances, making him famous. They made an indelible impression upon the participants:

Their luminous and dignified appearance, their serious de-meanor, and usually their original attire dazzled the partici-pants. All these phantoms brought with them some very unusual atmosphere, and they seemed to have a fatherly attitude toward all participants, with certain partiality toward some of them.[47] During such manifestations the medium was in deep trance, while the phantoms, very similar to real persons, exhibited an unusual vitality. When appearing, they gave the impression of "as if flowing down from above, and at the moment of disappearing they would again float up and dissolve in a luminous fog, most frequently emanated by themselves."[48] Manifestations of this type were often accom-panied by various fragrances which filled the seance room. These fragrances could be of: ozone, almond flowers, frank-incense, sandalwood, ambergris or mint.

I will present here one fragment from a seance which took place in Warsaw on July 11, 1924, and which was attended by Dr. Gustave Geley. The phantom of what was called an "Assyrian priest" appeared on that occasion. The seance was conducted by Okolowicz, and this is what he noted:

I remember his (that is, Dr. Geley's) joy when after creating some paraffin wax molds and after the appearance of phantoms in a subdued light, the phantom of the "Assyrian High-Priest" made an appearance in full splendor.[49]

A few moments later, steps were heard in the middle of the room. Almost immediately afterwards, a bright light flared, and those present clearly saw an Eastern-type apparition dressed in white, with a white head-covering and a shawl over the shoulders, covering the bare arms to the elbows. The figure illuminated itself with a flickering, luminous, greenish-yellow substance that spread over the fingers and palms. The brilliance of this light was incomparably greater than the light of the phosphorescent screen. It emitted lightly phosphorescent smoke with the scent of ozone mixed with the fragrance of mint and burned amber. The phantom illuminated his face several times by lifting his light-emanating hands. The characteristic features of the face were clearly visible. It was a figure of an ascetic-looking man in his prime: slender, with clear, bright eyes, and a long chestnut-colored beard coming down in two strands. The mustache was nearly invisible under the nose, but showed up well above the corners of the mouth where it blended with the beard. The figure made a noble and solemn impression, intimidating those present who, being enthralled by this living and magnificent display, did not dare to demand that it come closer and show itself to individual participants. In addition to illuminating its face, this phantom raised its hands high in front of himself and above the participants, making luminous signs of a triangle. The seance participants recognized in it the frequently appearing "Assyrian High Priest." It disappeared as suddenly as it appeared.[50]

As reported by Okolowicz, this phantom appeared twenty-nine times at various seances and with different participants present.[51]

Paraffin Wax Molds

A process which permits the determination of authenticity of the materialization and dematerialization phenomena in an indisputable manner was applied in the course of seances with Modrzejewski. It consists of making paraffin wax molds of materialized body parts of a phantom. This process was introduced in 1876 in the United States by a geology professor, Denton. First used by Reimer in Manchester and Oxley in London, it became widely used by other investigators later. Okolowicz described the method as follows:

> A receptacle containing molten paraffin (melting point is 51-55°C—depending on the content of specific hydrocarbons) on a hot water bath is placed near the medium. The materialized phantom is asked to immerse a few times a hand, foot, or even part of the face in the melted wax. A precise cast of the immersed member is formed on contact with air, or cold water—a container of which is placed near the molten paraffin bath. As the phantom's member dematerializes, it leaves the cast. Plaster of Paris is poured into it later, and when it sets up, it is placed in hot water; the paraffin wax melts. Thus a precise form of the phantom's body part is obtained.[52]

At the Institut Metapsychique International in Paris, a series of tests was conducted with Modrzejewski. All in all, nine casts were obtained. It suffices to see photographs of these casts of hands and legs to become convinced they could not have been done with normal hands and legs; their removal from the paraffin form two to three millimeter thick was not possible.

The French investigators, Charles Richet and Gustave Geley, who experimented with Modrzejewski used a means to secure against bringing previously prepared paraffin molds to the session. During the December 27, 1920 test in Warsaw, they secretly added a blue dye to the paraffin. The wax forms obtained in the course of the session there were blueish.

Another method employed by the French researchers relied on introduction of some cholesterol into the blue-dyed paraffin (five grams to about 1200 grams of molten paraffin wax). When dissolved in the paraffin wax, this substance does not change its color but can be subsequently detected through a chemical reaction. This reaction is based on dissolving a sample of the treated paraffin in chloroform and adding a small amount of sulphuric acid, a result of which is the wax slowly and gradually takes on a reddish and later brownish color. Plain paraffin does not give this reaction. This method also makes impossible the smuggling (if such were planned) of ready-made forms. During the session two forms were obtained (a child's leg and part of a young man's face), and a subsequently performed chemical reaction showed that the forms were not brought in but were made from paraffin wax prepared by Richet and Geley. There was neither a child at the seance nor a young man with similar features.

This briefly represents the phenomenology of phantoms manifesting during sessions with Modrzejewski, as described in the voluminous reports by Dr. Gustave Geley and Norbert Okolowicz. Many phenomena, however, occurred also outside the seance settings. The psychic life of Modrzejewski was surrounded by an impenetrable mystery, which he refused to discuss. He took the same position with reference to the question of psychic abilities. When questioned, he would briefly and unwillingly answer: "I don't know what it is." "Neither was he sure whether popularizing metaphysical phenomena would bring more harm than good."[53]

Mediumistic phenomena would constantly and stubbornly accompany him outside the seance. However, he surrounded these matters with total secrecy. Despite that, the untiring Okolowicz was able to make some splendid observations:

> Frequently, persons walking into Modrzejewski's room found him laying on an ottoman, surrounded by luminous mists and lights, which began to disappear at the moment of their entry. Such phenomena occurred frequently and after seances, and seemed to gain in strength when the participants were leaving.

> It happened several times that his acquaintances came to visit, having learned he was at home, but before entering his room, would peek through the cracked door so as not to wake him. They knew he spent sleepless nights working, thus every moment of sleep in the evening was refreshing. In such instances, they would sometimes notice one or more phantoms, and the medium among them, moving about in a lively manner. Some of those figures had been seen several times, other appeared more rarely. They were all perfectly materialized and gave the impression that their contact with the medium had a strictly personal character.[54]

What more can be said? These are incredible and astonishing things. How many problems are hidden within, how many unsolved mysteries....

Here is another observation recorded by Okolowicz. After the March 23rd seance, he noted changes in the weight of the medium, who entered a cataleptic trance and became completely rigid. Trying to move him, Okolowicz was surprised that the body became extremely light. Pressing down on the legs extending beyond the couch was sufficient to raise the body to a vertical position. Okolowicz repeated this a number of times, then he easily lifted Modrzejewski's body, feeling that he had lost two thirds of his normal weight (sixty-six kilograms was his normal weight). Finally, after prying open the tightly clenched fists, the medium returned to his normal state and the body regained its usual weight.

I will cite an interesting anecdote, related by Romana Dalbor, who knew Modrzejewski personally and attended his seances many times. She once had the opportunity to briefly converse with him on the topic of his mediumistic capabilities, and she wrote about it as follows:

> Modrzejewski was escorting me home after the seance. I mentioned to him how sorry I was that he himself was unable to see and to know what happened during a seance. He answered: "And how do you know what I am going through?" Then he suddenly added that two years after his death they can dig up his coffin, and convince themselves that his body is intact. He died during the German occupation; therefore, doing that was impossible. That was the only time he spoke on the topic. He never wanted these topics discussed in his presence, nor did he want to be questioned on the subject. He dismissed curious inquiries, or would answer with a joke. His coworkers at the bank related that after Modrzejewski had walked down an acacia-lined avenue, they were unable to stay with him in the same room because they would choke from the acacia fragrance.[55]

Dr. Tadeusz Sokolowski quoted the following story, told him by Modrzejewski:

> Serving as a volunteer in a certain regiment of dragoons, he was obliged to take part in a banquet, given by the officers in honor of a delegation from another regiment which had a number of Tartars. After a hefty libation, the somewhat inebriated Modrzejewski sat down with the Tartars and, as he remembers, conducted a lively conversation with them. The following day, his immediate superior told him he never suspected such knowledge of the Tartar language, and that the Tartar officers expressed their amazement. The no-less-surprised Modrzejewski admitted to the conversation but indicated he absolutely had no knowledge of the Tartar language. This was denied by his superior and the other officers, one of whom studied oriental languages. They also remembered that the regimental commander expressed his displeasure at the

fact that the group of officers, among whom Modrzejewski found himself, spoke a tongue not understood by all the banquet participants.[56]

Opinions of Seance Participants

Modrzejewski was internationally known. He took part in seances in Warsaw, Paris, Florence, Milan, and Vienna. His mediumistic manifestations were seen by about 350 participants.

Modrzejewski was never caught cheating. He never took honoraria for his work. Fifteen photographs were taken of his materialization manifestations, and forty-two photos of plaster of paris casts, obtained from paraffin wax molds.

Okolowicz took a poll of the seance participants, asking their opinion of the manifestations they had witnessed. His appeal was answered by many. I quote here a number of the most interesting statements:

Prof. Charles Richet:

> I hereby acknowledge that I participated, in Paris and in Warsaw, in a number of seances with Mr. T. Modrzejewski of Warsaw and I ascertained under good control conditions the following characteristic manifestations of a great mediumistic force: light phenomena, starting with merely points of light all the way to fairly strong lights of various shapes and colors; touching by materialized body members; rustling, sounds of steps; murmurs; sliding, levitation, movement of large and small objects, as well as the apport of objects present in the seance room but beyond the medium's reach; the formation of paraffin wax molds, which after being cast with plaster of paris, resulted in perfectly formed human hands and legs; materializations of hands, faces, heads and complete human figures, which illuminated themselves with their own light or with the aid of a phosphorescent screen.

H. McKenzie, honorary director of the British College of Psychic Science in London, ascertained the following:

> I hereby certify that in May 1922 I took part, in Warsaw, in one session with Franek Kluski, a medium, and I was a witness, under conditions of unquestionable control, to manifestations which attest to the very strong mediumistic properties of Mr.

Kluski. During the seances I ascertained: rustling and murmurs, as well as stomping; formation of paraffin wax molds which after casting with plaster of paris gave perfect casts of human hands; clearly materialized human heads, illuminated by their own light. These phenomena gave me the impression that Franek Kluski undoubtedly has the psychic force to create materializations of high quality and perfection which can be seen in the paraffin wax molds, five of which I obtained at the one and only session I attended. These were done under conditions which removed all my doubts as to the genuineness of the phenomena.

The next statement was made by the philosopher and historian, Adam Zoltowski, professor of the University of Poznan:

I hereby certify that in 1924, in Warsaw, I participated in two seances with Franek Kluski, the medium. Under conditions of normal control, I witnessed manifestations which demonstrate Mr. Kluski's strong mediumistic qualities.

In the course of the seance I ascertained: the appearance of light phenomena—from spark-like lights to nebulae; the touch of materialized human hands as well as very strong pressure and blows by the same; rustling, murmurs and the sound of stomping; the smell of ozone and fragrance of perfume which no one present wore; shifting, lifting, and dropping of both small and large objects; automatic striking of typewriter keys; whispers; totally clear materializations of hands, faces, heads, and entire human figures, which illuminated themselves through either their own source or by the phosphorescent screen.

None of the manifestations were known to me, except that of Cesare Battisti, the Italian hero, whose appearance was familiar to me through photographs. The phantoms strongly impressed me as unquestionably authentic and as possessing great strength.

My attention was drawn to the medium's dazed condition following the seance, a state hard to simulate.

Professor Henri Breuil of Paris stated this:

There were materializations of hands, faces, and heads, or more frequently busts or entire persons, some of which were luminous, or more frequently illuminated by the light of phosphorescent screens. On the 29th of April, from among the faces, I could clearly distinguish the medium's deceased daughter-in-law, whose photograph I saw after the seance. I find these manifestations impossible to duplicate through fraudulent methods. The placement of the table was such that it made it impossible for the medium and two persons sitting on his right to move. The other two persons were under my direct control.

Casimir Nencki, Ph.D., chemist, stated:

Among these (materialized) persons, without doubt, I recognized the phantom of Jadzia M. (twelve times) and Frances M. (four times) and others. The first one died in 1921, the other one in 1896 or 7. These phantoms impressed me as being complete materializations of persons known to me in life—which I could precisely ascertain with all my senses.

And Theodor Jakobsen, an engineer, said this:

Among the (materialized) persons I most certainly recognized twice the phantom of Mieczyslaw Arnd, who died December 15, 1922. These appearances gave me the impression of phenomena which cannot be reconciled with laws of nature as I know them, and which therefore must be ascribed to Modrzejewski's mediumistic abilities. After the seance, I was left with a deep feeling of having been in touch with a power that is for me a total mystery.

The industrialist Thadeus Osinski made the following observation:

From among the phantom figures, I without doubt twice recognized my deceased friend L. Nowakowski, who died in 1912. These manifestations made a great impression on me, they created within me the conviction that they stand on the threshold of great knowledge or mystery. Every intelligent human should feel the need for further studies of it.

Thadeus Boy-Zelenski, M.D., participated in the February 17, 1924 seance. Among others, he made the following comment:

With interest, I am observing the mold which the phantom left us. It is a thin and very delicate mold of the right hand, up to the wrist: two fingers are straight, three are bent. It looks like someone immersed a hand in molten paraffin wax and removed it, covered with a thin layer of the wax—except that it is impossible to remove a live hand from such a mold. It is the hand of a phantom, an "astral" hand.... My friend, the medium, is returning to the room; it is difficult to look at him—eyes vague, face swollen. He coughs—the handkerchief is full of blood. (It is not a serious hemorrhage, assures one of the doctors, but a temporary hyperemia.) Anyone seeing him in this state, could not consider the possibility of a fraud. Why would he be inviting us? One cannot doubt for a moment that we are face to face with a wondrous gift.

All other opinions are in the same vein. Not one of the respondents questioned any of the manifestations that had been described. I will end this review of statements made by participants in Modrzejewski's seances with one made by the recently deceased Prof. Tadeusz Urbanski. His statement was published early in 1984 in one of the publications of the Polish Academy of Science.

There is a certain fact, not connected with chemistry, from the days when I worked with Prof. Joseph George Boguski, which is worth noting. One day, my colleague from the laboratory, John Modrzejewski, turned to me with a proposal that I come to a spiritist seance. My first reaction was negative, for I heard a lot about the charlatans who hold seances for money. Modrzejewski, seeing my hesitation, told me in secret that the spiritist medium is his father, Teofil Modrzejewski, board member of one of the Warsaw banks, who appears at the seances under the pseudonym Franek Kluski, and that they are conducted by General Zaruski, assistant to Polish president Wojciechowski.... The seances were held strictly for the family and close acquaintances.

Excited by this explanation, I came to one of the seances, which took place at the Modrzejewski home on Krolewska Street. It was an unusual experience. The only illumination in the seance room, which was in the center of the home and therefore shielded from street noise, was a phosphorescent screen placed on a table with participants sitting around it holding hands to create a "chain." The medium fell asleep. Initially there were rays of light which appeared now and again. Then there came orange-scented wafts of air, and an ichneumon ran around the "chain" of participants. Seated in a chair, I was raised into the air by the Assyrian priest who appeared next. Heroic figures also appeared, for instance the Italian, Battisti, who was executed by the Austrians during the occupation of northern Italy in the 1860's.

The phosphorescent screen would float up into the air and illuminate the phantoms. Then the effects began to weaken, and again there were rays of light and wafts of air. Then the medium came out of the trance.

Modrzejewski left the room to rest, and the participants left, feeling weakened, especially on the following day. It was an after-seance reaction as everyone gave up some of his energy.

That was a great experience.[57]

I conducted interviews with five participants in Modrzejewski's seances, namely: Dr. Anthony Czubrynski, Mrs. Zofia Okolowicz, Prosper Szmurlo, Thadeus Urbanski, and Robert Walter. All were generous with their information and fully confirmed the authenticity of the materialization phenomena to which they were witness. Especially valuable were statements of Mrs. Okolowicz, who attended all sessions. Only the lack of space prevents me from quoting additional details.

Physical Mediumship in Russia

DR. LARISSA VILENSKAYA
MENLO PARK, CALIFORNIA

Since ancient times, many Russians—sophisticated highly-educated scientists and down-to-earth people in the street alike—believed in special powers of village seers, starets (elders) and shamans of Northern Asia.

Nineteenth-century anthropologists brought from Siberian tribes, like the Yakut, eye-witness observations of phenomena reportedly occurring in "magnetic trance." According to these anthropologists, a shaman enters the tent-like *yurta* with a drum and produces a rhythmic sound. The assembled people sing in cadence. Suddenly the shaman falls flat on the ground and remains in such a position, like a corpse, for several hours. No one is to touch him, since this could cause his death. After he awakens, he relates what he has seen in the various places he has apparently visited while in trance.[1]

Some shamans, such as those in the Chukotka peninsula and Altaian *yadachi*, were credited with the ability to influence weather: to cause and stop snow storms, rain or hail.[2] It was believed for a long time that the Lapp shamans possessed power over the winds. The Lapps tied three magic knots and when they untied one, moderate winds began; they unfastened the second, and stronger winds blew; when they loosed the third knot, a snowstorm or a thunderstorm struck.[3]

Despite wide-spread beliefs and a deep interest of the Russian culture in the "esoteric" and "supernatural," even then (not unlike nowadays) many limitations and obstacles deterred inquisitive minds from pursuing these interests. In the Middle Ages, witches were burned at the stake in Russia, just as they were in Western Europe.[4] In 1227, four witches were put to the flames in the court of an archbishop in Novgorod. In the beginning of the fifteenth century, ten sorcerers were slain in Pskov. In a tale written for Ivan the Terrible, fire was prescribed as the proper punishment for witchcraft.[5] The seventeenth-century writer George Kotoshikhin, a disgruntled government official who escaped to Sweden in 1664, wrote a report for his new employer, Swedish intelligence, in which he described witchcraft, among many things. The manuscript was published in the nineteenth century. He related that women were sometimes buried up to their breasts and left to die for their occult practices.[6]

Although these practices were abandoned in the "enlightened" eighteenth century, the Russian obsession with spiritualism and the occult sciences was strongly frowned upon, and at times forbidden outright by the Russian Orthodox Church. In the nineteenth century the situation started to change, a contemporary reported, albeit very slowly.[7]

Spiritualism as a doctrine was introduced into Russia in 1854 by those who had witnessed spiritual phenomena abroad and had become acquainted with the works of Allan Kardec. Unhappily, however, the advocates of spiritualism had to keep a low profile, Russia not yet enjoying a free press. Since the State Church did not allow publication in the Russian language of any books or pamphlets discussing spiritualism, it was, therefore, a subject only of private discussion among those who knew foreign languages. Furthermore, Russia had a penal code in which any Russian who stepped outside the pale of the Greco-Russian Church or who attempted to teach doctrines contrary to it was punishable by exile in Siberia. Happily, however, laws there were loosely observed.[8]

When I was working in parapsychology in the Soviet Union, from the late 1960s to late 1970s, a strangely similar situation existed. While serious official interest in the study of "psychic" phenomena developed, independent spiritual search by enthusiasts from the general public was virtually forbidden. Though one could easily expect to find oneself in Siberian exile for pursuing these interests, it is difficult to judge whether or not these bleak prospects represented a more real threat to us than to our predecessors of a century ago. Fortunately, a certain laxity of law-keeping continued throughout Russian history.

Due to this laxity (and/or to Divine Providence), I managed to work in the field of parapsychology while in the USSR, was fortunate enough to meet gifted psychics, observe their intriguing demonstrations, and discover accounts of physical mediumship in Russia in the last century. I managed to emigrate and establish my home in the USA in 1981. I present here a review of my findings. We shall travel into the past to observe some physical phenomena recorded in the nineteenth century, return to the present to discuss some contemporary Soviet psychics and try to glimpse the future of parapsychology, this utterly fascinating science, attempting to elucidate the mysteries of the mind.

Physical Mediumship in Pre-revolutionary Russia

In the second half of the nineteenth century, the reign of Tsar Alexander III, spiritualistic seances had the patronage of the royal family. Due to this interest of royalty and high society, a journal named the *Rebus* was founded for reporting mediumistic activities and spiritualistic seances all over Russia.[9] Among contemporary researchers of psi phenomena, credence is seldom given to experiences which occurred during seances, especially when only scarce details about the conditions are given. Due to the virtual lack of other sources about Russian mediumship, however, I will often refer to the *Rebus* which began in 1881 and published reports on strange occurrences and seances until 1917. The first editor of the *Rebus*, V.I. Pribytkov, remained in charge of the journal for twenty-four years. We will begin our review with a list of strange events in Russia of that time compiled by Pribytkov:

1. In 1881, in the home of M.I. Perov in Riazan, objects disappeared, including dishes from locked closets and tightly tied baskets. The seminarian Nazarevsky, who did not believe in the disappearances, was knocked to the floor by a thick object. No explanations were ever found.

2. In 1882 in Ufa, strange sounds caused a young student of a holy school for women to be placed in the hospital; however, the force

apparently remained and began answering questions with strikes for positive answers and rustles for negatives.

3. In 1883 in the apartment of Mr. Arkhangelsky in the town of Borisogleb of the province of Tambov, an unknown force hit the windows and floors so hard that objects in the room fell and broke.

4. In 1883 in Diagilev, near Riazan, all the utensils moved in a peasant's hut. A pot of water flew from a stove toward the village priest and threw water on everyone. The peasant burned his cottage with all his belongings.

5. In 1884, in the apartment of the former military officer Florensky in Kazan, potatoes flew out of a stove and dropped from the ceiling. After Florensky gathered all the potatoes and locked the oven, the door flew open and more potatoes "escaped." The police came to investigate, and the event recurred while they were there. Fortunately, these events finally ceased.

6. In 1884, in the apartment of Sukharov in Kazan, peas began falling from the ceiling when there were no peas in the house. That vegetable was joined by chips of bricks, boiled potatoes, underwear and military head gear. Then these objects jumped onto cabinets and tables. No explanation of these phenomena was found.

7. In 1885, at the cottage of the overseer Ivan Sokolov on the estate of Mrs. Leontiev in the province of Kazan, furniture and utensils moved about and "sailed" through the air; firewood flew from a passageway into a room and broke the inner pane of a double window. These events took place in the daytime and only during the presence of a 12-year-old girl.

8. In 1885, in the village of Koshka of the Province of Samara, a local judge and doctor were called to an apartment where they saw unusual happenings around a 12-year-old girl. They placed her in a corner of a room and watched closely. Soon a blanket placed over her rose in the air. Her clothing flew off. The doctor took her to the hospital for observation and the same phenomena recurred.[10]

Most of the above events appear to be poltergeist phenomena, and we intend to devote an entire section of this chapter to their contemporary manifestations. As we will see, the century that passed has little changed the habits of noisy ghosts or spirits (the literal meaning of "poltergeist" which English-speakers borrowed from German). If we strip the accounts of all indications of the period to which they belong, the similarities are indeed striking, frequently including the presence of a teenager considered to be an active agent or "focus" of poltergeist activity. Numerous phenomena of this kind, some witnessed by policemen and other officials, that reportedly occurred in various parts of Russia (e.g., the Ukraine, the central part, the Urals) in 1840-1894, were described in detail in Alexander

N. Aksakov's book, *Predvestniki Spiritizma* [Forerunners of Spiritualism], published at the end of the nineteenth century.[11]

As far as adult mediums and psychics are concerned, Russian researchers of that time seemed to believe there is no prophet in one's homeland and preferred to conduct their observations and seances with famous Western mediums, like Daniel Dunglas Home and Eusapia Palladino.[12] We can find only few descriptions of rather controversial seances with Russian mediums in the above-mentioned *Rebus* magazine and in publications by Aksakov, a Russian philosopher, author and researcher of mediumship.

One of the cases described in *Rebus*[13] involved a well-known hypnotist, O. J. Feldman. The sitting took place in the apartment of Mr. A. S. Zigmont, who met there with the wife of Dr. K.P. Ulezko and other persons on October 24, 1890. Zigmont, who furnished the account, noted that Feldman was not a spiritualist, but when he was present on that occasion, the phenomena were quite different from those the circle had experienced previously. Zigmont wrote that as soon as the circle was closed and everybody was seated at the long, rather heavy four-legged table, Feldman ordered loudly that when he had finished counting to ten the table should rise into the air with all four legs. Those present were amazed when Feldman's order was fulfilled at once. This was repeated time and again: different objects moved from place to place according to his command. When he ordered the bell to ring, it rose at once into the air and started ringing. In one word, whatever force was in action during the seance, it responded to Feldman's authority.[14]

Feldman was known to his contemporaries not only as a practicing hypnotist but also as a researcher who possessed a "truly inquiring mind... always eager for new experiments and never shy of scientific scrutiny."[15] A brilliant predecessor of contemporary researchers in enhancing natural faculties of a person under hypnosis, not unlike Soviet hypnotist Dr. Vladimir Raikov who has been working along similar lines in the 1960s-1990s, he designed and implemented truly remarkable experiments which suggested virtually unlimited potential of the human mind. In one of his tests, Feldman read to the subject (under hypnosis) several strophes from the *Iliad* (in Greek hexameter); the subject not knowing Greek repeated them afterwards without a single mistake in words or meter. Then half a page was read from a French book. The subject repeated it without mistake. In a third experiment Feldman gave his subject a difficult trigonometric problem which the latter tried to solve for several hours without success. Under hypnosis he solved it with remarkable ease, using a different formula and tackling logarithms without hesitation.[16]

The above-described, mediumship phenomena were clearly of

exceptional interest, but unfortunately we do not possess sufficient data to enable us to determine their authenticity. Feldman was primarily a hypnotist, but it would seem from the above description that he was acting as a medium, producing psychokinetic/levitation phenomena. Some authors believe the alleged phenomena were hallucinatory and had been produced by Feldman as an experiment demonstrating the power of hypnotic suggestion.[17] I wonder whether it is "easier" to make several people experience the same hallucination than to produce physical phenomena. When Soviet researchers began studying psychokinetic phenomena produced by Nina Kulagina (see Section 3), many also believed the observers were somehow hypnotized and hallucinating, until some experiments were recorded on film and shown to various audiences. Let us, however, return to other descriptions of ostensible physical mediumship of the last century.

The issue of *Rebus* of June 16, 1885 reported:

At Mrs. Makarov's several seances have been held. The medium Mr. Galitsky did not leave the group but sat in the middle of a circle. The phenomena that took place were:
1. A wide golden bracelet with a strong dangling lock was taken noiselessly from the arm of the medium. It was thrown on the floor and appeared unopened.
2. A box of matches was raised from a table and thrown on the floor.
3. A wedding ring which had not been taken off for several years was momentarily removed from the finger of the medium.
4. Several words were etched on legal paper lying on a table. No one present touched the paper.
5. The door leading to the neighboring room and tightly locked was briskly opened with a noise. This occurred several times. No one was in the neighboring room.
6. A rather small lady's suitcase lying on a couch was transferred over our heads into the other part of the room, passing through a cotton drapery which divided the room.
7. At the last two seances all those in attendance heard a voice not belonging to anyone present.[18]

Regretfully, the account did not name the seance participants and did not specify whether any precautions against fraud were taken.

The following account in *Rebus*[19] describes another quite incredible occurrence. The experiment took place at 2 p.m. on August 5, 1892 in

Tsarskoe Selo with five people present. Two of them were hypnotized and shortly afterwards a spot of light appeared near the right hand of one of the subjects. This became gradually wider and brighter and seemed to be an extension from his hand. It took a pencil from the table and wrote, "This is an astral body." Unfortunately, again we are not privy to the details of the experiment.

I was fortunate enough, however, to discover a more detailed description of seances with a Russian medium, named Nikolaeff, who was active at the end of 19th century.[20] It is an account of sittings held by members of the Russian Society of Experimental Psychology.

Nikolaeff was discovered by Prof. N.P. Wagner, a noted Russian researcher of mediumship at that time, who began experiments with him when Nicolaeff was a boy of 14. Many seances were held afterward and, as the record indicates, the 91st sitting conducted by the Society commission with this medium occurred on May 11, 1891. In 1893, the Society had ten sittings with Nikolaeff, one of which (held on April 27, 1893) is described in detail. The record emphasizes very strict precautions against possible fraud taken before this sitting (which was typical in this respect) conducted at the apartment of Dr. Kraevsky, one of the Society members.

Only two doors led into the dining room, i.e., the seance room—one from the study (where the commission members sat), the other (a glass door) opening into the hall. A thick shawl was spread during the sittings over the glass part of the door. The door itself was expressly locked and sealed with the Society's seal. Before the beginning of the seance and after its ending, the seals were expressly inspected. The only window in the dining room was covered over with a thick carpet whose edges were also sealed in such a way as to make it impossible to push it aside. All unnecessary furniture, pictures, etc., were removed from the dining room before the seance. There remained in it only an armchair for the medium, a sideboard whose door was locked and sealed, the dining table which was placed close to the door leading into the hall, a big sofa which stood in a corner, and a lamp hanging over the table in the center of the room. Before the beginning of the seance, the whole room, the furniture, the floor under the furniture were searched. The medium and the house servant were not permitted to enter the room before the seance.

Before being led into the seance room, the medium was first undressed completely in another room, his face and hands and his whole body were washed with soap. He was searched, and his mouth was examined. Afterward the clothes specifically ordered by the commission were examined and put on the medium's naked body. These consisted of a blouse and pants of black calico and a black smock without pockets. In this way none of his own clothing or linen remained on the medium. In some instances, the medium was allowed to wear his boots on his bare feet, the boots being examined first in the most detailed fashion to see whether there were any double welts, etc. On three sittings, the medium was asked to wear the host's slippers instead of the boots, but, as the record states, "the mediumistic phenomena did not in consequence cease nor was their usual character modified."[21] When the medium was being dressed, the Commission made sure that he did not have about him any white or light object— such as a handkerchief, socks, gloves, pieces of muslin or paper, etc.— which might have been used to simulate "the white self-luminous matter"[22] manifested during seances.

At the beginning of the seance, the medium was seated on a dark red armchair, the curtain was drawn, after which Nikolaeff fell into trance and spoke in the name of 'Vladimir,' his spirit-guide. When the trance was deep enough, the curtain was drawn aside, in accordance with Vladimir's directions. Vladimir also indicated the amount of light required, and the light in the study where the members of the Commission were sitting was diminished or increased accordingly. Although the light in the dining room was extinguished, the whole of the medium could be seen well in the light of the electric lamp covered with a shade in the study. The sitters could distinguish the features of his face and his fingers which lay on his knees.

When the curtain was carefully drawn aside at 10:55 p.m., a white spot of indistinct shape was visible on the medium's left shoulder (although, as we remember, nothing white was left on him after the careful search and a change of clothes). This spot grew more distinct a few minutes later, and it was simultaneously noticed that the medium's wrists had begun to emit a phosphorescent light and to be wrapped in a small luminous cloud. The acoustic phenomena began:

> The medium was fully motionless. Various sounds and raps began to be heard in the cabinet, increasing to such an extent they hindered all conversation. They sounded like druming by fingers now on wooden, now on soft parts of furniture; the blows against the soft seat of a sofa which stood apart from the medium [and on which no one was sitting] were, judging by the sound, quite identical with blows produced by a human palm. The blows quickly succeeded each other, at times growing more violent in accordance with the wishes of those present, after which still more various sounds were heard from corners of the room quite at a distance from the medium. In the right corner of the room, fourteen feet from the medium, a strong scratching as if of claws was heard.[23]

Soon the light phenomena began to intensify leading to apparent materializations:

> When the sounds had grown somewhat rarer and weaker, a little whitish cloud of indistinct shape appeared from behind the back of the medium's chair and was seen by all present. The little cloud began to grow bigger and to take an oblong form of a weakly luminous ray, with the outlines rather strongly marked. This ray moved about unceasingly, remaining all the time on the medium's left. Finally it moved on the medium's chest and took the shape of a long white stripe under his chin. A few seconds later it changed its shape to that of a human arm bared to the elbow. The "arm" rose above the medium's head, then moved behind the back of his armchair, close to the wall, and began to strike upon it quick, loud blows. Then this luminous arm—with fingers like protuberances— again moved behind the medium's armchair, then upon the soft seat of the sofa, and then upon the floor. The blows upon the sofa were of peculiar violence.[24]

Interestingly enough, further development of ostensible materializations was accompanied by dramatic acoustic and psychokinetic-like phenomena:

> ...The members of the Commission noticed in the air near the lamp a luminous arm which at once began to strike its glass shade.... The luminous hand soon began to fly about and to strike the lamp glass cover and the shade with such violence that it seemed as if these would fly into splinters. A kind of savage bell-ringing was taking place. Under the eyes of all those present the luminous vapor-like hand suddenly tore the silken shade from the lamp and tossed it through the opening in the curtain with such violence toward Dr. Lestchinsky that he involuntarily drew aside. After the silken lamp shade had thus flown out, the raps on the lamp grew weaker and a second luminous hand appeared on the medium's left. Both hands, still partially materialized, looked like two luminous rays coming out of the sides of the medium's body separated by small dark spaces. It seemed as if the medium, besides his own two hands, was now endowed with two other luminous hands moving in the air.... They often flew away from the medium and rapped violently either upon the medium's armchair or ...

upon the sofa. The blows on the seat of the sofa were so violent that they could be heard three rooms away as if the sofa were very violently beaten with a stick....

At the end of this period of the seance both luminous arms, with clearly materialized fingers, appeared before the medium and began to clap loudly, palm against palm. This was repeated several times, it being possible to follow distinctly the slightest movement of the luminous, clapping hands, the sound being identical to the sound of natural hand-clapping.

Then the right luminous arm, having stretched itself toward the heavy sofa, ... began to push it toward those present with a strength and adroitness hardly accessible to an ordinary man. Simultaneously the left luminous arm which had moved behind the medium's armchair set it in motion together with the sleeping medium toward the right side. The sofa stopped about one foot from the curtain. Several very loud and violent hand-clappings were heard in the air and the sitting ended.[25]

The account concludes with the following statement concerning the authenticity of the phenomena:

All these phenomena were of so sharp a nature that it became superfluous to talk about their being forged, since it was obvious to those present that the medium was asleep in sight of them all.[26]

Ostensible physical phenomena were also demonstrated by Russian mystic Helena P. Blavatsky. A world traveler, the first Russian woman to enter Tibet, and founder of the Theosophical Society in the United States, Blavatsky returned to Russia in the 1880s. *Rebus* described some unusual phenomena which reportedly took place during one of her seances in the city of Pskov.[27] As the seance participants discussed a reported ability of the British medium D.D. Home to make heavier objects lighter, and lighter things heavier, Blavatsky was asked whether she could do the same. She said she had done it at times and agreed to try but emphasized that she could not guarantee results.

"I shall look at this chess table," she said. "Whoever wishes to raise it now and afterwards, please do so." One of the young people went to the little table and raised it as if it were a feather. "Fine. Now place it back and walk away from it." In silence, Blavatsky did nothing but stared at the table. Later, not lowering her blue eyes, she motioned with her hand for the young man to lift it. He went to the table and assuredly seized the table by the leg. The table did not move. He took it with both hands. The table remained as if screwed to the floor. The young man sat down on the floor, grabbed a leg with both hands and energetically began to nudge the table with his shoulders. The table did not move.

An important page in Russian studies in mediumship is associated with Aksakov, who, in 1875, wrote of himself, "What pertains to me personally is this: having never denied the possibility of so-called spiritualistic phenomena and holding to the truth ... a person who is a witness in defense of the truth is obliged to do everything in his power to promote its investigation and acceptance. I steadfastly followed this path."[28]

Aksakov's open-minded approach was criticized by well-known Russian scientist, Prof. Dmitri Mendeleev, in a lengthy volume, *Materialy dlya Suzhdeniya o Spiritizme* [Materials for a Judgement on Spiritualism], published in St. Petersburg in 1876.[29] The volume described activities of a commission established by the Physical Society at the University of St. Petersburg in 1875 to investigate mediumistic phenomena. Members of the commission reportedly observed impressive physical phenomena, such as levitation of a table. A record of January 11, 1876 stated that when seance participants were lightly touching a three-legged table it unexpectedly rose into the air. According to the description, the table was somewhat tilted, and the leg closest to the floor was approximately ten centimeters from it. Then the table went down with such force that one of its legs broke.[30] These observations, however, failed to convince Mendeleev that the phenomena were genuine. Unlike Mendeleev, his colleague Prof. Alexander M. Butlerov, also a distinguished Russian scientist, was convinced of the reality of psychokinetic phenomena. In the 1870s he conducted observations and experiments in which seance participants were ostensibly capable of changing the weight of objects. Depending upon the wishes of the participants, the objects ordinarily weighing from two to 40 kilograms, placed on the scales, could reportedly become two to three times lighter or heavier, presumably due to PK-like effect. For me, the most impressive point is that the phenomenon was allegedly repeatable upon demand.[31] Butlerov also described his observations of levitation of heavy objects (tables) in seances without professional mediums.[32]

It is very difficult to find the right way between Scylla of excessive open-mindedness (bordering on gullibility) and Charibdis of excessive skepticism. Although each of the above descriptions of alleged physical phenomena is open to criticism, especially in the absence of precise details, the sheer number of these accounts reminds me of an old metaphor: you can easily break one straw, but it is much more difficult to break a bunch of straws. Throughout the past 20 years, I have read many dozens (if not hundreds) of accounts of this kind and witnessed many unusual phenomena; therefore, it becomes more and more difficult for me to maintain doubt. After observing several contemporary "physical mediums," I am ready to admit that, most likely, the emperor is indeed wearing some clothes. Let me describe some on these observations in more detail.

Contemporary "Physical Mediums" and Psychics in the USSR

Nina Kulagina

In early 1968, the Soviet press first wrote of the psychokinetic (PK) abilities of Nina S. Kulagina, also known by her maiden name as Nina (Ninel, Nelya) Mikhailovna. The housewife from Leningrad, then in her early 40s, mother of three children, could reportedly move objects without touching them, or "without the mediation of muscular exertion," as was written later in the *Great Soviet Encyclopedia*.[33] The objects included a compass needle, matches, cigarettes, empty matchboxes, and other wooden, metal, and plastic objects. These apparent psychokinetic abilities of Kulagina attracted the attention of numerous Soviet and Western researchers.[34] No Soviet psychic has probably been tested as extensively and thoroughly as Kulagina.

At first, the scientific community was more than skeptical, suspecting tricks and sleight-of-hand. In the spring of 1968, however, scientists from Moscow University and the Physical Institute of the USSR Academy of Sciences conducted experiments with Kulagina.[35] Then, experiments continued for three days at the Department of Physics of the Moscow University, headed by Rem V. Khokhlov, member of the USSR Academy of Sciences. Although the physicists were unable to explain the phenomenon of the movement of objects produced by Kulagina, some of which were placed under a transparent plastic cube, as well as other equally puzzling occurrences, they signed three experimental records that described the phenomena in detail. It should be noted that in some tests, the possible slit between the plastic cube (which covered the objects to be moved) and the surface of the table was thoroughly sealed with tape, and many other precautions against trickery were taken.

The phenomena observed by scientists in experiments with Kulagina from 1968 to 1978 included numerous manifestations of her apparent PK abilities. On many occasions and under controlled conditions, she demonstrated the movement of objects weighing up to 380 grams, at distances of up to two meters from the objects, without touching them and without using any other known physical means. She successfully moved objects of various shapes and materials placed on a flat surface. She could move single objects or several objects simultaneously, often in a desired or requested direction (sometimes the objects were moved simultaneously in different directions; at times selective movement of one object from the set was possible, spontaneously or upon the experimenter's request). By concentrating her gaze on a pan of laboratory scales, Kulagina could make the pan move down, while a load of up to 30 grams was on the other pan. By mental concentration, she could divide an air bubble in a glass-tube with water into two parts and move these parts to the separate ends of the tube. She also demonstrated levitating objects weighing up to thirty grams and "suspending" them in the air. She produced movement of objects in a partial vacuum, in water, and through various partitions and shields of paper, wood, ordinary and lead glass, transparent plastic, ceramics, sheet lead, aluminum, copper, steel, and other materials.

In some experiments, Kulagina exerted remote influence on various physical and chemical detectors. She changed the color of the liquid crystals dramatically. In these experiments, liquid crystal film was placed on transparent plastic, with a sheet of black velvet paper under the plastic. When a 20 x 25 mm liquid crystal film was placed within the proximity of the objects which were moved psychokinetically by Kulagina, in a few minutes cyclic changes in the color of the film were observed in reflected light. These changes lasted an hour or more. First, a dark green spot appeared in a corner of the film, then slowly spread throughout the whole area of the film. The green changed to dark blue and violet, and then to dark red and orange. These cycles occurred many times. Kulagina also demonstrated levitation of a light plastic ball. If, afterwards, the ball was placed in a glass together with the liquid crystal, without direct contact with it, similar cycles of color changes in the liquid crystal were observed.

In other experiments, phosphorescent powders, which usually emit light only after first being exposed to light, when influenced by Kulagina, began to luminesce in darkness; two substances which normally begin to react at a temperature of 70°C reacted at room temperature. When a scintillation detector was placed near objects to be moved by apparent PK, the readings of the detector were three times lower as compared to ordinary background activity, while PK movement of objects occurred. Kulagina also demonstrated exposing photographic light-sensitive materials and produced images in the shape of an imperfect cross, circle, square, and star by mentally "drawing" them on photographic paper placed in a black envelope. She also was able to expose photographic film shielded by lead sheets 1.5 mm thick and by ebonite 20 mm thick.

Kulagina demonstrated apparent PK influence upon biological systems in many experiments. In some of these tests, flies and other insects were placed in a box of transparent plastic. When Kulagina imagined a barrier in the way they were moving, the insects, as if they had encountered a real obstacle, changed the direction of their movement. The same phenomenon occurred with aquarium fish.

Kulagina worked with white mice and, at the experimenter's request, tried to suppress their vital functions. A few movements of her hands caused the mice to become motionless, as if dead. As soon as she removed her hands, they perked up and returned to normal. In laboratory conditions Kulagina's influence on an isolated frog's heart was tested. The frog's heart was placed in a physiological solution with electrodes attached to it to record the heart's activity. In normal conditions, an isolated frog's heart will continue to beat for 30 to 40 minutes (in some cases up to one and a half hours). When the heart stops, it can be activated by electro-stimulation. When Kulagina was asked to increase the frog's heartbeat, the intensive systoles were recorded during the period of one and a half to two minutes. Afterwards Kulagina was requested to stop the heart from a distance of about 1.5 meters, evoking in herself the state analogous to that when she was able to demonstrate PK movement of objects. Forty seconds later, the frog's heart stopped, and the electro-stimulation method appeared to be insufficient to activate it.

From 1978 to 1984, Kulagina's phenomena were studied by physicists from the Institute of Precise Mechanics and Optics in Leningrad, the Research Institute of Radio-Engineering and Electronics, and the Baumann Higher School of Technology in Moscow. According to their report, published in 1984,[36] the hands of Nina Kulagina emitted strong magnetic and acoustic impulses. The frequency of acoustic impulses recorded by piezoelectric sensors was in the range from 25 to 10,000 Hertz, and their magnitude was from 70 to 90 decibels. The intensity of the magnetic impulses that were measured, up to .027 Tesla, exceeded the intensity of the Earth's magnetic field about 100 times, while for ordinary individuals the intensity of the magnetic field is measured 100,000-10,000,000 times less.

In carefully controlled conditions, a laser beam was observed to attenuate noticeably under Kulagina's influence. The experimenters believed that she might in fact change physical properties of the gas (air, nitrogen, or carbon dioxide) in a cuvette through which the laser beam was passing. Kulagina's influence upon the gas-filled cuvette lowered the intensity of a 10.6 micrometer laser beam passing through it by up to 77 percent.

Numerous researchers noted that Kulagina produced PK effects while in the condition of great stress, accompanied by considerable loss of weight, increase in heartbeat rate, blood pressure, blood sugar, etc.

In the late 1970s, Academician Yuri Kobzarev of the USSR Academy of Sciences' Research Institute of Radio-Engineering and Electronics wrote: "I have become convinced that the phenomena demonstrated by N. Kulagina ('telekinesis'—the movement of objects without touching them)...are in no way tricks but essentially manifestations of unusual human capabilities. This conviction of mine, based on the results of experiments specially set up, is shared by many people, among them professors and academicians. (Signed) Yu. B. Kobzarev, August 7, 1978."

Unlike mediums of the last century, Kulagina needed neither a darkened room nor any other special conditions to demonstrate her powers. Many of her demonstrations were recorded on film. As with virtually every medium, the issue of fraud arose repeatedly, was rejected, and surfaced again. At least one researcher told me straightforwardly that he saw a thread while Kulagina was moving objects; another hinted at it as well. I met with Kulagina several times, saw her move objects, discussed her abilities and demonstrations with many researchers who worked with her and read descriptions of numerous experiments. I watched Kulagina move her hands across a table, and the cap of a pen (which I placed in front of her several seconds earlier and which she surely did not touch afterward) obediently moved toward her under her gaze. I observed her stand at a distance about four to five feet from a table with her hands down and move a thin tube suspended in liquid, making it change direction at experimenter's demand. I detected no threads or other tricks. I was not hypnotized, and I do not consider myself an uncritical believer. Still, I believe my own eyes, my observations, and my experience. That is all I can say about this controversial issue.

In 1986, a certain V. Strelkov, in his article in the magazine *Chelovek i Zakon* [Man and Law],[37] referred to earlier publications by journalist Vladimir Lvov[38] and accused Kulagina of fraud. Kulagina sued the magazine for defamation and won the case. In accordance with the Resolution of the Dzerzhinsky District Court of Moscow, the editorial office published a refutation of the statements insulting to Kulagina that accused her of charlatanism and fraud. This retraction appeared in *Chelovek i Zakon* in May 1988.[39] To my best knowledge, this is the first time in the USSR that a psychic sued a Soviet publication for defamation and won.

Kulagina died in the spring of 1990. I believe her gift could have been used more wisely to assist scientists in better understanding the psychokinetic phenomena if the studies with her had been conducted in a free, more open atmosphere by broader-minded researchers. At the same time, more should have been done to help her better utilize her unusual powers, to reduce stress, and to enhance the quality of her life. Science failed, the Soviet system failed, and we all failed to really appreciate and fully benefit from the wonderful gift bestowed upon her by nature.

Elvira Shevchuk

In early 1979, Elvira Shevchuk, a 40-year-old woman from the city of Kalinin (150 kilometers northwest of Moscow), an employee of the Kalinin Polytechnic Institute, demonstrated another psychokinetic phenomenon.[40] During her demonstrations, Elvira usually sat on a chair and held one end of a lengthy object, while the other end of the object touched the floor. In some of the tests it rested on a piece of glass placed on the floor. As Elvira slowly moved her hands away from the object, its upper end, remained "suspended" in the air. In some cases, there was a small gap between the lower end of the object and the floor (i.e., there was a real levitation of the object, though only to a small height). When Elvira removed one or both hands from the object, slight oscillations of the object were observed that gradually attenuated.

In the experiment I witnessed, Elvira first paced agitatedly around the room preparing herself for the test. Then she sat on a chair, and a wooden stick about forty centimeters long (provided by Dr. Pushkin) was placed on the floor within her reach. She took it gently in her hands, placed one end of it on the floor so that the stick formed an angle of approximately 45 degrees to the floor, and slowly moved away her hands. She left one hand at a distance of seven to ten centimeters from the object and moved the other one aside. The stick remained in this position of unstable equilibrium for over a minute.

An essential condition of these experiments was Elvira's insistence on being informed about the test a day before. As a rule, the knowledge of the forthcoming test caused changes in her psychological state. She became focused upon the upcoming experiment and manifested increased psychological tension. Elvira's behavior suggested that from the time she knew the date of the experiment until the time of the test she was preparing with a particular kind of "tuning in" for an activity that required a new and special system of psychological self-regulation and self-control.

General stress, associated with a transformation of the regulatory processes, reached its culmination at the moment the test began. Despite this stress, Elvira's participation in the experiment was the essential condition for recovering from stress and normalizing her condition. There were instances when researchers, observing her tension before the test, suggested postponing or cancelling the experiment. As a rule, she disagreed and tried to perform the test. If she failed, her recovery from the stressful condition was much slower than it was after a successful experiment, despite the fact that in successful experiments Elvira seemed to expend more energy.

In these experiments, Elvira worked with wooden rulers (from 20 cm to one meter long), a wooden stick with attached strips of thin paper, a metal knitting needle, a beaker containing colored liquid, and a tall glass filled with dry sand. She also performed a test with a strip of paper which behaved like the "suspended" rigid objects.

The number of tests was sharply limited since each test involved severe psychological stress, and Elvira required from a few days to one month to regain normalcy. Nevertheless, in systematic studies more than fifty successful tests were conducted. Each test was witnessed by several researchers, although Elvira's performance was smoother in the presence of familiar people who evoked positive emotions in her. The presence of unknown people created additional stress that sometimes led to failure of the test.

Some physical measurements were performed during the tests. No electrostatic fields in the area where Shevchuk worked with objects were detected. The effect could not be attributed to the presence of magnetic fields because nonmagnetic objects such as glass, wood, or paper were successfully suspended. For me, as for Dr. Veniamin Pushkin and several other researchers, the most interesting were not the physical correlates, but the psychological state of Shevchuk before and during the test. We believed that she was creating a "mental model" of the object. At the beginning of each experiment Elvira established contact with the object, at which time she appeared to be in an altered and highly stressful mental state. When I observed one of Elvira's demonstrations, I had an impression that she treated the object to be "suspended" as a living entity. From observations during the tests and from Elvira's descriptions, we concluded that differences in the weight of objects, at least in the range used in our tests (up to several hundred grams), did not affect the outcome of the experiment.

I see Elvira as a sincere and trustworthy individual who worked hard and selflessly to explore her unusual gift and to contribute to a scientific understanding of the phenomena.

Boris Yermolayev

While Shevchuk felt more comfortable when one end of a long object touched a solid surface, Soviet filmmaker Boris Yermolayev from Moscow repeatedly demonstrated a complete levitation ("suspension") of objects.[41] I was fortunate enough to observe one of his demonstrations. It was conducted at Dr. Pushkin's apartment with a half-dozen observers present. Having consumed some vodka, Boris started with a card-guessing game using ordinary playing cards. It proceeded so quickly that I had difficulty following the details. Therefore, I have to treat it merely as a game, not an experiment. Believing he was quite successful in this game, Yermolayev then asked one of the observers to give him an object to be suspended. Someone gave him an empty cigarette pack, I presented him with a match box with some matches in it, and a third observer produced a cigarette. Boris put the objects aside and held his hands with wide-spread fingers so that there was a distance of approximately 15 to 20 centimeters between his palms. In a state of great tension, he gazed at his hands, and small drops of sweat appeared on his forehead. Then he took the cigarette pack in his hands and stared at it, holding it with the fingers of both hands. Suddenly he took his fingers away, and nothing unusual happened—the object simply fell to the floor. Somewhat irritated, Boris took it in his hands again and repeated his preparation, staring at the pack and almost "talking" to it in an inaudible whisper. After several minutes, he moved his fingers away from the cigarette pack, which remained suspended in the air between his hands for approximately 30 to 40 seconds.

I saw no threads or strings attached to the object. I did not see any attempts to distract the attention of observers characteristic of magic trick performers. I am sure the objects given by the observers were not substituted by Boris for his own look-alike objects. It was frustrating that we were unable to change the conditions of the test and therefore were only observers, not experimenters. This was dictated by the fact that Boris was quite unsure of his ability to perform the demonstration upon demand and preferred to adhere to the conditions that had worked for him previously.

Boris described how, at the beginning of a test, he established a kind of contact with the object. He "persuaded" the object and "projected" a part of himself into the object. These experiments caused a high degree of stress in Yermolayev. Sometimes he was not successful and could not definitely foresee the result of the test. To predict a degree of success, Boris used a special method: before the test, he tried to identify playing cards (placed face down) by moving his hands 5 to 10 cm away from the card. He believed it was worthwhile not to proceed with the tests until he first achieved a high degree of success in identifying the colors of the cards.

Boris's behavior pointed to a gradual acquisition of an optimal state for PK demonstration. First attempts to suspend objects, as a rule, failed—the objects fell down, each time evoking a severe stress response in Boris. Afterwards he managed to "suspend" objects, but in his first successful attempts they were "suspended" only briefly. However, the "suspension" time increased with each attempt. Finally, a state was achieved in which

Yermolayev was able to perform the "whole cycle" wherein the time of "suspension" was equal to the time of his breath retention. The same pattern of change was observed in Boris's responses to interruptive sounds and lights. There is reason to believe this is associated with the increase in his capacity of self-regulation as he gradually developed his ability to control his state and interaction with the object.

This increase in regulatory abilities was especially clear when the researchers attempted to take flash photographs of the tests. In his first effort, the "suspended" object fell, and Boris had to repeat the attempt. After several attempts, however, the researchers could make three flash photographs during one "suspension," and the flashes did not cause either a fall of the object or a stress response in Boris.

A comparison of Yermolayev's behavior in apparent psychokinetic experiments with that of Elvira Shevchuk in analogous tests points to the similarity of their psychological condition. Both Yermolayev and Shevchuk needed particular psychological preparation for the tests. Their behavior indicated changes in their mental states during their efforts. Neither could reliably control their mental state and their performance. In both cases before the tests and during the "suspension" of objects they exhibited signs of severe emotional stress. This stress apparently was created by uncertainty regarding the outcome of the test and by the energy loss during the "suspension" of objects. Both individuals also experienced considerable negative after-effects following the tests and both required a period of time for return to a normal state.

Tests conducted by Dr. Veniamin Pushkin (then the head of the Heuristics Laboratory at the Research Institute of Psychology of the USSR Academy of Pedagogical Sciences) usually did not produce unfavorable effects on Yermolayev's health and well-being, although they caused noticeable emotional stress. Prior to the test, Dr. Pushkin managed to reduce Boris's stress through electric stimulation of some acupuncture points on his back. However, according to Boris, after some earlier psychokinetic demonstrations he fainted and felt sick. To avoid such reactions, Yermolayev needed the presence of friends who sometimes kept their hands close to his hands. One could hypothesize that the energy lost by the psychic was compensated by energy received from others.

A skeptic would probably say that it was easier to distract the attention of observers with other people around the magician. In the final score, I do not consider the "suspension" of objects demonstrated by Yermolayev to be a proven scientific fact. At the time, however, I was greatly impressed by it.

Ivan Dekhtyar and Yevgeny Rogozhin

During the pilot tests with Elvira Shevchuk and Boris Yermolayev the following facts were established:

(1) a process of the psychic's "tuning in" to the object to be influenced through purported PK powers and the psychic's psychological mobilization;

(2) an increase in the psychic's sensitivity and his or her arousal during the experiment;

(3) a decrease in motor activity and a feeling of physical weakness after the test;

(4) some correlation between the psychological characteristics of the subjects and the kind (and results) of their PK influence upon the object.

The following experiments with yet another psychic, Ivan Dekhtyar, conducted in the USSR in the early 1980s, confirmed these conclusions.[42] For six to eight minutes before "suspending" an object, Dekhtyar was engaged in psychological preparation that could be described as "conscious self-arousal." Afterwards, he felt that his hands "had enlarged" and an elastic "air cushion" appeared between them. When an object, for instance a tennis ball, was placed between his palms, he further experienced the sensation of "enlargement" of both the hands and the object. As this sensation increased, it was usually accompanied by a trance-like state. The subject also experienced buzzing in his ears. When his hands were moved away from the object, it was "suspended" in air between his palms. The distance between the palms was twelve to fifteen centimeters, and the duration of "suspension" was eight to ten seconds. As soon as the sensation of "enlarging elasticity" disappeared, the object fell. Physical weakness, trembling of hands, an increase of the pulse rate up to 130 beats per second, difficult breathing, increased appetite, and sleepiness were the consequences of the test.

Dekhtyar, a middle-aged bearded man with a tense face and penetrating eyes, is a teacher of handicrafts in a vocational school in the Ukraine. It should be noted that his demonstrations of "suspension" of objects were criticized in the Soviet press and on TV and dismissed by some observers as fraud. Some believed that thin shining "threads," allegedly noticed in a film about Dekhtyar, were tiny drops of water condensed in the unknown force field between his hands, and which sometimes gave an impression of "threads" under the bright floodlights used by filmmakers. Despite the controversy, I am not ready to dismiss Dekhtyar's demonstrations as easily as do some Soviet bureaucrats.

The obvious similarities of the "suspension" phenomenon by Yermolayev, Kulagina, and Dekhtyar, in my opinion, contribute an additional argument in favor of the authenticity of their performance. Furthermore, demonstrations of Yevgeny Rogozhin, a soft-spoken engineer and physician currently living on the Black Sea coast, also show amazing similarity to those described above.[43] Rogozhin was a graduate of an engineering college and a medical school. He demonstrated a number of unusual phenomena, including the power of suggestion and the levitation of objects. While playing chess, he could make his partner make a wrong move by holding a vivid mental picture of the partner doing so. He also could "suspend" a tennis ball between his hands by establishing a "mental contact" with it. It is a pity that more thorough studies of these people apparently have never been conducted, or, if they were, that they have never been reported in scholarly journals or other easily accessible scientific publications. The above-quoted reports in the popular press do not provide the opportunity to draw substantiated conclusions.

Inge Gaiduchenko and Others

Another intriguing new psychic is a 14-year-old girl named Inga Gaiduchenko who lives in Byelorussia, a republic in the Western part of the former Soviet Union. First reports about her PK-like abilities appeared in the Soviet press in 1989. According to these reports, various objects—not only metal, but also paper, plastic, wood, and glass—easily and rather firmly stick to her palms, attracted as if by a magnet. For this the girl does not even need to concentrate hard; it is enough for her to keep her palms in vertical position, and copybooks, pens, forks, and knives "hang" on them. Inga's most surprising demonstration is "suspending" a large pan to which dumbbells, two kilograms each, and a hammer are attached. Dr. Vladimir Kalkun, a neurologist who studied Inga's abilities, and other researchers have reported that it is a genuine manifestation of "mind-over-matter" powers.[44]

According to reports from the USSR, Inga discovered her remarkable skill when she was six. "One day," her mother remembered, "she came in with one hand held above her head, and a book was hanging from it as though it were glued. She was giggling and said: 'Can I go to school this way?'" Inga thinks her special talent is funny. When she began taking piano lessons, she recalls: "The keys stuck to my fingers and I couldn't tear them away."

Maria Kletskova, principal of her public school, said: "Her powers are a mystery. She's been tested and retested. Scientists are in agreement that she produces some sort of magnetic radiation, but they are unable to detect its source."[45] This does not explain, however, the attraction of china, books and other nonmagnetic objects.

I was also informed that another girl, a 10-year-old, who demonstrated similar abilities, was discovered in the Ukraine.[46] In this connection, I would like to mention a recent report by a Soviet newspaper of a 13-year-old Hungarian boy named Mark, who apparently acquired psychokinetic abilities after an encounter with ball lightning.[47] The strange uninvited guest that entered a keyhole of their apartment during a thunderstorm did not harm the teenager. Mark only sensed some strange "itching" in his fingers after the incident. Soon thereafter, however, he was given a book about Uri Geller that described Geller's metal-bending. Afterwards, the boy reportedly demonstrated the ability to bend spoons, to move a compass needle, to stop and start watches, and even, according to the reports, to stop the closing doors of a streetcar by using the powers of his mind. Thus, the phenomenon of "mini-Gellers" reported in this country and in Western Europe seems to manifest in the USSR and Eastern Europe as well.

I wrote the above lines about two years ago. Since then, many more individuals with abilities to "attract" objects were discovered in Russia. Among them was a 22-year-old woman Saniya Karymova from the city of Tomsk in Siberia. According to published reports, various objects—made of glass, plastic, metal or wood—are attracted to her palms, lips, collarbones and feet.[48] Biophysicist Dr. Alexander P. Dubrov and physicist Andrei A. Berezin of the Research Institute of Theoretical Problems of the USSR Academy of Sciences in Moscow described similar experiments with a woman named Khurjan A. Davletova from the town of Khiva in Uzbekistan.[49] Another individual with psychokinetic abilities, recently studied by Dr. Dubrov, is Yuri P. Tkachenko from the town of Sochi in the Black Sea area. Tkachenko reportedly can hold up to fifty kilograms (!) of objects which mysteriously remain "stuck" to his chest as long as he wants, without any effort, stress or fatigue on his part.[50] Other individuals who exhibit this ability include: Anatoly M. Kupriyev, who demonstrated holding objects on his spine; the Falandysheva family—Zoya P. Falandysheva, 67 years old, her daughter, 38, son, 32, grandchildren, five, ten, and 27 years old, and great-grandson (a four-year-old boy) from the town of Ryazan; M. Mikautadze, M. Khazaradze, and Eka Sharashidze from Tbilisi; a retired peasant woman, Ye. Udivanova from Kuibyshev province; a 10-year-old girl Kristina Gyularyan from the town of Kaliningrad, Moscow province; five-year-old Sasha Mamontov from Magadan region and many others.[51] One laboratory, the Magnitobiology Laboratory in Tbilisi, headed by Dr. Revaz V. Khomeriki, found hundreds (!) of individuals who demonstrate this ability.[52] Many of the individuals who "attract" objects also claim to possess healing abilities.

One of Khomeriki's subjects, named Khazaradze, from a distance of sixty centimeters increased or decreased the heart beat of a frog by ten to twenty beats per minute. In studying some of these "human magnets" (as they are often called in the Soviet press, although they can "attract" objects other than metal; the American press would probably coin the name "human Velcros" for these individuals), Khomeriki found that while ordinary people usually have a difference in temperature between the center of the palm and the tip of the middle finger not more than 1.5°C, these individuals showed several times greater temperature difference. He believes the wide-spread appearance of these phenomena may be caused by ecological factors, e.g., radiation, electromagnetic fields, or some kinds of environmental pollution. Most researchers in Russia with whom I discussed this hypothesis disagreed with Khomeriki. They believe we all possess such latent ability, although to a different degree, and publications about Inga Gaiduchenko (who probably was endowed from birth with a stronger, more pronounced ability of this kind) lowered or eliminated some kind of a psychological barrier which had prevented individuals from manifesting these abilities. In addition, the phenomenon is not totally new. Khomeriki himself stated that he observed it with healer Alexei Krivorotov twenty years ago.[53]

During my trip to Russia in the fall of 1991, I was introduced by Dr. Dubrov to Klara S. Surkova, a retired M.D. living in Moscow. She readily demonstrated to me the phenomenon of "attraction" of objects. Most of the objects were mine (rings, lipstick, coins, paper clips, etc.), while some were brought by Dr. Dubrov and his friend Eugene. Before the demonstration, Klara washed her hands without our asking her to do so. Then she took my rings and put them on her bare skin in the collar-bone area. The three rings remained "stuck" there while I busied myself taking pictures. Afterwards Klara continued working with objects placing them on her hands, arms, and forehead, where they remained "stuck" for minutes on end—usually as long as she desired. She did not make any extraneous movements and did not try to distract our attention.

The most interesting observation was that I was also able in Klara's presence to "attract" the objects the same way. I could place a coin, lipstick, or rings on my forehead or "stick" them to my fingers held vertically; they remained "stuck" as if held by a strong superglue. Some objects (the rings and the lipstick) were touched by Klara before I worked with them, and some (the coins) were not. This ability was active in the presence of Klara Surkova and disappeared afterwards.

Whatever the nature of the phenomenon is (Dr. Dubrov talks about biogravity), the subjects seem capable of generating enough force to hold quite heavy objects. Nikolai Suvorov is able to hold three irons on his chest. Dr. Dubrov gave me a detailed record of an experiment with Yuri Tkachenko. The record, dated December 12, 1990, and signed by twelve researchers present during the test, stated that Tkachenko could place a steel plate weighing thirty kilograms on his chest, then an assistant (chosen by the researchers and not by Tkachenko) placed another plate, weighing twenty kilograms, on top of the first one, and Tkachenko held them until the assistant took the plates down. The experiment was videotaped and both plates and the surface of Tkachenko's chest were examined before the demonstration, and no "secrets," "hidden devices" or glue were found.

Khurjan Davletova and Saniya Karymova demonstrated holding a piece of glass (approximately 45 to 50 cm long and about 20 to 25 cm wide) "stuck" to their two hands, or sometimes to even one hand, held horizontally. It turned out that a significant force was required to remove it from the hand(s). However, when Davletova said she was "giving" the piece to the person who tried to take it, the glass became "unstuck" instantly.

Dubrov indicated that the effect could also be demonstrated in water.[54] Saniya Karymova was reported to demonstrate an "attraction" of toothbrushes and tubes of toothpaste to her hands while holding them under tap water.[55] Karymova said that being wet is helpful, and when she is wet, the surface of her entire body can "attract" objects, while otherwise she can do it only with her hands, forehead, lips and collar-bones.

Poltergeist Cases in the Soviet Union

The great Russian poet Alexander Pushkin wrote in his diary on December 17, 1833, the following:

> ...In the city they are talking about a strange occurrence. In one of the houses belonging to the directorship of the court horsestable, furniture took it upon itself to move and jump. The matter went to the officials. Prince V. Dolgoruky started an investigation. One of the clerks called a priest, but during the service, chairs and tables did not want to stand peacefully. Various interpretations are going around.[56]

The above lines were written at a time when spirits and devils were an obsession in Russian society. The materialistic Soviet state does not believe in spirits, ghosts, and demonic forces. However, these or other equally enigmatic forces which cause poltergeist phenomena do not fail to manifest themselves there from time to time despite the hostile, materialistic atmosphere.

Poltergeists in the Ukraine

The Soviet press rarely acknowledges something as strange, mysterious and unexplained as poltergeists. To date, only a limited number of cases have merited its attention, one dating back to the end of the 1920s, and the others as recent as 1990.

The incident, which took place in 1926 in the suburbs of the city of Kiev, found its way into the pages of the Ukrainian newspaper *Proletarskaya Pravda*.[57] In the early 1970s, I unearthed this article from the depths of Moscow's Lenin Library and, together with an account of an eyewitness to the event, submitted it for publication to the *International Journal of Paraphysics*.[58] The case developed as follows:

On the evening of November 20, 1926, strange phenomena began to occur in a small house. Three women were in conversation when various objects began to fly into the room from the adjacent kitchen. First a log fell from the stove, followed by the frying pan, the salt cellar, the milk bottle and the soap dish. The women were so alarmed that one of them summoned the chief of the local police. When objects continued to fly in his presence, he immediately telephoned for reinforcements. After the arrival of other policemen who witnessed the objects flying around the room, one of them drew his revolver and shot at invisible "tricksters" responsible for the disturbance; fortunately no one was hurt. One of the women, a 50-year-old house guest, was detained by the police and subsequently released. The incident was brought to the attention of scientists who described it as a case of "telekinetic" or "psychokinetic" phenomena.

This 65-year-old case came to my mind after reading a detailed account of another one, which took place in the Soviet Union in 1987. It also happened in the Ukraine, this time in the town of Yenakiyevo of Donetsk province. The active agent of the case discussed in several Soviet newspapers is most likely the 13-year-old teenager Alexander K.[59]

The most interesting feature of the case is that, along with the spontaneous movement of objects (as heavy as a cupboard, refrigerator and washing machine), numerous instances of spontaneous combustion were observed. Some of them occurred in the presence of police and firemen. As usual, tricks were suspected, but not discovered. Spontaneous fires continued in the boy's apartment, along with blown fuses and electric bulbs (even those which were not connected to the electric circuit). A round hole of unknown origin appeared in the window glass, its edges melted as if by a blow torch.

The boy's parents were in despair: nine large fires and many small ones were started in the apartment. When the family temporarily moved to the apartment of relatives, the fires continued there. Once the boy's favorite attache case caught fire while at school, and everyone—the teacher and students—struggled to put the fire out. The police could not find the "magicians" and "tricksters" whose participation they suspected and finally turned to scientists.

Alexander was studied at the Department of Theoretical Problems of the USSR Academy of Sciences. The scientists, of course, could not explain the phenomena. Another researcher, M. Dmitriyev, Professor of Chemistry from the Laboratory of Physico-chemical and Radiological Studies, came up with the idea that the nature of the forces causing the spontaneous combustion is similar to that associated with ball lightning. Then the opinions divided: while some believed these forces were triggered by the boy's specific mental state and some kind of "psychic energy" associated with it, others maintained that the phenomena of spontaneous combustion were caused by ordinary ball lightning, without any connection to the human mind. However, they could not explain how ball lightning could cause movement of heavy objects and again had to resort to the "hypothesis" of "tricksters"—and the discussion came to a dead end.

I looked with great interest through all of the available reports about the Ukrainian case and found many features common to poltergeist cases observed and documented in the West—from electrical disturbances, as in the famous Rosenheim case in West Germany,[60] to spontaneous combustion, as in a relatively recent case in the Brazilian town of Suzano.[61] A poltergeist case involving spontaneous combustion in a town in the Ural mountains was described in detail by Russian researcher Aksakov as early as the last century.[62] In ancient mystery rituals, it was believed that, as a divine manifestation, water could produce fire. The ancients believed water to be a symbol of love and fire to be symbolic of creativity. It is still for skeptics to doubt and for open-minded researchers to determine whether these beliefs are a product of the "primitive" consciousness of ancient people, or of the extraordinary powers of the human mind capable of manifesting the fire of creativity, the fire of faith and probably the real fire of psychokinesis.

Poltergeists in Moscow Suburbs

I found that the contemporary poltergeist case in the Ukraine was not the only recent occurrence of this kind in the Soviet Union. Several other cases were described in the Soviet press:[63]

"Sideboards have been turning over, bedside tables tumbling and kitchen utensils have been flying around with no apparent reason for the second month in the Roshchin family's house in Nikitskaya village, 80 km outside of Moscow, in the Klin region.

"It all started with electric fuses. They were normal fuses and the usual electric meter. The fuses blew frequently. The disc of the meter would start to revolve at a maddening rate, piling up rubles for power not consumed. This happened in late December and did not cause any panic.

"In January, the fuses started playing tricks again, the heating battery tap got unscrewed, and a kind of halo appeared around the meter. The phantasmagoria reached its peak in February: heavy objects started to fall down, a table did a somersault, upper parts of sideboards slid down from their bases, a fridge was found lying on its side. A sugar bowl traversed the room and smashed a window pane five meters away followed by a meat mallet and a jar. . . . The fuses blew again. Twelve-year-old Alyosha was sent to the neighbor's house, and a table was somersaulting there too."

Yevgeniya Albats, the author of the above-mentioned article,[64] referred to another similar occurrence in the village of Kommunarka a year ago: again it was a teenage boy, who also lived with his grandparents, his parents were also divorced, and again objects were flying around.

Meanwhile, strange phenomena in the Klin region continued:

"During the breaks in these wild and increasingly more bizarre supernatural goings-on, hens started clucking, two of them fell ill and quickly died. Their flesh was blue. The village was disturbed, candles were lit at the church, the approach of night was dreaded."

The events developed further according to the usual scenario; local police were summoned. They first laughed, then came to the house:

"They searched through the garret and basement (they had no warrant, of course), looking for evidence of moonshining. Nothing was found. Representatives of the authorities came and saw no traces of criminal activity either. The Roshchins asked for a guard to be put at their house. Everyone was understanding, but refused to stay there at night.

"A quiet month followed. But on Monday, the 16th of March ... a bedside table fell, and electric fuses blew three times in a row."

Again scientists were summoned. Researchers from the Institute of Earth Magnetism, Ionosphere and Propagation of Radio Waves of the USSR Academy of Sciences insisted that the electric phenomena could be caused by magnetic disturbances, but had no comments about flying objects. Enthusiasts of "parascientific phenomena" explained to the journalist:

"Alyosha ... has a strong biological energy field, and, consequently, can (unaware of it) exert influence on objects, i.e., lift, hurl them, and so on. True, he was not always present when the cupboards were falling over, but, as it turned out, that was not necessary, for 'an influence at a distance is quite possible.' ... Similar things can occur only once in a lifetime and only with children no older than 15 years of age. That's the reason why it is not easy to register and analyze the phenomenon."[65]

The article ends with the usual unsolved question of whether it is a "miracle" or sleight-of-hand. I asked myself why was it that no poltergeist occurrences were published in the USSR for almost 60 years, and suddenly three of them appear within several months and yet another in 1988 in the city of Gorky.[66] First I thought the Ukrainian case, which received broad publicity might fire people's imagination and trigger other cases (assuming these forces can somehow be triggered by people's minds). Examining all my data, however, I found that the first publication about the Ukrainian case occurred in April 1987; the Moscow region cases started in 1986 but went unpublicized until the new Soviet policy of *glasnost* (openness) permitted publishing such news. Thus, it seems possible that poltergeist cases were occurring in Russia for all these years, but no word came to print.[67]

A recent poltergeist case investigated by Soviet police was described in detail by Victor Kabakin, staff worker of the Ministry of Internal Affairs of the USSR.[68] Manifestations observed in the house of the Solodkovs family included unexplained fires, spontaneous movement of objects ("a writing-set stand flew out of the cupboard and crashed through the window") and disturbances in the operation of the telephone, radio, and electric bell. The poltergeist "focus" was apparently their 14-year-old son named Vladik. The case was examined both by scientists and by police. Parkhomov, a PhD in physics and mathematics, stated:

> I brought along films in opaque packing, a recording device for registering electric signals and other instruments which can detect the slightest change in electric field. They recorded a point when the character of the field changed drastically. Almost simultaneously I observed a synchronous movement of two of the hands of the recording device. The film which lay behind the door frame darkened more than twice as intensively as the control film. I cannot explain all this for the time being.[69]

The police first resorted to a usual hypothesis of tricksters, but had to abandon it after careful investigation. The article concludes as follows:

> [Police] investigator Barinov wanted more than anything to avoid an unjustified conviction (which, unfortunately, had happened before in similar cases) for a non-existent crime. Having carefully studied all possible versions of the Solodkovs' case, he came to the conclusion that he had come across a real but little studied phenomenon. The criminal case

was closed. This is the first case in the USSR when state institutions officially recognized the existence of poltergeists.[70]

The Controversy Continues

I believe the teenagers who are found to be the "focus" of poltergeist activity are unwitting mediums and psychics, and their mediumistic powers are completely out of their conscious control. Mediums and contemporary psychics are in partial control and often are able to produce the phenomena upon demand. Shamans can access altered states of consciousness at will and therefore have more complete control. However, they are hardly good experimental subjects because they view themselves as mediators between the sacred and the profane; they are inclined to fulfill the needs of their community rather than the "whims" of scientists.

I believe the future of parapsychological research is in studying macrophenomena rather than applying intricate statistics to demonstrate microphenomena. I also believe that the more open-minded a researcher is, the more impressive phenomena he or she will be able to observe and document. Although open-mindedness does not exclude rigorous precautions against possible non-paranormal causes and outright fraud, the fact (now recognized by physicists) that the observer most likely influences the outcome of the experiment emphasizes the significance of the attitude of the researcher.

Today, scientists and writers continue to ponder the "pros" and "cons" of which phenomena are most likely genuine and which are not. I believe I made a modest contribution to this discussion. I also would like to point out that it is an unrealistic task to assess the status of parapsychological research (studies of physical phenomena in the Soviet Union included). It is virtually impossible to ascertain the truth of endless rumors about very serious but secret research and unsubstantiated newspaper accounts. Because of my personal experience, I am in a better position than most Westerners to do so, but I feel I failed nonetheless. I also probably failed as a scientist who attempted to conduct research there. Too often I could only observe and not experiment—primarily because the phenomena were so tenuous and elusive and the mental balance (or imbalance) of the psychics at times was so precarious and unstable. I believe, however, that despite my failure as a scientist, I probably succeeded as a human being committed to growth and understanding. I encountered the unusual, baffling phenomena with an open mind; I continue to do so, and I hope I will not change my ways in the years to come.

Psychic Phenomena in China

ZHU YI YI
SHANGHAI, THE PEOPLE'S REPUBLIC OF CHINA

*M*ore than ten years have passed since the phenomenon of reading through the ear was discovered in Sichuan Province, the People's Republic of China, in March 1979. During this period, we, along with more than a hundred other scientists, have done a lot of research on paranormal phenomena. This research has verified that human beings have such abilities. We think they are potential abilities of mankind.

Reading through the ear has received extensive interest in many fields of science in China. Specialists in diverse fields, including medicine, physiology, chemistry, electronics, computer science, biophysics, biochemistry, nuclear physics, electromagnetism, intelligence, Chinese medicine, psychology, brain science, sonics, and electricity are among those in nearly a hundred universities and institutes studying phenomena associated with the human body.

Results of this work include the following:

1. The existence of paranormal phenomena associated with the body—including paranormal reading, seeing, and writing; thought transfer; the movement of objects; and the passage of matter through matter—has been demonstrated at the bar of modern science. These tests meet the requirements of modern physics, modern biology, and modern psychology. Subjects were tested double-blind under conditions of complete control, with reliable and repeatable results obtained at a significant statistical level.

2. Physical mechanisms of the phenomena have been investigated.

3. The physiological conditions of subjects involved in paranormal activity have been measured. It has been discovered that the rhythms of the heart and breath are faster, the rate of blood flow is increased, and some unusual brain activity occurs.

4. Subjects have been found to produce a kind of radiation which acts upon such materials as nuclear emulsion film, unexposed photographic film, photographic paper, etc. This radiation can be measured by thermoluminescent dosimeters, and it registers on infrared detectors, semiconductor devices, video recorders, and biological detectors.

5. The application of psi to industry, agriculture, and mining has been studied.

Psi research is receiving more and more attention from the Chinese people. The famous scientist, Professor Qian Xuesheng, pointed out that paranormal abilities are the most advanced human capacities. And we warmly predicted that a breakthrough in research would bring about a new scientific and technological revolution and a second Renaissance in the history of humankind. What a high estimation and what a high prediction this is!

We report only actual performances here. We would like to communicate them in order to make people appreciate the magical ability of which the human body is capable. These performances may surprise you, as they did us when we first encountered them.

We do not have any wild expectations that you will come to believe in paranormal abilities through reading this report; we realize that it is difficult to accept the existence of such phenomena on the basis of reading alone. By the time we came to accept the existence of a new ability, we had always gone through the process of repeated observation and consideration. But perhaps this report will prepare you to experiment with your own hands and brain. It includes accounts of the kind of phenomena that

Chinese scientists have researched. Although only a few short stories are presented, not only are they the talk of the town, they will cause you to feel the energy which will contribute great forces to the world when the secret potentials of the human body have been exposed.

The real names of most subjects are given in this report, but pseudonyms are used in the cases of a few persons who did not wish the events of their childhoods to be known. We think readers will pardon us.

We will be very pleased if this brief report arouses your interest in the extraordinary abilities associated with the human body in China.

Like X-Rays

The experimenter enclosed the samples in envelopes and adopted various security measures to prevent the subjects from reading them by normal means. For example, some samples were put in tea cans with double tops; some were sealed in glass test tubes; some were closed in a black plastic box. Sometimes the samples were wrapped in more than ten papers, and so forth. But no matter what means were used to protect the samples, it seemed that the psychics could identify the words written on them.

Some observers said that the subjects had "penetrating eyes." This gave the researchers an idea. They lead the subjects not only to "penetrate" hidden samples but parts of the human body as well. A short time later some psi subjects could "penetrate" the human body like X-rays.

There was a gentleman, Mr. Yao, in the Science Committee of the city of Xuan Chen, An Hui Province. He was wounded during the war and a piece of shrapnel was still in his body. Few persons in his group knew about this piece of shrapnel. Mr. Yao had heard of psi, but he did not believe in it. It was too strange to believe.

One day, two associate professors, Xu Xinfang and Xia Xuguan, in the teacher's Institute of An Hui, brought a 12-year-old girl named Hu Lian to visit Mr. Yao. These two professors were working in the field of biology. They talked with Mr. Yao about psi functioning and told him that the psychics could not only identify words but could also "penetrate" the human body like an X-ray machine. Mr. Yao said he did not believe it and asked whether he could see it demonstrated sometime. Professor Xia said that Hu Lian had the ability to "penetrate" the human body; she could try it just then. Mr. Yao felt very excited, though incredulous. He asked Hu Lian whether she would try to "penetrate" his body.

Hu Lian asked Mr. Yao to sit down. She stood facing him and stared at him for a while. Then she faced his back and listened. Finally she said to Mr. Yao: "Uncle Yao, there is a piece of something which is light and shiny in your body." She pointed out the position of the thing in his body, and drew its shape.

Mr. Yao was very excited when he heard Hu Lian say she had seen a piece of something in his body, and when she pointed out its position he was astonished. When he saw the picture she had drawn, however, he said: "No, no, not this shape." In his memory, the piece of shrapnel was of a different shape. But Hu Lian insisted that the "shiny thing" was in the shape she had drawn; she repeated this several times and seemed to feel certain she was right.

The two continued to argue. Then Mrs. Yao said to Mr. Yao: "I remember we kept the X-ray negative. Why don't we get that and check it?" Mr. Yao recalled they had kept two of the X-ray negatives. We went into the back room in a hurry and found the X-rays which he had kept for twenty years. He checked the picture Hu Lian had drawn against the negatives. The shape was almost identical, and the picture was almost the same size as the object on the negative. Mr. Yao had to laugh and felt Hu Lian's head and said: "I'm sorry. I'm wrong! See my poor memory!" Hu Lian said with a smile: "See, I'm right! I did see clearly!" After this event, Mr, Yao had to believe in psi and to believe in it from the bottom of his heart.

From that time onward Mr. Yao always talked about Hu Lian's "penetrating" the shrapnel when people talked about psi. He said: "I did not know Hu Lian before, and the girl could not have done anything to trick me. I really believe psi ability exists. This is a new scientific field that is worth researching!"

Psi Can Be Trained

News of "reading through the ear" was published in the *Sichuan Daily* in March, 1979. Between then and the end of 1979, other researchers and I in Shanghai found more than thirty newspaper reports of psychics. So many reports made us think deeply about psi. If psi ability was rare, why did more than thirty psychics appear in only a few months? Other researchers and I talked with psychics and observed them. After some period of observation, we had the impression that they were not unusually strong physically, nor were they unusually intelligent; they were very common people. The question arose whether psi was a potential human ability and whether other common people could be trained to express psi.

Several professors at Beijing University were the first to study the psychic effect. They did extensive tests with 10-year-old children in a primary school. They randomly tested both boys and girls. Surprisingly, 60 percent of the juveniles who had been taught and trained to produce psi were able to read through the ear. When the results of the research were published in the *Nature Journal*, it brought a much more extensive response in China. Researchers in many Chinese cities and towns trained psychics and the success rate was between 40 and 60 percent.

Shanghai researchers did their psi training with juveniles in the districts of Nan Shi, Hong Kou, Zha Bei, Xu Hui, Chang Ning, and Jia Ding. They got successful results. Sometimes 30 percent of the pupils demonstrated psychic ability after only one training session. At times, after several sessions, the success rate reached 90 percent.

The discovery of the generality of psi training effects indeed verified the existence of psychic ability. At the same time the discovery provided the fundamental condition for the research on paranormal abilities.

One Tumor or Two?

One of my closest friends, Ms. Yang, my classmate at Fu Dam University, came to Shanghai on business. When she heard I was testing psychics one Sunday, she visited me immediately, hoping one of the psychics could see into her abdominal cavity. I asked a girl, Xiao Zhang, who was in her third grade of middle school, to do the test for her. After a while Xiao Zhang said: "There are two tumors in auntie's womb. A big one is in deep and a small one is next to it."

My friend only half believed this because she had seen doctors in two hospitals not long before and had been told that there was indeed a tumor in her womb. But only a single tumor had been diagnosed. She had agreed to have an operation for the removal of the tumor. I asked her to let me know the outcome of the operation, which she promised.

When she returned to Beijing, Ms. Yang went back to the hospital. She told the doctor a psychic girl had said there were two tumors, not just one. She related what the girl had said about the sizes and positions of the tumors. The doctors disputed the diagnosis but agreed to examine the tumor again with an ultrasonic wave test. The test was witnessed by several doctors who had heard about the psychic diagnosis. They were astonished by the results of the ultrasonic scan: there really were two tumors; one big, the other small. Moreover, they were positioned as the psychic had described. Later the doctors performed an operation on Ms. Yang. Of course, two tumors were removed from her womb.

Ms. Yang wrote me saying that previously she could not understand why I was so interested in psychic phenomena. But after her experience, she understood why I continued the research no matter what other people, including family, friends, and colleagues, had to say. She hoped to assist in research in this new field. She said she was thinking of making a career in it, and this gave us great encouragement.

Reading Through the Ears

At the beginning of 1979, a small bit of news was passed from one family to another, from one person to ten, from ten to a hundred. Soon it was known by every family in the small mountain village in Da Zhu County, Sichuan Province. People were very excited about this. What had happened in this small village?

A small boy named Ching Xiao Ming met his classmate Tang Yu on a clear afternoon in the end of 1978. They were walking and talking happily. Suddenly Tang Yu stopped Xiao Ming and said, "Xiao Ming, is a packet of Fai Yan cigarettes in your pocket?" Amazed at the sudden question, Xiao Ming remarked to himself that Tang Yu was showing off his amazing ability again.

Tang Yu often played the game of "guess the words" with his classmates. He could guess the words correctly every time. He was No. 1 in the game at school. On this occasion, Xiao Ming did not like Tang Yu's pride and said: "You're wrong, I don't have any cigarettes in my pocket."

Tang Yu called: "Nonsense, let me check; you do have a packet of cigarettes in your pocket. And it's Fai Yan brand! I can see it clearly."

Xiao said: "How can you see it? Where do I have it?"

Tang suddenly caught hold of one of Xiao's pockets and shouted: "It's right here!"

Xiao then took out a packet of Fai Yan cigarettes. Tang told Xiao he suddenly had seen the cigarettes in his pocket, not by using his eyes, but through his brain. He said that when he played "guess the words," he just put the small paper with the words on it in his ear, and the words would appear in his mind. He just needed to concentrate on the paper. For Xiao, it was as if he were hearing a tall tale. But he remembered the game of "guess the words" and recalled seeing Tang Yu put the paper in his ear.

It was wonderful! Xiao ran to school with Tang and told their teacher what had happened. The teacher knew that Tang was champion of "guess the words," but she had not given it much attention, since it was just a children's game. However, after hearing Xiao's description, she wondered whether it was true or not. It was best to do a test.

The teacher wrote some words on a piece of paper and rolled it until it formed a small ball, then asked Xiao and Tang to come in. She put the paper ball in Tang's ear and told him he was not allowed to touch it with his hands. Less than two minutes passed before Tang shouted out: "Teacher, you have written, 'I am Tang Yu,' four characters, haven't you?" The teacher was surprised at how true it was! She went to the room next door and wrote several more messages, rolled them into very small balls, then put them one by one into Tang Yu's ear. It only took Tang one minute, sometimes as little as 20 seconds, to identify the words on each of the papers. The messages were such as "Da Zhu County, Sichuan Province, China," "I am a student," "Science Technology Culture," "My ears can read the words," "Pig, horse, cow," "3 x 18 = 54," etc. Tang's ears even recognized pictures of a baby's head and of a small animal the teacher had drawn.

The news travelled so fast that many people living nearby came to Tang Yu's house to ask him about his ability to read through his ears. The small mountain village was excited, and Tang Yu's house was full of people. Tang's father and brother were farmers, and were very kind to the people whether they knew them or not. Tang nicely demonstrated his ability for the visitors. The news quickly spread beyond the confines of the village. It reached the *Sichuan Daily*, where the reporter Mr. Chang Nan Ming heard it and decided to see it with his own eyes. He went to the division of Jing Jing, only to learn that Tang Yu had been sent to the county where he was to attend a test.

Mr. Chang and other people were there for the test. They wrote many messages on small pieces of paper and rolled them into balls, sometimes folding them first. They checked every ball to make sure the words on them could not be read by normal means. Then they put the paper balls in Tang's ear and asked him to read the words on them. Tang sat surrounded by the crowd and read the messages one by one until he had read them all correctly. He even read the twenty words of a well-known poem from the T'ang dynasty. It was too wonderful to believe. They were trying to decide the best way to verify it was true.

The next day, they talked it over with Tang and he agreed to do the test in the dark. In a dark room with the electric light turned off, only a little moonlight shone through the window. Those present could recognize some things in the room indistinctly, but they could not read any characters in a newspaper. Tang Yu nevertheless recognized all the words on ten paper balls as they were put into his ears one by one. He told everyone what color the words were and what kinds of pens they used: some had used a fountain pen, some a ballpoint pen, some a pencil, some a Chinese brush. Those present found it hard to comprehend. But they clearly saw there was no dishonesty, no magic; it was true beyond doubt.

Tang Yu said he had felt electricity in his hands, and words appeared in his brain when he tried to read the words on the paper balls. When a ball was put in his ear, it seemed as if there were a screen in his brain, the words projected on it distinctly. If the tests were conducted in a very quiet environment or if he was very happy, the words were especially clear. Tang not only read words which he knew but could also recognize Chinese characters and English letters which he had not learned; he wrote or drew them on paper.

Mr. Chang Naiming wrote that although these phenomena could not be explained so far, they were without a doubt real. He wondered whether other boys might be able to do the same, whether science might be interested in research in this area. He wrote an article that appeared under the headline, "Discovery of a Boy with the Ability to Read through his Ears in Da Zhu County," in the *Sichuan Daily* on March 12, 1979. This was the first story about reading through the ear in China, and it brought quite an unexpected response in many Chinese cities and provinces. Since then, people with similar abilities have been discovered thoughout the country. Mr. Chang Naiming's article raised the curtain on research on the exceptional abilities of the body in China.

I Can Do It Too

After the news of reading through the ear was published in *Sichuan Daily*, the *Beijing Technology* newspaper reprinted it at once and carried it to a much wider audience. Among them was a family in Che Gong Zhuong, Beijing. The father, Mr. Lao Wang, was the officer of a factory and the mother a factory worker. Their three daughters and their son were students. One evening in April 1979, Mr. Leo Wang and some of his friends were talking about the story in *Beijing Technology*, expressing surprise and wonder. Suddenly the third daughter, then aged eleven years, shouted: "It is not praiseworthy! I can do it too."

Her mother thought her impolite to interrupt while the friends were talking and chastised her. Wang Bing felt wronged by her mother's criticism and shouted again: "I can do it, really!" Her older sister Wang Qiang then said to her: "You may not shout when they are talking. Let's go to the room next door. If you can do it, you show me, all right?" The two girls retired to the small inner room. Wang Qiang took out several small pages and wrote some words on them, rolled them into balls, and put them in Wang Bing's ears. She watched her sister attentively. After a short time, Wang Bing recognized the words exactly. Wang Qiang then shouted excitedly: "Mom, mom, my sister really can do it. She can read words through the ear!"

Her parents and their friends stopped talking, and went into the small room. They asked Wang Bing to do the test again. They repeated the test several times, and she was right every time. After a while Wang Qiang also decided to try. She took a ball, put it into her ear and went to a quiet corner. Unexpectedly, the words "shined" in her mind frequently. The two sisters Wang Bing and Wang Qiang became very famous during the early research on phenomena associated with the human body. Later, they not only performed the test with the paper balls in their ears, but under their armpits as well.

We met the family in July 1979. Because there was criticism in some newspapers about reading through the ear, we and several scientists did the test with special precautions. We went into a small room where the two sisters were sitting at a small table. We surrounded them on four sides, with two people on each side. The distance between us and the subjects was only forty centimeters. We put the test sample in the girls' hands, and they placed their hands under their armpits. After fifteen minutes, both had recognized the words on the papers. We were too prudent to trust a test done in their home, we then asked them to repeat the test the next day at the Xin Jiang hotel where we were staying. Their parents agreed with pleasure.

The next afternoon, the two girls came to Xing Jiang hotel in the company of their parents. There were two beds and eighteen monitors in a 16-square-foot room. It was too crowded to walk. Two people at the end of the corridor, at least twenty meters away from the room, wrote the words. This second test also was quite successful. The decision was made to hold a third test in Beijing several days later.

It was a very hot July in Beijing in 1979. I brought the two sisters into the room in which nineteen people were waiting; it was very hot. I had a pair of white cotton gloves in my baggage. If the subjects wore gloves in which we had put the test samples, it would be impossible to read the words by normal means.

If the subject's gloved hand were put under her armpit, she certainly could not steal a glance at the words. All the monitors approved of this idea. The scientists put the gloves on the two girls, put the samples in the gloves, and tied the gloves to the girls' wrists with nylon cord. Then the girls placed their hands under their armpits. It was extremely fast this time: in only ten minutes, Wang Bing said she had recognized the words. She drew a picture of a square with a dot in it and a second dot above it. When the monitor took out the sample, he found she was exactly right! The picture as drawn had only a square with a dot in the center, but the paper had a second dot above the square—the result of the experimenter's having folded the paper before the ink was dry.

Wang Qiang also performed well. She drew a picture of a square with an X in it and an inverted triangle above, the color red outside and blue inside. In these tests, the girls not only read the words and drew the pictures, they also identified the colors. They did six tests each under these critical conditions, and each one was successful. All of the monitors and scientists who attended the tests believed in the results from their hearts. The tests increased their confidence in psi research and their determination to study the exceptional abilities of the body.

Reading Through the Foot

It was a day in February 1980. The first symposium on psi research was taking place in Shanghai Science Hall. "Un-eye sight" was performed for the delegates. "Un-eye sight" (or eyeless sight) means seeing things, including pictures, by other than the eyes. More than ten young people or students were sitting in the front of the hall.

An old professor sat in the first row of the audience, and a 12-year-old stood beside him. The old man was physics professor Chen Hankui of East China University Teacher's College. The young man was psychic subject Zhao Hong from the city of Changzhou. Why did Professor Chen bring Zhao to his side?

Professor Chen had spent his professional life in physics. He had not encountered any psi phenomena in his lifetime, so he felt very strange, surprised and noncomprehending when he first heard about it. He certainly could not believe it easily. He thought the test shown in the hall might not be valid, and he hoped to conduct a test himself. So he asked Zhao Hong to come to his side. He had prepared his own sample. Nobody else knew what was on it. He was very happy when Zhao Hong told him he could recognize the words even though the sample was put under his foot. Because he could keep watch on Zhao Hong's eyes very easily, he put the sample into Zhao Hong's shoe, then Zhao Hong stood on the sample.

As the test continued minute after minute, Zhao Hong appeared very relaxed, sometimes talking with other people. The professor kept an eye on him. After twelve minutes, Zhao Hong said he recognized the character for "physics"—two Chinese characters in black. Professor Chen bent and took out the sample, which was still folded very well. He opened the paper and showed the word "physics" written in Chinese characters with a black ballpoint pen. He asked Zhao Hong how he could have seen the word. The boy said: "When the sample was under my foot, I concentrated on it. After a while it seemed that there was a TV screen in my brain, and a stroke appeared on it very clearly. It was just like that."

Professor Chen said very excitedly that he must now believe in psi because nobody had seen the sample which he himself had prepared. And during the test Zhao Hong had not even looked at his foot. Something real had happened. The professor said again that although one could not yet explain how these unusual and wonderful phenomena might happen, it was always the case that the phenomena came first, and the theory came later, after many important discoveries. If we identify and verify these phenomena today, then we can research them in the expectation of being able to explain them some day.

Reading Through Chewing the Words

We now knew that psychics could read through the ears, feet, hands, armpits and other parts of the human body. Now I will tell you of another strange way of reading words.

In a psi research symposium, the psychic Xiao Ping heard someone talking in whispers, and he felt that some people distrusted the tests. He suggested to the monitors that they do a test as follows: have members of the audience write words on papers which could be rolled into balls, which he would put into his mouth. With the paper ball in his mouth, he would not be able to touch it and could not see it either. In this way they could believe the test.

A man of middle age came out of the audience at this time. He introduced himself as a senior researcher in an institute and said his purpose in attending the symposium was to see psychic functioning himself. If he put the test sample in the subject's mouth himself and removed the sample after the subject had perceived the words—assuming neither the subject nor anyone else touched the sample—under these conditions, he would believe the test. Xiao Ping opened his mouth and put his hands behind his back. The senior researcher removed a small paper ball from his pocket and put it into Xiao Ping's mouth. Then he sat facing Xiao Ping, the distance between them only 50 centimeters.

Surprisingly, Xiao Ping chewed continuously. The man was anxious about it. He asked Xiao Ping: "What are you chewing?" Xiao Ping said: "What I am chewing is the paper ball you gave me just now." He chewed and chewed, and after fifteen minutes wrote on a piece of paper four words in Chinese characters: "mountain, town, wind, rain." He noted the words "mountain" and "wind" were written by a red ballpoint pen, the word "town" was written by a black ballpoint pen, the word "rain" was written by blue ballpoint pen.

At that time the senior researcher took the little paper ball from the tip of the boy's tongue. He used a soft paper to dry the ball, and tried to unfold it, but the paper had already changed into pulp and did not have any recognizable words. The writing was blurred and could not be made out at all. Nevertheless, the senior researcher said sincerely: "I really believe it today because I saw it myself! I prepared the paper ball at my home yesterday; the words and colors perceived by the boy are exactly right. Although the paper has changed into pulp, I can guarantee that it is right! But I really do not understand the boy's performance. If the writing had already blurred, how could he perceive the words? This phenomenon is really worthy of research, it seems to me." His speech was warmly applauded.

Xiao Ping's psi abilities were accidentally discovered. At first he perceived the words through his ear or hand. In testing he would occasionally put the sample into his mouth, and while he was chewing the paper ball, he would suddenly see the words. He wrote the words immediately and spit the paper from his mouth to check it, and it was right. In this way we discovered Xiao Ping's ability to perceive the words through chewing.

Sitting in the Right Place

The express train from Beijing to Shanghai was under way. In one of the sleeping cars were two sisters, Wang Qiang and Wang Bing. They would attend the first Chinese symposium on psi research in Shanghai.

The girls were accompanied by their mother and a researcher, and they felt a little bored. The researcher thought of a game the sisters could play. He took out two small paper bags made of Kraft paper. The bags were sealed so that it was impossible to see the contents by normal means. He asked the sisters if they could see the things in the bag.

Each girl chose one of the bags and held it in her hand, then reached the hand under her armpit. Only one minute later Wang Bing called: "Uncle, you are tricky, there are very small pieces of paper in it." Wang Qiang said: "No, there are words on these pieces." The researcher let the girls bet who would perceive the words first. Seven minutes later, Wang Bing said three words, "take the train," were on the pieces of paper, written in blue, but the characters had been cut, each part in irregular shape. Wang Qiang recognized the words at this time: two words "light moon" in Chinese characters, in black. The two characters were cut into five parts. She described the shape of each part.

The researcher unsealed the small paper bags, and they saw that the pieces of paper were piled one upon the other. Eight pieces of paper were in Wang Bing's bag, and five pieces of paper were in Wang Qiang's bag. The three of them put all of the pieces of paper together. It took eleven minutes to reassemble them in their original shape. That means the two sisters perceived the words through their psi faster than the time they spent putting the pieces of paper together. The successful tests signify a new psychic functioning. The two sisters arrived in Shanghai and the first symposium on psi research with their new psychic power and their beautiful flow of psi wide open.

It is surprising that the subjects could recognize the words on the scraps of paper. According to common knowledge, this is an impossible feat. It is especially strange because some Chinese characters, if reversed, mean different things. Even with the characters cut, the psychics could still recognize them clearly and exactly in their original form.

According to the subjects, the psychic ability to put the characters together occurred in the brain. When the first scrap of paper appeared in the brain, then the second scrap appeared and automatically moved to find the right position adjacent to the first. The third scrap appeared, found its position, and so on, until all the pieces were in place. This ability to "sit in the right seat" is difficult for any intelligent machine to perform. Psi is really inconceivable.

The Discovery of Psychic Movement Ability

In early 1980, I received a letter from a youth who lived in the countryside, the county Si Hong, Jiang Su Province. He told us he had bought a watch he liked very much until he discovered his watch was often either much faster or sometimes much slower than others. He had the watch checked by a jeweler, but no problem was detected. After repeated requests to have it repaired, the shop gave him a new watch but it was not long before he began to notice the same problem with the new watch. This so annoyed him that he sold the watch and bought another of a different brand. But this new watch, also, sometimes ran fast, sometimes slow.

The young man changed watches again, and again, but every one of the watches he had on his wrist had the same problem. Even stranger, these same watches, on other people's wrists, ran correctly. He did not know what made this happen to his watches. His fellow villagers said he must have some strange illness. Then he happened to read a news story about paranormal abilities of the body. He wrote to us to ask whether his strange illness might be psychic functioning and whether the trouble might be resolved with our help.

In May of the same year, Mr. Zhu Runlong, who was the Secretary-General of the Chinese Somatic Science Association, went to the youth's hometown specifically to meet him. The young man, 19 years old at that time, was very simple and honest, with an introverted disposition. He told Mr. Zhu anxiously that he had had the strange illness for over a year. In order to check the young man's reports, Mr. Zhu had brought two watches which had run accurately for several years. The first experiment was made that morning. Mr. Zhu put five watches on the young man's body—one on each wrist, one on each ankle, and one on his neck. Two of the five were electronic watches. The young man sat down on a chair and kept his body, his hands and feet, motionless. After one hour all the watches were still running accurately, and the young man said he did not know why none of them were acting up as usual.

That evening the test was repeated. This time, after 40 minutes, something amazing happened. One of the ankle watches was running thirty-seven minutes fast, whereas the watch worn on his neck in front of his chest was twenty-five minutes slow. The experiment was repeated the next day. The two watches brought by Mr. Zhu sometimes ran fast, sometimes slow, keeping bad time. Only the electronic watch went regularly.

When Mr. Zhu visited the young man's neighbors, they verified the strange occurrences and told Mr. Zhu that when they had first heard of the strange watch illness, they asked the yong man to show them his watch every day for some period of time. That meant he had performed the test thousands of times. Whatever the brands of watches—including those of Radar, Enneigo, and Urmiga, made in Sweden, or Chinese brands—they malfunctioned on his wrist. Nobody could understand why these strange things were happening.

When Mr. Zhu returned to Shanghai, we published a report called "Information on Psychic Functioning." As a result, psi researchers designed many new tests with very good ideas, including experiments to test psychics' abilities to affect watches through the power of thought. The first successful test was made in Kun Ming Province.

At first the test was conducted under the following conditions. The watch was covered by a handkerchief, one of the subject's hands was held and the other hand was not permitted to touch the watch. After five to thirty minutes, the subjects would feel some change in the watch. When the monitors opened the handkerchief, they found the watch was indeed running either faster or slower than the correct time.

On another occasion I invited four youngsters to attend a science meeting to demonstrate their psi abilities. The researchers brought four china cups with tops and put three or four watches in each cup. The watches came from the meeting delegates randomly during the test. They placed the four cups before each of the four subjects. Some of the subjects held the cup with two hands, others put their hands on the tops of the cups. But none of them removed the tops. After seven minutes, a girl named Xiao Yan said that of the four watches in her cup, only two were running; one was a golden lady's watch, the other was black with a leather band. The monitor removed the top of the cup and took out the watches. It was true: the golden lady's watch was three hours slow and the black watch with the leather band was two hours and fourteen minutes fast. After a while they found the watches in the other subjects' cups also were keeping poor time—either faster or slower than they should be. Later some psychics could make the watches change time when they were a meter away, with no contact between them and the watches. One even made the date counter move forward by several days.

Associate professors Zheng Tianming, Luo Xing, and Zhu Mingling at the University of Yun Nan designed a test in which the subjects would be asked to move clock hands with the power of thought. They took out the mechanism of the clock, which was placed on a table seventy centimeters away from the subjects. The subjects faced the back side of the clock, and the monitors faced its front. The monitors could see the movement of clock hands clearly. I was fortunately able to observe these tests in the laboratory of the University of Yun Nan several times. You can understand my surprise when I saw the clock hands turn around very quickly without any physical manipulation.

We saw a wonderful performance shown by another subject. Four or five watches were placed on the table before the subjects. When the subjects gave a "puff" to the watches with a slight bow of the head the hands of these watches turned around quickly, just like a paper windmill, a kind of children's toy.

My dear readers, don't you think the discovery of these phenomena is important? The discovery of the malfunctioning watches gave Chinese researchers a good idea. They began looking into psychic movement ability. It wrote a new page in Chinese psi research. Since that day much research has been done on psychic movement ability in China. It has brought a new way of testing extraordinary abilities associated with the human body.

How the Copper Wire Got Curved

Two brothers were studying at the same school in Shanghai. One day we went to the school to conduct psi tests and discovered that both boys were psychics. They became good cooperators in later tests.

The older brother, named Chen Jei, was 18 years old; his younger brother, Chen Lei, was 16. They were asked to attend an experimental attempt to curve a copper wire which had been placed in a test tube. The glass test tubes were five centimeters long and one-and-a-half centimeters in diameter. Each test tube held a copper wire of three centimeters in length and half a millimeter in diameter. The top of the tube was plugged with a rubber cork. When Chen Jei and Chen Lei held the tubes, they could bend the copper wires into the shapes U, V, or O by using their psychic abilities.

Chen Jei said he did not know why the copper wire was curved in his tube. He only knew there was a copper wire in his mind when he saw the wire had become curved. But the younger brother said that he needed to think in order to curve the wire into some special shape; then the wire moved into that shape. Not only could these wires be curved but also wires of other metal, such as lead.

The purpose of training psychics to accomplish many different psychic functions is to verify the existence of psi by objective means in order to create a solid foundation for research into its nature. The fact that subjects can bend metal wire raises the question of whether this is made possible by some "force." What kind of "force" might this be? How big a "force"? With these questions in mind, the researchers designed tests in which the forces, if they did indeed exist, could be measured and recorded by instruments—the first step in researching the mechanism of psychic functioning.

The Dancing Screw and Nut

As ability to set watches with the power of the mind was discovered, psi research was gathering more and more interest. Many discoveries concerning psi were too surprising to believe. If psychics could cause watches and clocks to malfunction, could they move other things?

It was in the Harbin Institute of Technology that Professor Guan Shixu and others had performed the tests moving watch hands successfully and repeatedly. They wondered what other actions the psychic mind was capable of achieving. One day two girls, Wu Ming and Huang Hongnao, were invited to a test in their lab. By chance, they found a screw and a nut in Wu Ming's pocket. The professors got the idea that if the subject could set the nut on the screw and twist it, it would demonstrate a new capability of the psychic mind.

They placed a screw and nut into each of two glass test tubes. Then they set a cap into each tube. They asked Wu Ming and Huang Hongnao, both of whom had strong psychic abilities but neither of whom had done this test before, to do the experiment. Although the girls were young, they realized the test was an important one in psi research. After half an hour passed with no result, the two girls appeared a little anxious. The professors asked them kindly how they were feeling. The girls said the screws and nuts were dancing about the test tubes, but the nuts could not be set on the screws. This description gave the professors an idea: the test should be easy at first, then harder later. Why didn't they start by asking the girls to take the nuts *off* the screws, rather than putting them on? This test would be easier because the mind could focus on a single point.

The tests continued. Every nut was wound onto the corresponding screw for five turns, and the screw with the nut on it was put into test tube, which was then plugged with a rubber cap. Each girl had the one test tube in each of her hands. This time the test went faster. Huang Hongnao was the first to report that her nut had moved two turns; almost at the same time little Wu Ming said her nut had moved too. The professors thought they were hearing fairy stories, but fifteen minutes later both Hongnao and little Ming said they had removed the nuts from the screws. The professors took the test tubes from their hands and found the nuts and screws separated from each other.

After several days' practice, the professors asked the girls again to set the nuts on the screws; this time it did not take much time for them to accomplish the task. The two girls were very happy.

The Spring City's Yang Li

After the report of psychic moving ability was published, we received some letters in which similar phenomena were reported. In order to check these reports, we went in groups to cities and towns in various provinces. At the end on 1980, I travelled from Shanghai to the spring city of Kun Ming in deep winter. I had no sooner arrived in the city, when I was affected by the beautiful sights and the fresh air. The tiredness and boredom caused by the long trip disappeared at once. I went to the university of Yun Nan first and did a series of inspections with researchers there.

First I inspected a 13-year-old girl named Yang Li who had been doing psychic tests for over a year. Her father, Mr. Yang, worked in the Kun Ming Library. Yang Li demonstrated the "unlock" trick for us first. Mr. Yang explained that one day he could not find his key to the padlock on the door, so they could not get into the room. He suddenly had a fantastic idea and asked his daughter Yang Li to open the door without using the key. Unexpectedly, she succeeded.

We were very interested in that, and asked the girl to demonstrate this ability. There were two ways to do the test. The first was; the door was locked with the key in the lock. The second was; the door was locked, and the key removed. We began with the first. I locked a padlock on the door and left the key in the keyhole. Yang Li and I stood facing the door from the distance of about a meter and a half. After thirty minutes the door still had not been opened. Mr. Lang said it usually took five to fifteen minutes for Yang Li to open the door. I thought perhaps Yang Li felt tense because I was a stranger to her. I suggested we rest for a while.

During the rest Yang Lu and I became friends, and the tension abated. When the test resumed she seemed much more relaxed. Now, after only eight minutes, Yan Li told us the lock had been unlocked. I went to the door quickly and discovered it unlocked! The key was still in the keyhole. Mr. Yang saw that the test was successful and suggested we do the second test while Yang Li was in a good mood.

The second test began. I locked the door and put the key in the pocket of my coat. Yang Li stood about two meters from the door. This time it took only five minutes before she said the lock had been opened. I searched for the key and noted it was still in my pocket. When I went to the door, I saw the lock really was unlocked.

During the course of the test, Professor Zheng Tianming, Professor Luo Xinfu and I monitored the test very carefully; there was no negligence on our part. But I still wondered how the task could have been accomplished so fast, so unbelievably. I suggested a retest using a lock I had brought from Shanghai. Yang Li happily responded. Not only did I place the padlock on the door and lock it, I also took the key from the lock and placed it in my pocket, holding it tightly throughout the test.

Yang Li stood about two meters from the door. She talked with her father and others and appeared to be very relaxed. After about twelve minutes had passed, Yan Li stood motionless with her head hung. Another two minutes passed, and Yang Li looked up and said that the lock had been opened. My hand grasped the key in my pocket even more tightly—the only key to the lock. We found the lock truly unlocked; the bottom of the lock had been turned a quarter of a turn. My hand had held the key from the test's beginning to end. Faced with this fact, I had to accept the "unlock" psi ability demonstrated by Yang Li.

The Cigarette with Wings

Yang Li told me her best psychic ability was "remove the cigarette." When she told me the story, I recalled a letter from Mr. Yang in which he related that his daughter could make a cigarette "spread like wildfire"— in other words, disappear without a trace. Sometimes the cigarette moved to the window, sometimes to a chair, sometimes it disappeared and was never seen again.

We had not dared believe it when we received the letter several months ago; at that time a lot of people did not even believe in the extrasensory ability of "reading through the ear." Even among researchers, there were those who did not believe in the ability to set clocks with the power of the mind. Who could believe such a strange story? More importantly, a given extrasensory function could only be accepted after repeated tests. I told Mr. Yang my opinion directly. When he heard my negative opinion, Mr. Yang said with a smile: "I agree with your position. We believe it because we have done more than a hundred tests and they were very successful."

They told me about some of the tests Yang Li had completed. In Kun Ming the cigarettes were put into a paper cylinder box, holding fifteen or one hundred cigarettes each. They put the cigarettes, which they had just counted, into the paper box, they hid the box. Yang Li could remove one cigarette, two cigarettes, even more, one after another, with her mind alone. Sometimes a cigarette which had disappeared from the box could be found in a drawer, in a cabinet, or under a bed. Sometimes they could not find the cigarette at all. They did not know where the cigarettes had gone.

After hearing this description, it was still hard to imagine—unbelievable, without witnessing the tests myself. The next day I asked Yang Li to demonstrate her ability. I put twenty-five cigarettes I had marked into the box and placed thelid on the box myself. I asked Yang Li to sit down on a sofa one meter away from the table and two meters away from the cabinet, and I placed the cigarette box on the table. After forty minutes, Yang Li told me she had removed one cigarette. Opening the box quickly, I found only twenty-four cigarettes. One cigarette had disappeared without anyone having touched the box. It seemed the cigarette had grown wings. We know magicians use their skills, props and cover-up to make things seem to disappear. But in this test I used cigarettes I had counted myself, and I placed the lid on the cigarette box. During the test Yang Li did not touch the cigarette box. How did the cigarette disappear? It was impossible to understand.

Nowhere Are There Flying Flowers in the Spring City

It was Sunday—only two days until New Year's Day, 1981. To spend the last two days of 1980, a year worthy of remembrance in the history of Chinese psi research, I invited two girls, Su Liping and Shao Hongyan, to Yang Li's home to perform some tests. Both girls, twelve years old, had trained under Professors Luo Xinfun and Zheng Tianming. They had done tests for over two years. Professors Luo and Zheng came to attend the test, too.

When the professors arrived, they asked me what I thought of the "taking out the cigarette" test. I told them directly: "I dare not believe everything, but since I can't disprove it so far, I am in a contradictory state." They laughed aloud upon hearing this and said that almost everyone, upon first seeing the test, had the same reaction.

While we were talking, Hongyan asked Professor Luo what "taking out the cigarette" was. When the professor explained how Yang Li removed cigarettes from a paper box, the girls said they wanted to try it too. Inasmuch as the children wanted it, of course, we were very interested in attempting the test. Then it occurred to me that if they could remove cigarettes, might they be able to take out other things?

I had been living in Kun Ming for several days. This nice city experiences spring four seasons of the year. Wherever we went were colorful, beautiful flowers—brilliant red camellia, and many light yellow flowers, the winter jasmine fully blooming on the branches, and many other flowers I could not name—in every garden of every family, in the streets, in the fields, and everywhere. I have liked fresh flowers since I was very young. When I came to Kun Ming, I really enjoyed the sightseeing described in a famous Chinese poem, "Nowhere are there flying flowers in the spring city." So I said without thinking, "You may take the fresh flowers here!"

Professor Luo, Professor Zheng and I gave four china cups to Yang Li, Sun Liping, Shao Hongyan and Chen Ling—one cup for each girl—and put caps on the top of each. We told them to choose any flower they liked to put in the closed cup, and each of us focused on one cup. After a while Liping shouted with surprise: "It's really coming out!" Tenseness and wonder appeared on her face, convincing us she did not know what she had done. We opened her cup, and, indeed, found there a fresh jasmine bud.

Was it true? Was it possible? Liping was surprised, very excited and happy. The encouragement from everyone made her want to repeat the test, and Hongyan, Chen Ling and Yang Li were confident after seeing Shu Liping's success. All four of them focused their minds on the cups. After a while, they shouted one after another: "I have it, I have it!", "It's coming, it's coming!", "It's really coming!" We opened the cups to find something in each cup: one had a piece of leaf, one had a fresh flower bud, one had a colorful paper card. They were successful!

The researchers were amazed. They looked at each other and seemed to ask: Is it true? Is it possible? When we asked the four girls to repeat the test, we checked their pockets first to be sure they were empty. Then we asked them to transport jasmine buds into their cups. Within thirty minutes, the four girls managed to transport no fewer than thirty-five fresh flower buds from the winter jasmine to the closed cups. One even had two buds. Morever, besides the thirty-five jasmine buds, in Liping's cup was a camellia bud.

When Mr. Yang saw one of the jasmine buds, he seemed to recognize it, and we noticed that he appeared a little tense. He immediately went to the balcony of his house. He came back with a flower pot in his hands, and pointed with a mixture of surprise and discouragement to the jasmine branch planted there. He said:

> I planted this famous and expensive jasmine three years ago, and it budded for the first time this year. I liked it very much. Who would have thought they would pluck my jasmine bud— my only jasmine bud?" He was very sad but at the same time very happy. He added: "None of us went to the balcony, none of us left this room, but the flower disappeared from the branch and appeared in the cup. The test really was successful. Although my jasmine plant won't be able to open again this year, the flower of moving things through psi really is opened."

This test, in which subjects were asked to move and remove things through psi, is one of the most wonderful I have seen—something I will never forget. The four girls' facial expressions of surprise, fascination, excitement, and happiness still appear in my mind. It will encourage us to explore the human body's exceptional abilities.

Written by Idea

Xiong has the psychic capacity to write with her thoughts or ideas. The experiments we conducted were as follows:

Experiment 1: Xiong sat before a table upon which were placed three pens with red, blue and black ink respectively, and a sealed box containing a blank sheet of paper. The experimenter ordered Xiong to write what she wished in an assigned color of one of the three pens, but without touching it. When Xiong claimed to have finished her writing, the experimenter opened the box and discovered that on the blank paper was writing in the assigned color.

Experiment 2: Conditions were the same as Experiment 1, except that the pen was held by an experimenter, standing two meters away from the subject, instead of being placed upon the table. After Xiong claimed to have finished writing, the experimenter discovered that there was writing on the paper sealed in the box which would have been written by that particular pen.

Experiment 3: The purpose of this experiment was to verify that the psychic was able to use the power of her mind to write in an assigned place. A page number was given, and a notebook was wrapped so tightly it was impossible for the subject to open. Xiong was asked to write on page 37 with a pen which was locked by the experimenter in a sealed box. Xiong was successful in this trial. She wrote with no pen on the assigned page which she was unable to touch.

Through the Bottom

Zhang is a youth who can make the tablets contained in a hermetically sealed glass bottle drop through its bottom without cracking the bottle.

The experiment was as follows:

Under close watch by the experimenters and the audience, a glass medicine bottle from the pharmacy containing one hundred red tablets was handed to Zhang after having been weighed precisely. Zhang held the bottle toward himself repeatedly while tracing his forefinger round the body as if he wanted to dig something out of it. Suddenly it seemed as if Zhang was nervous, and with the bottle in his right hand, he knocked it several times lightly against the surface of the table. A red tablet dropped through the bottom of the bottle. Knocking once more, three more red tablets appeared. He continued knocking, and the tablets dropped down continuously until the experimenter ordered him to stop. After that, one could see that Zhang ran his hands against the surface of the table as if they were very hot.

The experimenter examined the bottle quite carefully. There was not a crack or any damage to it. In a word, the bottle was sealed as it had been. The experimenter counted the tablets; a total of thirty-five tablets had dropped through the bottom of the bottle, and the number of tablets remaining in the bottle was exactly sixty-five. The experimenter claimed that the experiment was strict and trustworthy.

What sort of force must be involved that can make tablets go through glass without a crack!

Notes

Chapter 1

1. de Goes, 1937.
2. Besterman, 1935.
3. Dingwall, 1961.
4. Medhurst, 1972.
5. Besterman, 1935.
6. Dingwall, 1936.
7. Murphy & Ballou, 1960, Chapter 7.
8. Besterman, Theodore, Letter to the author, Nov 7, 1973.
9. Driesch, Hans, Letter to W. H. Salter, Nov 28, 1928.
10. Imbassahy, 1935, pp. 243-247; see also Walker, 1934.
11. Playfair, 1975, pp. 78-110.
12. Stein, 1991; see also Playfair, 1992.

Chapter 2

1. More information about Eusapia Palladino can be found in Carrington, 1909, 1931, 1954; Feilding, Baggally, & Carrington, 1963; Alvarado, 1982; Cassirer 1983a, 1983b; and Tietze, 1972a, 1972b.

2. More information about Gustavo Adolfi Rol and other Italian mediums can be found in Dettore, 1979; Di Simone, 1973; Fidano, 1986; Giovetti, 1982a, 1982b, 1986.
3. Cerchio Firenze 77, 1978, 1980, 1984, 1986, 1988.

Chapter 3

1. A more extensive version of this paper was published in *Proceedings of the Society for Psychical Research*, Vol. 57, Part 214, January 1989, pp. 54-148.
2. Kvaran, 1906, p. 8.
3. Kvaran, 1934.
4. Nielsson, 1922b, p. 450.
5. Nielsson, 1924a, p. 233.
6. Thordarson, 1942, pp. 1-2.
7. Nielsson, 1922b, p. 452.
8. Nielsson, 1924b, p. 167.
9. Thordarson, 1942, p. viii, 3-8.
10. Nielsson, 1922a, p. 10.
11. Nielsson, 1922b, p. 451.
12. Kvaran, 1934 (authors' translation from Icelandic).
13. Nielsson, 1919b, p. 344.
14. *Ibid.*
15. Nielsson, 1922b, p. 451.
16. Kvaran, 1959, pp. 68-70.
17. Nielsson, 1924a, p. 235.
18. Nielsson, 1922a, p. 30.
19. Hannesson, 1924b, p. 243.
20. Nielsson, 1924a, pp. 234-235.
21. Hannesson, 1910, p. 208.
22. Kvaran, 1934.
23. Thordarson, 1942, p. 4.
24. Nielsson, 1922b, p. 452.
25. Nielsson, 1925, 1930.
26. Hannesson, unpublished notes, 12th Dec. 1908 - 15 Feb. 1909, p. 7.
27. Thordarson, 1942.
28. Kvaran, 1906, pp. 20-22.
29. Thordarson, 1942, pp. 97-98.
30. Auduns, 1948, p. 108.
31. Kvaran, 1906, pp. 8-11.
32. Kvaran, 1906, p. 11.
33. *Ibid.*, p. 16.
34. *Ibid.*, p. 18.
35. Nielsson, 1919b, p. 344; Kvaran, 1906, pp. 12-16.
36. Kvaran, 1906, pp. 16-18.

37. *Ibid.*, p. 18 (authors' translation from Icelandic).
38. *Ibid.*, p. 19.
39. *Ibid.*
40. Nielsson, 1919a, p. 3.
41. Kvaran, 1906, p. 17.
42. Nielsson, 1919a, p. 3 (authors' translation from Icelandic).
43. Kvaran, 1906, pp. 20-21.
44. Nielsson, 1922b, p. 452.
45. Kvaran, 1906, p. 20.
46. Nielsson, 1922b, p. 452.
47. Kvaran, 1906, pp. 20-21.
48. *Ibid.*, pp. 21-22.
49. *Ibid.*, p. 21.
50. *Ibid.*
51. *Ibid.*, p. 22.
52. *Ibid.*
53. Nielsson, 1922b, p. 452.
54. *Ibid.*
55. Thordarson, 1942, p. 97.
56. Kvaran, 1906, pp. 22-23; Nielsson, 1922b, p. 453.
57. Kvaran, 1906, p. 22.
58. *Ibid.*, pp. 22-23.
59. Nielsson, 1922b, p. 453.
60. *Ibid.*
61. Kvaran, 1906, p. 23; 1910, p. 45.
62. Nielsson, 1922b, p. 453.
63. Kvaran, 1906, p. 23; 1910, p. 45; Nielsson, 1922b, pp. 454-455.
64. Nielsson, 1922b, p. 454.
65. Kvaran, 1910, p. 45; Nielsson, 1922b, p. 455.
66. Kvaran, 1906, p. 23 (authors' translation from Icelandic).
67. Nielsson, 1919b, p. 344.
68. Nielsson, 1919b, p. 344; 1922a, p. 13; 1922b, p. 455.
69. Kvaran, 1906, p. 24 (authors' translation from Icelandic).
70. Nielsson, 1922a, p. 13.
71. Nielsson, 1919b, p. 344; 1922b, p. 455.
72. Hannesson, 1908-9, p. 9.
73. Kvaran, 1906, pp. 24-25.
74. Nielsson, 1922a, p. 12.
75. Kvaran, 1910, p. 45; Nielsson, 1922b, p. 455.
76. Kvaran, 1906, p. 24 (authors' translation from Icelandic).
77. Nielsson, 1919b, p. 344; 1922a, p. 13; 1922b, p. 455.
78. Kvaran, 1910, p. 46.
79. Kvaran, 1906, pp. 25-26 (authors' translation from Icelandic).
80. Kvaran, 1910, p. 45; Nielsson, 1919b, p. 344; Thordarson, 1942, p. 13.
81. Kvaran, 1906, p. 26.
82. *Ibid.*; Kvaran, 1934.

83. Thordarson, 1942, pp. 12-13.
84. Nielsson, 1922b, pp. 453-454; see also Nielsson, 1922a, pp. 17-18;
85. Kvaran, 1934.
86. Kvaran, 1906, p. 38.
87. Kvaran, 1906, pp. 27-32; 1910, p. 45.
88. Kvaran, 1906, pp. 27-32 (authors' translation from Icelandic).
89. *Ibid.*, p. 31.
90. Nielsson, 1919b, p. 344.
91. Nielsson, 1922a, p. 19.
92. *Ibid.*
93. Kvaran, 1906, p. 32.
94. *Ibid.*
95. Thordarson, 1942, p. 23.
96. Nielsson, 1919a, p. 75.
97. Nielsson, 1919b, p. 344.
98. Kvaran, 1906, p. 38; Nielsson, 1919a, p. 19; 1922b, pp. 455-456).
99. Aksakow, 1894; Carrington, 1906-7; Hyslop, 1907.
100. Fodor, 1966, pp. 115-116.
101. Kvaran, 1910, p. 46.
102. Kvaran, 1906, pp. 40-41.
103. *Ibid.*, p. 41.
104. *Ibid.*, p. 37.
105. *Ibid.*, pp. 40-42.
106. *Ibid.*, p. 42.
107. *Ibid.*
108. Nielsson, 1924a, p. 234.
109. Kvaran, 1910, p. 47.
110. Nielsson, 1922b, p. 456.
111. Kvaran, 1934; Nielsson, 1922a, p. 20.
112. Thordarson, 1942, pp. 102, 109.
113. Kvaran, 1910, p. 47 (authors' translation from Icelandic).
114. *Ibid.*
115. Kvaran, 1934.
116. Thordarson, 1942, p. 99 (authors' translation from Icelandic).
117. *Ibid.*, pp. 99-100.
118. *Ibid.*, p. 100.
119. *Ibid.*
120. Kvaran, 1910, p. 46.
121. Nielsson, 1919b, p. 344; 1922a, p. 22; 1922b, p. 458.
122. Nielsson, 1919b, p. 344.
123. Nielsson, 1922a, p. 22.
124. Nielsson, 1922b, p. 459.
125. Kvaran, 1910, pp. 48-49.
126. Kvaran, 1934.
127. Thordarson, 1942, p. 4.
128. *Ibid.*, p. 104.

129. Nielsson, 1919b, p. 350; 1922a, pp. 23-24.
130. Nielsson, 1919b, p. 350.
131. Rev. Jakob Jonsson, personal communication, 1984.
132. Tarchini, 1947.
133. Nielsson, 1930, p. 179.
134. Nielsson, 1930, p. 181; 1925, pp. 96-97.
135. Nielsson, 1925, p. 97.
136. Nielsson, 1930, pp. 182-184; Thordarson, 1942, pp. 24-32.
137. Thordarson, 1942, p. 31.
138. Nielsson, 1925, p. 99.
139. Nielsson, 1922b, p. 462; 1924a, p. 235.
140. Nielsson, 1922a, pp. 27-28.
141. Nielsson, 1922b, p. 462; 1924a, p. 235.
142. Hannesson, 1910, 1911.
143. Hannesson, 1924b; see also Hannesson, 1951, 1973.
144. Gissurarson & Haraldsson, 1989, pp. 102-105.
145. Hannesson, 1951, pp. 27-31.
146. Hannesson, 1924b, p. 248.
147. *Ibid.*
148. *Ibid.*, pp. 248-249.
149. Hannesson, 1951, p. 35.
150. Hannesson, 1924b, p. 250.
151. *Ibid.*
152. *Ibid.*, p. 252.
153. Hannesson, 1951, p. 39.
154. *Ibid.*, pp. 40-45.
155. Hannesson, 1924b, p. 253.
156. *Ibid.*
157. *Ibid.*, p. 254.
158. Nielsson, 1922b, p. 463.
159. Hannesson, 1924b, p. 255.
160. *Ibid.*, p. 256.
161. *Ibid.*, p. 272.
162. See especially Dingwall, 1947; Thurston, 1952, pp. 15-18.
163. Hannesson, unpublished notes, 1908-9, pp. 1-12.
164. Hannesson, 1910, 1911.
165. Hannesson, 1924b, pp. 258-260.
166. *Ibid.*, p. 258.
167. Excerpts from Hannesson's unpublished notes, 1908-9, pp. 1-6; a complete account of this seance was published in Gissurarson & Haraldsson, 1989, pp. 112-114; authors' translation from Icelandic.
168. Hannesson, 1924a.
169. Adapted from Hannesson, 1924a, p. 226.
170. *Ibid*, pp. 218-222.
171. *Ibid.*, p. 220; authors' translation from Icelandic.
172. *Ibid.*, p. 221.

173. Hannesson, 1924b, p. 260.
174. Nielsson, 1924a, p. 29.
175. Nielsson, 1922b, p. 464.
176. Thordarson, 1942, pp. 63-65.
177. *Ibid.*, pp. 82-85.
178. *Ibid*, p. 83.
179. *Ibid.*, pp. 57-58.
180. *Ibid.*, p. 48.
181. Kvaran, 1910, p. 49.
182. Nielsson, 1924b, p. 454.
183. Thordarson, 1942, pp. 54-56; see also Kvaran, 1910, p. 49.
184. The Experimental Society kept extensive Minute Books of Indridason's seances. They still existed in 1942 when Thordarson was writing his book on Indridason, but were since then thought to have been lost. In the autumn of 1991, after our original report was published (Gissurarson, & Haraldsson, 1989), they were found among the belongings of Rev. Audun's wife who had passed away at that time. The contents of the books do not appear to bring about any changes to the material we have published so far. An article on the Minute Books is in preparation for the *Journal of the Society for Psychical Research.*
185. Nielsson, 1924a, p. 238.
186. Home's phenomena as reported in Dunraven (1924), Crookes (1972) and Zorab (1970) were examined for the construction of this table.

Chapter 4

1. Imich, 1932.
2. *Ibid.*
3. *Ibid.*
4. Tabori, 1950, p. 31.

Chapter 5

1. This is a chapter from Dr. Bugaj's (1990) book. Section 5 about phantoms of animals is written by Dr. Alexander Imich.
2. See *Revue Metapsychique*, Bulletin de l'Institut Metapsychique International, 1921, 1922, 1923; in particular, *Revue Metapsychique*, 1923, pp. 27-39; see also Geley, 1922a, pp. 505-528.
3. Geley, 1922b.
4. Geley, 1925, pp. 214-303.
5. Okolowicz, 1926.
6. Niemojewski, 1921, p. 109.
7. Szczepanski, 1936, pp. 100-116.

8. Lipski, 1976, pp. 537-538.
9. von Gulat-Wellenburg, von Klinckowstroem, & Rosenbusch, 1925, pp. 402-411; Moser, 1935, p. 722.
10. Lipski, 1976, p. 538.
11. Okolowicz, 1926, p. 285.
12. *Ibid.*
13. Geley, 1925, p. 225.
14. Geley, *ibid.* pp. 226-227.
15. Heuze, n. d., p. 138.
16. Okolowicz, 1926, p. 455.
17. *Ibid.*, p. 378.
18. Ochorowicz, 1913.
19. Ochorowicz, 1909, p. 237.
20. Okolowicz, 1926, p. 457.
21. Ochorowicz, 1913, Vol. 3, p. 388. It should be pointed out that psychics do not observe rules. The one I have been associated with was conscious and active during violent appearances of a materialization; as a matter of fact, she never experienced a trance state (editor's note).
22. Okolowicz, 1926, p. 465.
23. *Ibid.*
24. *Ibid.*, p. 437.
25. von Schrenck-Notzing, 1914a, 1914b.
26. Okolowicz, 1926, p. 437.
27. *Ibid.*, p. 475.
28. *Ibid*, p. 478.
29. *Ibid*, p. 480.
30. *Ibid.*
31. *Ibid.*, pp. 308-309.
32. *Ibid.*, p. 481.
33. Geley, 1925.
34. Okolowicz, 1926.
35. *Ibid*, p. 493.
36. *Ibid.*
37. Geley, 1924.
38. Niemojewski, 1921, pp. 138-139.
39. Okolowicz, 1926, p. 498.
40. *Ibid.*, p. 503.
41. *Ibid.*, p. 505.
42. *Ibid.*, p. 88.
43. *Ibid.*, p. 116.
44. Geley, 1925; Okolowicz, 1926.
45. Okolowicz, 1926, pp. 90-91.
46. *Ibid.*, p. 190.
47. *Ibid.*, p. 514.
48. *Ibid.*, p. 515.
49. *Ibid.*, p. 207.

50. *Ibid.*, p. 212.
51. *Ibid.*
52. *Ibid.*, p. 409.
53. *Ibid.*, p. 290.
54. *Ibid.*, pp. 310-311.
55. Dalborowa, 1973, p. 16.
56. Sokolowski, 1948, pp. 102-103.
57. Urbanski, 1984, pp. 7-8.

Chapter 6

1. Zielinski, 1968, p. 80
2. Basilov, 1984, p. 15; Czaplicka, 1914, p. 200; Hultkrantz, 1978, p. 37.
3. Kharuzin, 1889, p. 41.
4. Karamzin, 1892, Vol. III, p. 105; Berry, 1984a, p. 5.
5. *Moskovityanin*, 1840, #1, p. 249.
6. Florinskii, 1957, Vol. I, p. 302; Berry, *op. cit.*
7. Britten, 1884, p. 350.
8. Berry, 1984b, p. 145.
9. Berry, 1985, p. 107.
10. quoted in Berry, 1985, pp. 108-109.
11. Aksakov, 1895.
12. See the chapter by Dr. Paola Giovetti in this volume.
13. Zigmont, A.S., *Rebus*, No. 45, 1890; quoted in Zielinski, 1968, pp. 31-32.
14. quoted in Zielinski, 1968, pp. 31-32.
15. *Ibid.*, p. 19.
16. *Ibid.*, p. 20.
17. *Ibid.*, p. 32.
18. quoted in Berry, 1985, pp. 109-110.
19. Bodisco, 1893, p. 21; quoted in Zielinski, pp. 32-33.
20. Perovsky-Petrovo-Solovovo, 1945, pp. 261-266.
21. *Ibid.*, p. 262.
22. *Ibid.*
23. *Ibid*, p. 263.
24. *Ibid.*, pp. 263-264.
25. *Ibid*, p. 264-265.
26. *Ibid.*, p. 265.
27. *Rebus*, 1883, #41, p. 366; quoted in Berry, 1985, pp. 111-112.
28. quoted in Berry, 1985, p. 114.
29. *Materialy dlya Suzhdeniya o Spiritizme*, 1876.
30. *Ibid.*, pp. 31-32.
31. Butlerov, 1875, pp. 332-333.
32. *Ibid.*, pp. 335-337.
33. Zinchenko & Leontiyev, 1974, p. 192.
34. Ullman, 1974; Keil, et al., 1976; Vilenskaya, 1981.

35. Kolodny, 1986; 1991, p. 111.
36. "Scientists...", 1984; Volchenko, et al., 1984.
37. Strelkov, 1986.
38. Lvov, 1971, 1974.
39. "The editorial...", 1988; see also *Tekhnika-Molodezhi*, Nos. 5, 6, 7, 1988.
40. Zlokazov, Pushkin, & Shevchuk, 1980/1982, pp. 15-17.
41. *Ibid*, pp. 18-19.
42. Naumov & Mikhalchik, 1983.
43. Kolodny, 1988.
44. Buldyk, 1989.
45. Nelander, 1990.
46. Vilenskaya, 1991, p. 30.
47. Gerasimov, 1990.
48. Lebedeva, 1990; Dubrov & Berezin, 1991; Dubrov, 1992.
49. Dubrov & Berezin, 1991.
50. e.g., Rudsky, 1990; Dubrov, 1992.
51. Orlov, 1990.
52. *Ibid.*, p. 28.
53. *Ibid.*, p. 27.
54. Dubrov, 1992.
55. Lebedeva, 1990, p. 36.
56. quoted in Berry, 1984b, p. 151.
57. "A miracle...," 1927.
58. Vilenskaya, 1972.
59. Dorofeyev, 1987; Ivchenko & Lisovenko, 1987; Lisovenko, 1987; Vilenskaya, 1988.
60. Bender, 1968.
61. Andrade, 1975, 1988.
62. Aksakov, 1901, pp. 322-337 (with reference to *Rebus*, Nos. 43-48, 1886).
63. Albats, 1987, p. 9.
64. *Ibid.*
65. *Ibid.*
66. Arefiyev, 1989, p. 12.
67. The above accounts about poltergeists in the USSR appeared, in part, in Vilenskaya, 1988, and in Vilenskaya & Steffy, 1991, pp. 34-35.
68. Kabakin, 1991.
69. *Ibid.*, p. 155.
70. *Ibid.*

References

Aksakov, A. N. (1895). *Predvestniki spiritizma* [Forerunners of spiritism]. St. Petersburg (in Russian).

Aksakov, A. N. (1901). *Animizm i spiritizm* [Animism and spiritism]. St. Petersburg (in Russian).

Aksakow, A. N. (1894). Ein epochemachendes Phanomen im Gebiete der Materialisationen. *Psychischen Studien, 21,* 284-299, 337-353, 385-399, 435-449, 478-490 (in German).

Albats, Yevgeniya. (1987, April 5-12). A flying sugar bowl, or a sensation in the making. *Moscow News,* No. 13 (3261), p. 9.

Alvarado, Carlos S. (1982). Note on seances with Eusapia Palladino after 1910. *Journal of the Society for Psychical Research, 51*(791), 308-309.

Andrade, Hernani Guimarães. (1975). The Suzano poltergeist. *Proceedings of the Second International Congress on Psychotronic Research* (pp. 174-175). Monte Carlo.

Andrade, Hernani Guimarães. (1988). *Poltergeist: Algumas de suas ocorrencias no Brasil* [Poltergeist: Some Occurrences in Brazil]. São Paulo, Brazil: Editora Pensamento (in Portuguese).

Arefiyev, Alexander. (1989, March 27-April 2). A byl li malchik? Malchik—byl [And was there a boy? A boy was indeed]. *Nedelya,* No. 13(1513), p. 12 (in Russian).

Auduns, J. (1948). *Agrip af sogu salarrannsoknanna*. Reykjavik: Leiftur (in Icelandic).

Basilov, Vladimir N. (1984). *Izbranniki Dukhov* [The Chosen of the Spirits]. Moscow: Politizdat (in Russian).

Bender, Hans. (1968). An investigation of "poltergeist" occurrences. In *Proceedings of the Parapsychological Association*, No. 5, 31-33.

Berry, Thomas E. (1984a). Seances for the Tsar: Spiritualism in Tsarist society and literature. Part I. *The Journal of Religion and Psychical Research*, 7(1), 5-16.

Berry, Thomas E. (1984b). Seances for the Tsar: Spiritualism in Tsarist society and literature. Part III. *The Journal of Religion and Psychical Research*, 7(3), 141-230.

Berry, Thomas E. (1985). Seances for the Tsar: Spiritualism in Tsarist society and literature. Part V, Section I. *The Journal of Religion and Psychical Research*, 8(2), 106-118.

Besterman, Theodore. (1935). The mediumship of Carlos Mirabelli. *Journal of the Society for Psychical Research*, 29(520), 141-153.

Bodisco, Constantin A. (1893). Astralnoye telo [The Astral Body]. *Rebus*, No. 2, p. 21 (in Russian).

Britten, E.H. (1884). *Nineteenth Century Miracles or Spirits and Their Work in Every Country of the Earth*. New York: Lovell.

Bugaj, Roman. (1990). *Eksterioryzacja—istnienie poza cialem* [Exteriorization—existence beyond the body]. Warsaw: SIGMA NOT (in Polish).

Buldyk, N. (1989, July 2-9). Sorceress from Byelorussia. *Moscow News*, No. 26(3378), p. 5.

Butlerov, Alexander M. (1875, November). Mediumicheskiye yavleniya [Mediumistic phenomena]. *Russkiy Vestnik* [Russian Herald], pp. 300-348 (in Russian).

Carrington, Hereward (1906-1907). An examination and analysis of the evidence for 'dematerialization' as demonstrated in Mns. Aksakof's Book: A case of partial dematerialization of the body of a medium. *Proceedings of the American Society for Psychical Research*, 1, 131-168.

Carrington, Hereward. (1909). *Eusapia Palladino and her phenomena*. New York: Dodge.

Carrington, Hereward. (1931). *The story of psychic science.* New York: Ives Washburn.

Carrington, Hereward. (1954). *The American seances with Eusapia Palladino.* New York: Garrett/Helix.

Cassirer, Manfred. (1983a). Palladino at Cambridge. *Journal of the Society for Psychical Research, 52*(793), 52-58.

Cassirer, Manfred. (1983b). The fluid hands of Eusapia Palladino. *Journal of the Society for Psychical Research, 52*(794), 105-112.

Cerchio Firenze 77. (1978). *Per un mondo migliore* [For a better world]. Rome: Edizioni Mediterranee (in Italian).

Cerchio Firenze 77. (1980). *Le grandi verita* [The great truth]. Rome: Edizioni Mediterranee (in Italian).

Cerchio Firenze 77. (1984). *Oltre il silenzio* [Beyond silence]. Rome: Edizioni Mediterranee (in Italian).

Cerchio Firenze 77. (1986). *La fonte preziosa* [The precious source]. Rome: Edizioni Mediterranee (in Italian).

Cerchio Firenze 77. (1988). *Dai mondi invisibili.* Rome: Edizioni Mediterranee (in Italian).

Crookes, W. (1972). Sittings with Daniel Dunglas Home. In R. G. Medhurst, K. M. Goldney, & M. R. Barrington, *Crookes and the spirit world.* Great Britain: Souvenir Press.

Czaplicka, M. A. (1914). *Aboriginal Siberia.* Oxford: Clerendon Press.

Dalborowa, Romana. (1973, March 25). A jednak ciekawe... [And yet interesting]. *Stolica* [Capital], Warsaw, *28*(12/1320/) (in Polish).

de Goes, Eurico. (1937). *Prodigios de biopsychica obtidos com o medium Mirabelli* [Bio-psychic wonders obtained with the medium Mirabelli]. São Paulo: Cupolo. (in Portuguese)

Dettore, Ugo. (1979). *L'uomo e l'ignoto* [Man and the unexplored]. Milano: Armenia (in Italian).

Dingwall, E. J. (1936). *Journal of the Society for Psychical Research, 29*(520), 169-170. The Mediumship of Mirabelli (Letter to the Editor)

Dingwall, E. J. (1947). *Some human oddities: Studies in the queer, the uncanny and the fanatical.* London: Home & Van Thal.

Dingwall, E. J. (1961). *Journal of the Society for Psychical Research, 41*(708), 80-82. Book reviews.

Di Simone, Giorgio. (1973). *Rapporto dalla dimensione X* [Report from X-dimension]. Rome: Edizioni Mediterranee (in Italian).

Dorofeyev, G. (1987, May 31) Pod sledstviyem... chudesa [Miracles . . . under investigation]. *Sotsialisticheskaya Industriya* [Socialist Industry], Moscow (in Russian).

Dubrov, Alexander P. (1992). Bioprityazheniye [Bioattraction]. *Nauka v SSSR* (Moscow), No. 2 (in Russian).

Dubrov, Alexander P., & Berezin, Andrei A. (1991, February). "Tvoi tainstvennyye ruki" ["Your mysterious hands"]. *Priroda i Chelovek*, Moscow, No. 2, pp. 59-60 (in Russian).

Dunraven, Earl of. (1924). Experiences in spiritualism with D.D. Home. *Proceedings of the Society for Psychical Research, 35,* 1-284.

[The editorial office answers]. (1988, May). *Chelovek i Zakon* [Man and Law], No. 5 (209), p. 70 (in Russian).

Feilding, Everard, Baggally, W.W., & Carrington, Hereward. (1963). *Sittings with Eusapia Palladino and other studies.* Introduction by E.J. Dingwall. New Hyde Park, NY: University Books.

Fidano, Demofilo. (1986). *Un medium esce dal mistero* [A medium from mystery]. Trento: Edizioni Reverdito (in Italian).

Florinskii, M. T. (1957). *Russia: A history and an interpretation.* New York: MacMillan.

Fodor, N. (1966). *Encyclopedia of psychic science.* New Hyde Park, NY: University Books.

Geley, Gustave. (1922a). Experiences de materializations avec M. Franek Kluski. In *Le Compte Rendu Officiel du Premier Congres International des Recherches Psychiques a Copenhague*, Aug 26 - Sept 1921 (pp. 505-528). Copenhague (in French).

Geley, Gustave. (1922b). Materialisations-Experimente mit M. Franek Kluski. In von Freiherrn von Schrenck-Notzing, *Die neueren Okkultismusforschung im Lichte der Gegner.* Leipzig (in German).

Geley, Gustave. (1923). Experiences de la Societe Polonaise d'Etudes Psychiques avec Monsieur Franek Kluski. *Revue Metapsychique*, 27-39 (in French).

Geley, Gustave. (1924, November/December). [New experiments with the medium Franek Kluski]. *Revue Metapsychiques*, No. 6 (in French).

Geley, Gustave. (1925). *L'Ectoplasmie et la clairvoyance. Observations et experiences personnelles* (pp. 214-303). Paris (in French).

Gerasimov, V. (1990, April 30). [Bending spoons by looking at them]. *Pravda*, No. 120 (26203), p. 6 (in Russian).

Giovetti, Paola. (1982a). *Arte medianica* [Mediumistic art]. Rome: Edizioni Mediterranee (in Italian).

Giovetti, Paola. (1982b). PK and metal-bending in Italy. *Psi Research, 1*(3), 22-24.

Giovetti, Paola. (1986). *I misteri intorno a noi* [Our inner mysteries]. Milano: Rizzoli (in Italian).

Gissurarson, L. R., & Haraldsson, E. (1989). The Icelandic physical medium Indridi Indridason. *Proceedings of the Society for Psychical Research, 57*(214), 54-148.

von Gulat-Wellenburg, W., von Klinckowstroem, Carl, & Rosenbusch, Hans. (1925). *Der physikalische Mediumismus* (pp. 402-411). Berlin (in German).

Hannesson, G. (1910, December 21). *Nordurland*, pp. 207-209 (in Icelandic).

Hannesson, G. (1911). *Nordurland*, January 21, pp. 9-10; January 28, pp. 15-16; January 31, pp. 17-18; February 4, pp. 23-24; February 11, pp. 26-27; March 18, pp. 46-47 (in Icelandic).

Hannesson, G. (1924a). Tveir fundir hja Tiraunafelaginu. *Morgunn, 5*, 217-226 (in Icelandic).

Hannesson, G. (1924b). Remarkable phenomena in Iceland. *Journal of the American Society for Psychical Research, 18*, 239-272.

Hannesson, G. (1951). I svartaskola. *Morgunn, 32*, pp. 20-46, 143-163; first published in *Nordurland* in 1910-11; see also in *Satt* below (in Icelandic).

Hannesson, G. (1973). *Satt, 21*, pp. 9-14, 34, 43-46, 71, 79-82, 102-104, 115-116, 139 (in Icelandic).

Heuze, Paul. (n.d.). *Czy umarli zyja? Ankieta o stanie obecnym nauk metapsychicznych* [Do the deceased live? A poll regarding the current state of metapsychic studies]. Translated from French by Jozef Wasowski, Warsaw (in Polish).

Hultkrantz, Ake. (1978). Ecological and phenomenological aspects of shamanism. In V. Dioszegi & M. Hoppal (Eds). *Shamanism in Siberia* (pp. 27-58). Budapest: Akademiai Kiado.

Hyslop, J. H. (1907). Replies to Mr. Carrington's criticism of M. Aksakof. *Journal of the American Society for Psychical Research, 1,* 605-611.

Imbassahy, Carlos. (1935). *O espiritismo a luz dos fatos* [Spiritism in the light of the facts]. Rio de Janeiro: F.E.B. (in Portugues).

Imich, Alexander. (1932, July). Bericht uber zwei Sitzungen mit einem neuen Medium [Report about two seances with a new medium]. *Zeitschrift fur Parapsychologie,* pp. 289-295 (in German).

Ivchenko, L., & Lisovenko, N. (1987, May 27). ["Wonder" in Yenakiyevo: What scientists think about it]. *Izvestia* [News], Moscow, No. 147 (in Russian).

Kabakin, Victor. (1991, October). Some devilry for you. *Sputnik,* No. 10, pp. 152-155.

Karamzin, N. M. (1892). *Istoriya Gosudarstva Rossiiskogo* [History of the State of Russia]. St. Petersburg: Ye. Yevdokimov (in Russian).

Keil, H. H. J., Ullman M., Pratt, J. G., & Herbert, B. (1976). Directly observable PK effects: A survey and tentative interpretation of available findings from Nina Kulagina and other known cases of recent date. *Proceedings of the Society for Psychical Research, 56,* 197-235.

Kharuzin, Nikolay. (1889). O noydakh u drevnikh i sovremennykh loparey [About the "Noids" in Ancient and Contemporary Lapps], *Etnograficheskoye Obozreniye* [Ethnographic Review] (Moscow), *1,* 36-76 (in Russian).

Kolodny, Lev. (1986, August). Chto zhurnalist mozhet? [What can a journalist do?...]. *Zhurnalist* [Journalist], No. 8, pp. 42-44 (in Russian).

Kolodny, Lev. (1988, December 8). Nado li strashitsya sharika? [Should one fear a small ball?]. *Moskovskaya Pravda* (in Russian).

Kolodny, Lev. (1991). *Fenomen D i drugiye* [Phenomenon D and Others]. Moscow: Politizdat. (in Russian)

Kvaran, E. H. (1906). *Dularfull Fyrirbrigdi*. Reykjavik: Isafoldarprentsmidja (in Icelandic).

Kvaran, E. H. (1910). Metapsykiske fanomener paa island. *Sandhedssogeren, 6,* 42-51 (in Icelandic).

Kvaran, E. H. (1934, December 6). Fra landamaerunum. *Morgunbladid, 21,* p. 291 (in Icelandic).

Lebedeva, Yelena. (1990, September). Tvoi tainstvennye ruki [Your mysterious hands]. *Priroda i Chelovek,* Moscow, No. 9, pp. 36-37 (in Russian).

Lipski, Jan J. (1976). Modrzejewski Teofil. In *Polski slownik biograficzny* [Polish biographical dictionary] (Vol. XXI/3, pp. 537-538). Wroclaw (in Polish).

Lisovenko, N. (1987, April 11). Pozhar po "...sobstvennomu zhelaniyu"? [Fire as you like it!] *Izvestiya* [News], Moscow, No. 101, p. 4 (in Russian).

Lvov, Vladimir. (1971). *Po nevidimym sledam* [Following invisible tracks], Leningrad (in Russian).

Lvov, Vladimir. (1974). *Fabrikanty chudes* [Fabricators of miracles], Leningrad (in Russian).

Materialy dlya suzhdeniya o spiritizme [Materials for a Judgement on Spiritualism]. (1876). St. Petersburg (in Russian).

Medhurst, R. G. (Ed.). (1972). *Crookes and the spirit world*. London: Souvenir Press.

A miracle in the Sapernaya settlement. (1927, June 2). *Proletarskaya Pravda* (Kiev), No. 123, p. 5 (in Ukrainian).

Moser, Fanny. (1935). *Der Okkultismus, Tauschungen und Tatsachen*. Munchen (in German).

Murphy, Gardner, & Ballou, Robert. (Eds.). (1960). *William James on psychical research*. New York: Viking.

Naumov, E. K., & Mikhalchik, A. A. (1983). Some aspects of practical application of psychotronics in the USSR. *Psi Research, 2*(3), 34-44.

Nelander, John. (1990, May 29). Inga, the human magnet. *Globe*.

Nielsson, H. (1919a). Um svipi lifandi manna. In Haraldur Nielsson, *Kirkjan og Odaudleikasannanir*. Reykjavik: Isafold, pp. 1-40; also in Haraldur Nielsson, *Lifid og Odaudleikinn*. Reykjavik: Isafoldarprentsmidja, 1951 (in Icelandic).

Nielsson, H. (1919b). Wonderful boy medium in Iceland. *Light*, October 25, p. 344; November 1 & 8, pp. 350, 353.

Nielsson, H. (1922a). Egne Oplevelser paa det Psykiske Omraade. In Haraldur Nielsson, *Kirken og den Psykiske Forskning*. Copenhagen: Levin og Munksgaard (in Danish).

Nielsson, H. (1922b). Some of my experiences with a physical medium in Reykjavik. In C. Vett (Ed.), *Le Compte Rendu Officiel du Premier Congres International des Recherches Psychiques a Copenhague*. Copenhagen, pp. 450-465.

Nielsson, H. (1924a). Remarkable phenomena in Iceland. *Journal of the Americam Society for Psychical Research, 18*, 233-238.

Nielsson, H. (1924b). Poltergeist phenomena in connection with a medium observed for a length of time, some of them in full light. In *L'Etat Actuel des Recherches Psychiques d'apres les Travaux du 2me Congres International tenu a Varsovie en 1923 en l'Honneur du Dr. Julien Ochorowicz* (pp. 148-168). Paris: Les Presses Universitaires de France.

Nielsson, H. (1925). Poltergeist phenomena. *Psychic Science, 4*, 90-111.

Nielsson, H. (1930). Reimleikar i Tilraunfelaginu. *Morgunn, 11*, 171-198; also in Haraldur Nielsson, *Lifid og Odaudleikinn*. Reykjavik: Isafoldarprentsmidja, 1951, pp. 87-113 (in Icelandic).

Niemojewski, Andrzej. (1921). *Dawnosc a Mickiewicz* [The past and Mickiewicz]. Warsaw (in Polish).

Ochorowicz, Julian. (1909, Aug 16). Les phenomenes lumineux et la photographie de l'invisible. V. Les phenomenes lumineux chez Eusapia Paladino. *Annales des Sciences Psychiques, 19*(15/16) (in French).

Ochorowicz, Julian. (1913). *Zjawiska mediumiczne* [Mediumistic phenomena]. Warsaw (in Polish).

Okolowicz, Norbert. (1926). *Wspomnienia z seansow z medium Frankiem Kluskim* [Recollections of seances with Franek Kluski]. Warsaw: Ksiaznica Atlas (in Polish).

Orlov, Vadim. (1990, October). Objects stick to people: What would that mean? *Tekhnika-Molodezhi*, pp. 27-29 (in Russian).

Perovsky-Petrovo-Solovovo, Count. (1945). Nikolaeff: A little-known Russian physical medium. *Proceedings of the Society for Psychical Research, 47*(169), 261-266.

Playfair, Guy Lyon. (1975). *The flying cow: Research into paranormal phenomena in the world's most psychic country.* London: Souvenir Press (U.S. edition: *The unknown power.* New York: Pocket Books).

Playfair, Guy Lyon. (1992). Mirabelli and the phantom ladder. *Journal of the Society for Psychical Research, 58*(826), 201-203.

Rudsky, L. (1990, December 19). [Lifted on his chest]. *Rabochaya Tribuna,* Moscow, p. 4 (in Russian).

von Schrenck-Notzing, A. Freiherrn. (1914a). *Der Kampf um die Materialisations-Phaenomene. Eine Verteidigungsschrift.* Munchen (in German).

von Schrenck-Notzing, A. Freiherrn. (1914b). *Materialisations-Phaenomene. Ein Beitrag zur Erforschung der mediumistischen Teleplastie.* Munchen (in German).

Scientists study phenomena of Nina Kulagina. (1984). *Psi Research, 3*(3/4), 66-73.

Sokolowski, Tadeusz. (1948). Animizm czy spirytyzm [Animism or spiritism]. *Lotos, 8* (4) (In Polish).

Stein, Gordon. (1991, March). The amazing medium Mirabelli. *Fate,* pp. 86-95.

Strelkov, V. (1986, September). [Resurrection of Drakula, or who spreads mysticism], *Chelovek i Zakon* [Man and Law], No. 9 (189), pp. 28-46 (in Russian).

Szczepanski, Ludwik. (1936). *Mediumizm wspolczesny i wielkie media polskie,* [Contemporary mediumship and the great Polish mediums]. Krakow (in Polish).

Tabori, P. (1950). *Harry Price: The biography of a ghost hunter.* London: Atheneum Press.

Tarchini, P. (1947). La smaterializzazione del corpo del medio nelle sedute medianiche [Materialization of the medium's body during a mediumistic seance]. *Luce e Ombra, 47,* 44-51 (in Italian).

Thordarson, Th. (1942). *Indridi midill.* Reykjavik: Vikingsutgafan (in Icelandic).

Thurston, H. (1952). *The physical phenomena of mysticism.* London: Burns Oates.

Tietze, T. R. (1972a, January/February). Eusapia Palladino, medium. *Psychic,* pp. 8-13, 38.

Tietze, T. R. (1972b, March/April). Eusapia Palladino, medium. *Psychic*, pp. 40-45.

Ullman, Montague. (1974). PK in the Soviet Union. In W.G. Roll, R.L. Morris, & J.D. Morris (Eds.), *Research in Parapsychology, 1973*. Metuchen, N.J.: Scarecrow Press.

Urbanski, Tadeusz. (1984). Zapiski do autobiografii naukowej [Notes to a scientific autobiography]. *Kwartalnik Historii Nauki i Techniki PAN* [Quarterly on History of Science and Technology of the Polish Academy of Sciences] (Warsaw), *29*(1) (in Polish).

Vilenskaya, Larissa. (1972). Spontaneous phenomena in the USSR. *International Journal of Paraphysics*, *6*(5), 222-225.

Vilenskaya, Larissa. (1981). Psycho-physical effects by N. Kulagina: Remote influence on surrounding objects. *Parapsychology in the USSR* (Vol. III, pp. 12-25). San Francisco: Washington Research Center.

Vilenskaya, Larissa. (1988). Poltergeist cases in the Soviet Union. *ASPR Newsletter*, *14*(2), 10-11.

Vilenskaya, Larissa. (1991). Firsthand observations of PK-like activity in the USSR. *Exceptional Human Experience*, *9*(1), 24-31.

Vilenskaya, Larissa, & Steffy, Joan. (1991). Firewalking: A new look at an old enigma. Falls Village, CT: The Bramble Company.

Volchenko, V.N., Dulnev, G.N., Krylov, K.I., Kulagin, V.V., Pilipenko, N.V. (1984). [Measurements of extreme values of physical fields of the human operator]. In *Tekhnicheskie Aspekty Refleksoterapii i Sistemy Diagnostiki* [Technical Aspects of the Reflex Therapy and Diagnostic System] (pp. 53-59). Kalinin: Kalinin State University (in Russian).

Walker, May C. (1934). Psychic research in Brazil. *Journal of the American Society for Psychical Research*, *28*(3), 74-78.

Zielinski, Ludmila. (1968). Hypnotism in Russia 1800-1900. In E.J. Dingwall (Ed.), *Abnormal hypnotic phenomena: A survey of nineteenth-century cases* (Vol. 3, pp. 2-105). London: J. & A. Churchill, .

Zinchenko, V.P., & Leontiyev, A.N. (1974). Parapsychology. *Bolshaya sovetskaya entsiklopediya* [Great soviet encyclopedia], 3rd ed., Moscow, (Vol. 19, pp. 192-193) (in Russian; English translation by Macmillan, 1978, pp. 258-259).

Zlokazov, V. P., Pushkin, V. N., & Shevchuk, E. D. (1982). Bioenergetic aspects of the relationship between the image of perception and perceived object. *Psi Research, 1*(3), 11-21 [Translation from Russian; the original was published in [*Questions of psychohygiene, psychophysiology, and sociology of labor in coal industry and of psycho-energetics*], Moscow: Scientific and Technological Mining Society, 1980].

Zorab, G. (1970). Test sittings with D.D. Home in Amsterdam. *Journal of Parapsychology, 1*, 47-63.

Glossary*

Altered state of consciousness (ASC) A pattern of awareness that is qualitatively different in overall mental functioning from one's ordinary waking pattern.

Apport From Latin *apportare*, to carry to (a place). A physical object which has been *paranormally* transported into a closed space (room or container), suggesting the passage of matter through matter, i.e., through intervening material objects.

Automatic writing Spontaneous writing without the writer being consciously aware of what is being written.

Direct voice A phenomenon associated with *physical mediumship* in which an isolated voice without visible source is heard during a seance.

Direct writing The paranormal production of a written message, as, for example, a pen writing by itself.

Discarnate entity From Latin *dis-*, away, apart, and *caro (carnis)*, flesh. A disembodied being, as opposed to an incarnate one; the surviving soul, intelligence or personality of a deceased individual; a spirit.

Double-blind tests Tests in which both the *testee* and the experimenter (test-administrator and other test participants) are without knowledge of cues or other information which would reveal the true target (information) to be identified *paranormally* by the psychic.

---

* In compiling the Glossary, the following sources were used: Mitchell, Edgar D. *Psychic Exploration: A Challenge for Science* (New York: G.P. Putnam's Sons, 1974), Thalbourne, Michael A. *A Glossary of Terms Used in Parapsychology* (London: Heinemann, 1982), and Nash, Carroll B. *Parapsychology: The Science of Psiology* (Springfield, IL: Charles C. Thomas, 1986).

Entity, see *Discarnate entity*.

Extrasensory perception Paranormal cognition, the acquisition of information about an external event, object or influence (mental or physical; past, present or future) other than through any of the known sensory channels.

Healing, mental (psychic) Healing apparently brought about by such non-medical means as the laying-on of hands, prayer, etc., and inexplicable according to contemporary medical science.

Levitation The raising of persons or objects without any apparent agency as required by known physical laws of motion and gravity.

Materialization A phenomenon of *physical mediumship* in which living entities or inanimate objects take form. While many reports on materialization describe the appearance of living organisms or parts of them, other psychics materialize a great variety of artifax.

Medium A person who purportedly is in communication with *discarnates*, or who acts as a channel for discarnates to communicate through *direct voice, automatic writing*, or other means. A mental medium receives messages from the deceased and transmits them to the living. A physical medium can, in addition, produce all kinds of physical effects, including *materializations*. In some countries medium is a synonym for psychic.

Mediumistic Involving or pertaining to *mediumship* or *mediums*.

Mediumship The practice of skills associated with mediums.

Paranormal Term applied to any phenomenon which in one or more respects exceeds the limits of what is deemed physically possible based on current scientific assumptions.

Parapsychology Term coined by philosopher-psychologist Max Dessoir in Germany in the 19th century and adopted by the distinguished psychologist William McDougall to refer to the scientific study of *paranormal* (or *psi*) phenomena. Parapsychology is the branch of science that deals with behavioral or personal exchanges with the environment that are extrasensorimotor, i.e., not dependent on the senses (*extrasensory perception*) and muscles (*psychokinesis*).

Physical Mediumship, see *Physical Phenomena*.

Physical Phenomena Term referring to those phenomena of *mediumship* which involve the production of ostensibly *paranormal* physical events.

Poltergeist From the German literally meaning "noisy ghost." Various *paranormal* manifestations involving unexplained movement, breakage of objects, lighting of fires and a variety of other phenomena. The phenomena usually seem to depend upon the presence of a particular individual, frequently an adolescent or child.

Psi A general term, proposed by B.P. Wiesner and seconded by R.H. Thouless, used either as a noun or adjective to identify *paranormal* processes and paranormal causation. The two main categories of psi are paranormal cognition (*extrasensory perception*) and paranormal action (*psychokinesis*), although the purpose of the term "psi" is to suggest that they might simply be different aspects of a single process, rather than distinct and essentially different processes.

Psychic As a noun, "psychic" refers to an individual who possesses *paranormal* ability of some kind and to a relatively high degree; as an adjective, it is often applied to *paranormal* events, abilities, research, etc., and thus means "concerning or involving *psi*," or "parapsychological."

Psychokinesis (PK) The direct influence of mind on a physical system without the mediation of any known physical energy or instrumentation. Sometimes also called telekinesis.

Raps Percussive sounds, often heard during *mediumistic seances* or *poltergeist* occurrences and sometimes tapping out an intelligible message, said to be produced by *paranormal* means.

Seance A meeting of persons, generally, but not always, with a *medium*, for the purpose of generating *paranormal* phenomena or receiving communications from the deceased.

Shaman From German *Schamane*, derived from Russian *shaman*, derived from Tungusic *saman*. A tribal medium, healer and priest (as originally exemplified by Siberian tribes) accredited with *paranormal* powers, who can access altered states of consciousness at will. Shamans are mediators between the sacred and the profane; they receive messages which they encode for those who are not so receptive and they use symbols and rituals to express the ineffable.

Sitting, see *Seance*.

Spiritism Another term for *spiritualism*.

Spiritualism A concept based upon the belief that humans survive death, and upon the practice of communicating with deceased persons, usually via a *medium*.

Survival of death The concept of continued conscious existence after bodily death. In the framework of this concept, immortality (eternal existence) is neither implied nor ruled out.

Trance From old French *transe*, "passage," ultimately derived from Latin *transire*, "to go across." An *altered state of consciousness*, induced or spontaneous, in which the individual is oblivious to his/her situation and surroundings. Trance apparently gives access to many ordinarily inhibited capacities of the mind-body system. There are a variety of trance states, not just a single state.

About the Authors

Dr. Roman Bugaj, born in 1922, received his M.A. in chemistry at the University of Warsaw in 1951. He was the head of the laboratory of analytical chemistry of the same university from 1947 to 1961. In 1964 he received his Ph.D. in Humanistic Science. From 1972 to 1983 Dr. Bugaj was Assistant Professor at the Institute of Teacher Education and Director of the Institute of Natural Sciences. His additional specialty is history of science.

Dr. Bugaj has been an early organizer of the parapsychological movement in Poland and is currently vice president of the Polish Psychotronic Society. He is quite active in the field, writing, lecturing, and doing research, mostly with PK subjects. He authored seven books, including *Occult Sciences in Poland in the Time of Renaissance* (Wroclaw/Krakow/ Warsaw/Gdansk, 1975/1986, also published in German translation in Knittingen, 1970-1971) and a great number of articles and papers on parapsychology, chemistry, alchemy and occult sciences. The chapter about the famous Polish medium Teofil Modrzejewski, also known under the pseudonym of Franek Kluski, is translated from the second edition of his book, *Eksterioryzacja—Istnienie Poza Cialem* [Exteriorization—Existence Beyond the Body] (Warsaw: SIGMA NOT, 1990/1992).

Dr. Paola Giovetti Tenti, staff writer of *Luce e Ombra* (a leading Italian parapsychological periodical founded in 1900), syndicated writer for the national press weekly publications, is also a lecturer appearing frequently on TV. Between 1981 and 1990, she published ten books (many translated into foreign languages) about near-death experiences, healers, paranormal graphic art, interviews with scientists, contacts of parents with deceased children, Theresa Neumann, angels in world tradition, and Findhorn. Her *Dictionary of Parapsychology* and *History of Parapsychology* are in press. In this book Dr. Giovetti is writing about two Italian mediums, Gustavo Adolfo Rol and Roberto Setti. The first one, a well-to-do socialite, speaks several languages, loves art and literature. Himself a painter, his house is full of precious objects. Einstein had the chance to witness phenomena produced by Rol, who is by the way extremely difficult to reach. Roberto Setti is another miraculous psychic: he has spirit-guides and produces materializations, lights, fragrances and automatic writing with messages from deceased persons, often with profound philosophical meaning.

Dr. Loftur R. Gissurarson obtained his Ph.D. under Professor Robert L. Morris of the Koestler Chair and Dr. John Beloff, University of Edinburgh, with an experimental project involving computers and psychokinesis. He graduated in psychology from the University of Iceland, where he studied under Professor Erlendur Haraldsson, and wrote his thesis on the phenomena of the Icelandic physics medium Indridi Indridason. At present Dr. Gissurarson is a contract lecturer at the University of Iceland and chief psychologist at the Affairs of the Disabled in Reykjavik. He is the author of about forty scholarly papers on the study of extrasensory perception and psychokinesis published in English, Icelandic, German, and Italian in such journals as *Personality and Individual Differences, European Journal of Parapsychology, Journal of Parapsychology, Journal of the Society for Psychical Research, Luce e Ombra*, and others.

Dr. Erlendur Haraldsson, psychology professor at the University of Reykjavik, Iceland, is one of the leading authorities on parapsychology. Among his more than 150 publications are four books, including *At the Hour of Death* (together with Dr. Karlis Osis, 1977), a study of deathbed visions made in the USA and in India, published in fourteen countries, and most recent, *Modern Miracles: An Investigative Report on Psychic Phenomena Associated with Sathya Sai Baba* (1988), the result of a ten-year study in India.

In this book, Dr. Haraldsson writes about the great Icelandic medium Indridi Indridason. His psychic capacities appeared suddenly when, at the age of 22, he participated in a table-tilting seance, fashionable at that time. The study of mechanical, acoustic, olfactory, optical phenomena, including materializations and a dematerialization of his left arm, produced by this young printer's apprentice, were interrupted by his premature death at the age of 29.

Dr. Alexander Imich is a chemical consultant, a contributing editor to *Psychological Abstracts*, to *Parapsychology Abstracts International*, and in the past to *Chemical Abstracts*. His articles were published in British, French, German, Italian, Indian, and USA periodicals. Imich describes adventurous personal experiences with a little known but powerful Polish medium, Matylda S. This music teacher's late psychic career started after the death of the well-known Polish medium Jan Guzik. Matylda produced all types of paranormal phenomena: levitations and apports, including an apport of a living man; acoustical, including a direct human voice; olfactory; and optical, including a black materialization. Due to the medium's strong irrational conviction, the geographic location of seances seemed decisive of success or failure of her performances. Seances were held in three Polish cities and in London, where she was invited by Harry Price to participate in experiments in the National Laboratory of Psychical Research.

Guy Lyon Playfair, graduate of Cheltam College and Pembroke College, Cambridge, England, was born in India and lived for 14 years in Brazil. As a free-lance writer, he was connected with *Time, The Economist,* Associated Press and others. Author of nine books, including *The Unknown Power, This House Is Haunted, Medicine, Mind and Magic,* and *The Flying Cow,* he writes about the Brazilian psychic, Carlos Mirabelli, who produced powerful and multifaceted phenomena indoors and outdoors, in full daylight, stirring the imagination of the country and confirmed by hundreds of prominent Brazilian personalities, including the president of the republic. Some materializations that appeared with Mirabelli carried full human figures who walked, talked, breathed. and and had normal pulse and other attributes of living people. Sometimes they lasted for more than half an hour, were recognized by the participants and behaved like their deceased relatives, were touched or embraced by the participants and carried on significant conversations. In his normal state of consciousness Mirabelli spoke Portuguese and Italian; he also knew little French. But in the trance state he delivered serious dialogues in twenty-six languages and produced automatic writing in twenty-eight. Mirabelli was certainly one of the most prominent psychics known.

Dr. Larissa Vilenskaya was born in Latvia, studied physics and psychology in Moscow, USSR, and knew personally many famous Soviet psychics. In 1981 she emigrated to the U.S. and in 1982 founded and edited *Psi Research,* a quarterly journal devoted to parapsychology in the USSR, Eastern Europe and the People's Republic of China. Dr. Vilenskaya is an international lecturer, a leader of firewalking workshops and the recipient of a Swiss parapsychological prize. She is the author (or co-author) of over 70 publications in several languages, including such books as *The Golden Chalice, Parapsychology in the USSR,* and *Firewalking: A New Look at an Old Enigma.* After describing the mystical arena of the last century, Dr. Vilenskaya presents several of the contemporary psychics, such as Kulagina, Yermolayev, Davletova, and others.

Zhu Yi Yi is a graduate in biology from the Shanghai Fu Dan University. She is the staff writer of *Ziran Zazhi* (Nature Journal), a member of the Standing Council of China Somatic Science Association, Secretary General of the Shanghai Somatic Science Association, and Honorary Member and Deputy Secretary General of Shanghai Qigong Association. She is the author of *Superman in China* (Wen Hua Publishing House, 1987) and co-author of *Survey of Human Parapsychology Studies in China* (1988). In this book, Ms. Zhu relates experiments she conducted with several Chinese youngsters producing astonishing psychokinetic phenomena, often quite original and never previously observed.